THE HERITAGE OF
NORTH AMERICAN STEAM RAILROADS

THE HERITAGE OF
NORTH AMERICAN STEAM RAILROADS

FROM THE FIRST DAYS OF STEAM POWER TO THE PRESENT

BRIAN SOLOMON

The Reader's Digest Association, Inc.
Pleasantville, New York/Montreal

To The Memory of Joseph R. Snopek

A READER'S DIGEST BOOK

This edition published by The Reader's Digest Association
by arrangement with Amber Books Ltd

Copyright © 2001 by Amber Books Ltd

Editorial and design by
Amber Books Ltd
Bradley's Close
74–77 White Lion Street
London N1 9PF

Project Editor: Jill Fornary
Design: Jeremy Williams
Picture Research: Lisa Wren

READER'S DIGEST PROJECT STAFF

Project Editor: Nancy Shuker
Senior Editor (Canada): Andrew Byers
Contributing Project Designer: Jane Wilson
Editorial Manager: Christine R. Guido

READER'S DIGEST ILLUSTRATED REFERENCE BOOKS

Editor-in-Chief: Christopher Cavanaugh
Art Director: Joan Mazzeo
Director, Trade Publishing: Christopher T. Reggio
Senior Design Director, Trade: Elizabeth L. Tunnicliffe
Editorial Director, Trade: Susan Randol

        Library of Congress Cataloging in Publication Data
Solomon, Brian, 1966-
    The heritage of North American steam railroads : from the first days of steam power
to the present / Brian Solomon.
      p. cm.
    ISBN 0-7621-0327-2
    1. Railroads--North America--History. 2. Railroads--United States--History. 3.
Railroads--Canada--History. I. Title: Reader's digest the heritage of North American
steam railroads. II. Title.

TF22 .H47 2001
385'.097—dc21   2001019434

Printed in Italy

1   3   5   7   9   10   8   6   4   2

CONTENTS

THE BIRTH OF NORTH AMERICA'S RAILROADS

Inspired by English railway pioneers, early proponents of the steam locomotive in North America used home-grown technology to develop their own engines, tailor-made for the challenging terrain of a huge continent.

The railway era dawned in Europe just as the United States' territory was expanding, and it was the advent of the railway that helped this developing nation to achieve its greatness as an industrial world power. In the early 19th century, railways represented the cutting edge of technology. They attracted keen minds from many fields and

◄ **The advent of the steam locomotive was crucial to the rapid settlement and development of North America. In this timeless scene, Sierra Railroad No. 28 steams up the roundhouse at Jamestown, California, in preparation for its daily run.**

encouraged progress toward a "modern" world as the Industrial Revolution took hold. The emergence of the railway helped the United States to grow faster than any other country in history. The building of railways also enabled its northern neighbor, Canada, to bind together remote and sparsely populated regions into a cohesive national entity. Throughout North America the railroad did more than connect existing population centers – it was the primary catalyst for new settlement. The railway's ability to move people and goods quickly across great distances made it vital to the development of the United States and Canada.

▲ Seen here at Coalbrookdale, Shropshire, England, in the mid-19th century, this Newcomen Colliery Winding engine dates from the 1790s. Newcomen steam engines were large, ponderous machines used in industry.

The elements of the steam railway as we know it (including rail systems and powered engines) evolved in Britain and Europe during the early years of the Industrial Revolution. Primitive animal-hauled tram railways had been used for centuries in mines and quarries to help transport stone, coal, and other heavy raw materials. These lines were rarely more than a few miles in length and were crudely constructed using light wooden rails and wooden wagons.

The power of steam had been known since the 1st century AD, but there had been no serious attempts to harness it in a steam engine until the early 1700s. The Cornishman Thomas Newcomen improved an air-actuated pump design by introducing steam into the cylinder. Thus the first stationary steam engines were born. Newcomen engines, as they were known, were ponderously slow, huge machines that operated at low pressure (roughly 10lb per sq in). They were employed all over Britain, most often as pumping engines. Over the next century, a number of talented and industrious men set out to improve upon the Newcomen engine. Most notably, James Watt, from Scotland, greatly increased its efficiency and successfully converted its reciprocating (back-and-forth) motion into rotary motion. Watt's improved engine was much better suited to heavy industrial applications than Newcomen's. By the mid-18th century, engineers and inventors also began to ponder the concept of steam propulsion, not just in Britain, but in France and the United States, too. The Frenchman Nicholas-Joseph Cugnot is credited with building in 1769 the first steam-powered wagon, an awkwardly designed three-wheeled contraption that has been described as a "tea-kettle on wheels." Its only claim to fame is that of being the first steam-propelled vehicle, as its operation was very inefficient, with the device tipping over on its inaugural run.

During the last quarter of the 18th century, other inventors toyed with the idea of steam carriages, but without lasting success. The American inventor John Fitch was among these pioneers of steam propulsion. As well as building a series of steamboats, he also constructed a working model of a steam locomotive engine that ran on tracks. Fitch is believed to have proposed the building of a railway line across the Appalachian Mountains many years before such an effort was seriously undertaken.

The first successful steam locomotive is generally credited to another Cornishman, Richard Trevithick, who built a full-sized locomotive engine using relatively high-pressure steam (approximately 50lb per sq in) in 1803–04. This locomotive debuted at the Pen-y-Darran Iron Works on February 13, 1804, and is now known as the Pen-y-Darran engine. Trevithick went on to adapt his high-pressure engine design to various uses and inspired others to perfect his invention. Within a decade several industrial tram lines in Britain were using steam locomotives of various designs to supplement animal power on their railways.

One of the most talented early locomotive builders was George Stephenson, who is today called the "Father of the Railway." He quickly gained a reputation as one of the most skilled engineers in Britain. Among his most significant contributions to the railway was convincing the pioneer Stockton & Darlington line to employ steam power instead of relying strictly upon animal propulsion. The Stockton & Darlington Railway, using steam power, opened on September 27, 1825, setting an important precedent for all future railways. Stephenson went on to build an even more significant railway, the internationally renowned Liverpool and Manchester, often considered the first "modern" steam railway.

▼ The opening of George Stephenson's Stockton & Darlington Railway in Britain on October 27, 1825, sparked a railway revolution in Britain. It was the first steam-powered public railway. Earlier railways were no more than industrial tram lines.

▲ The innovative *Rocket*, with which Robert Stephenson (inset) won the Rainhill Trials of 1829, greatly influenced most successful locomotive designs. It is seen here in its later state, much altered from the original. Today the engine is preserved in York, England.

These prototype lines were relatively quickly copied and adapted around the world. On both these lines, Stephenson adopted a track width, or gauge, of 4ft 8½in (1,435mm) – roughly the inside measurement of the 5ft (1,520mm) width tram railway tracks in use at that time. This gauge had been used for many tram lines. Sometimes referred to as the Stephenson Standard gauge, it ultimately became the standard track width throughout Britain and in many other countries around the world, including the United States and Canada. In the early years of the railways, the question of gauge gave rise to fierce debates, and the Stephenson gauge did not always prevail. The argument for a wider gauge had merit. Such a gauge would allow for larger railway cars and increased capacity, and also offer greater stability, particularly desirable at higher speeds. Unfortunately, a broad gauge would be considerably more expensive to construct. Hence Stephenson's standard became a reasonable compromise in most places.

THE RAINHILL TRIALS OF 1829

Prior to the opening of the Liverpool and Manchester Railway, the owners held a widely celebrated competition to select the best type of locomotive for service. The contest was held on a section of level tangent (flat, straight) track at Rainhill, several miles east of Liverpool, and is known today as the Rainhill Trials. By the late 1820s, there were a number of locomotive manufacturers in Britain and there were

▼ The opening of the Erie Canal in 1825 greatly benefited the port of New York, and demonstrated the advantages of good interior transport. This steam-powered canal boat is pictured at Macedon, New York, east of Rochester, circa 1890.

an estimated 50 steam locomotives in daily service, the majority of these on industrial tram lines. Contestants at the Rainhill Trials included machines built by Timothy Hackworth and George Stephenson's son Robert. Robert Stephenson's entry, a fast engine named the *Rocket*, was the winner. It amazed the public by achieving a top speed of 29mph (47kph). While the *Rocket* quickly became world famous for its achievements, it proved even more significant by setting fundamental technological precedents that would greatly influence subsequent steam locomotive development in Britain and around the world. This marvelous machine combined the three principal elements incorporated in most successful steam locomotive designs: forced draft from exhausting steam, a multi-tubular fire-tube boiler, and direct linkage between the cylinders and driving wheels. Early locomotives used some, but not all, of these features; many had complex linkages between the cylinders and driving wheels, reducing their efficiency. Some employed vertical cylinders and rocking beams to transmit power to the drive wheels, while others used

systems of gears. Today, Robert Stephenson's brilliant solution to developing a better locomotive seems obvious, but in its time the *Rocket* was truly revolutionary. Today, Britain honors the Stephensons' contribution to the railways with its five-pound note, which features a portrait of George and a picture of his son's most famous locomotive.

AMERICAN RAILWAY VISIONS

While the British can rightfully claim to have had the first practical steam-powered railways, the United States was only a few years behind. The visionary American steam pioneer John Fitch had the idea of locomotive-powered railways before Trevithick built his successful engine. While Fitch died in obscurity, his concepts inspired others, and the railway notion simmered in the minds of progressive thinkers for a generation. Early railway promoters such as Col John Stevens of Hoboken, New Jersey, faced enormous hurdles to convince politicians, potential investors, and the general public that railways were a viable and practical transportation solution. In those days, improved post roads and canals were offered as the best alternatives for the country. In 1812 Stevens published a paper entitled *Documents Tending to Prove the Superior Advantages of Railways and Steam Carriages Over Canal Navigation* to encourage investigation into the possibilities of steam railways. The

inventor Oliver Evans was another early proponent. At roughly the same time as Richard Trevithick was demonstrating his Pen-y-Darran locomotive in Britain, Evans showed his steam-powered *Orukter Amphibolis* in Philadelphia; this was an amphibious vehicle capable of operating both on land and in water. A decade later he proposed building steam-powered railway lines into the interior of the country. It is significant that such interest in railways existed at that time in the United States, which was then primarily an agricultural nation with a population of roughly 7.5 million people.

In 1815, John Stevens chartered to build a railway that would effectively connect New York and Philadelphia

---

In 1815 Stevens made the bold step of chartering to build a railway across New Jersey that would effectively connect New York and Philadelphia via ferries on either end of the line. He was a generation ahead of his time, and his early vision was not fulfilled. He did not give up, however. A decade later, Stevens built a small demonstration railway on his Hoboken estate. He employed a diminutive, crudely constructed steam locomotive to haul a carriage with flanged wheels. This is believed to have been the first operating steam locomotive in the country.

Around the time John Stevens was demonstrating his locomotive, an estimated 37,000 miles (59,544km) of post roads had been built in the United States. In addition, Britain had been developing its canal network since the mid-18th century, and this inspired the United States to build its own canals. The first American canals

◄ The Baltimore & Ohio was among America's earliest railroads. It was chartered in 1827 and construction began on July 4, 1828. Solid stone markers, or mileposts, were set along the line every mile to indicate the distance from Baltimore.

▲ The Baltimore & Ohio's first terminal was located at Ellicott Mills, Maryland, which is today the oldest railway station in the United States. This view shows the ticket counter, with correspondence to Relay – an intermediate station – visible on the left.

opened in the 1790s, and by 1835 some 2,600 miles (4,184km) of canal had been completed. Early canals were typically short runs designed to bypass difficult stretches of natural waterways, such as rapids. The first were located in New England along the Connecticut River. Later, more extensive canals were built, such as the famous Erie Canal, which connected the Hudson River with the Great Lakes, offering a continuous navigable waterway into the country's interior. New York City enjoyed the advantage of the Erie Canal and captured the lion's share of this lucrative interior-bound traffic, bringing riches to the city and state of New York.

After the completion of the Erie Canal, the other large eastern seaboard ports began exploring a variety of canal and railroad schemes to improve their access to the nation's interior. Railway plans were favored by ports that lacked natural east–west waterways and where land routes west entailed difficult mountain crossings. New York was blessed by its geography, giving it a near water-level route to the west – a route that in time would prove an ideal path for the state's own railway line.

Despite early ideas for building railways and a clear need for better westward transportation, the decision to actually lay track did not come easily. During the 1820s, the prospect of railways in the United States sparked heated controversy. Canals were established, proven, and readily accepted, while railways were regarded as untested and even dangerous. Stevens and other railway enthusiasts suggested running trains at speeds of 20 and 30mph (32 and 48kph), much faster than horse-drawn carriages could travel. These speeds seem slow today, but at that time many people considered them impossibly fast, even reckless. A

result in a variety of unpleasant maladies. This dubious new machine belched steam and black smoke; it hissed, whistled, and roared; it frightened dogs and horses, small children, the elderly, and the faint of heart. Nevertheless, whenever the steam locomotive came to town, it was invariably the center of attention, as people gathered to look at it, to ride behind it, and to experience the awesome power of this potent symbol of progress.

Despite public curiosity, early railway promoters in North America had a difficult time convincing people of the advantages that railways offered, in part because the United States had not enjoyed the benefits of tram lines and steam technology to the same extent as Britain. Most Americans had never seen a stationary steam engine, and the whole concept of steam power seemed entirely strange to them. Railway promoters were hindered at every turn. Investors considered their schemes preposterous, and established financiers regarded railwaymen as fools. Opposition was eventually overcome, but it never disappeared, and throughout the railroad era, railways faced varying degrees of opposition.

THE FIRST US RAILWAYS

By the mid-1820s the first serious efforts at building railways in the United States got underway. These followed the opening of George Stephenson's pioneering Stockton & Darlington line in Britain. The very first railway to open in the United States, albeit with animal power rather than steam, was Gridley Bryant's three-mile (4.8km) long tram line, which debuted in Quincy, Massachusetts, on March 4, 1826. It was built for the primary purpose of moving heavy granite blocks from a nearby quarry to be used

▲ In the early days, inclined planes, or portage railways, were used to transport goods over mountainous terrain. Cables drawn by stationary steam engines pulled cars up the plane, as seen here in Pennsylvania's Lehigh Valley.

contemporary skeptic by the name of Wood wrote: "…nothing can do more harm to the adoption of railways than the promulgation of such nonsense as that we shall see locomotives travelling [sic] at the rate of 12 miles per hour . . ." He echoed a commonly felt opinion that anything moving faster than approximately 10mph (16kph) was simply *too* fast.

Pseudo-scientific publications claimed that traveling at high speeds (20mph/32kph or more) would

WORKING ON THE RAILROAD
BOILER EXPLOSIONS

Great power must be harnessed with great care to prevent unleashing a terrible destructive force. Inventor James Watt cautioned against the use of high-pressure steam, yet most steam engines – and consequentially nearly all locomotives – built after 1800 used high-pressure steam. The danger he feared was the risk of a boiler explosion, destroying the engine and possibly killing its crew and anyone unfortunate enough to be standing nearby. Boiler explosions can be triggered in a number of ways, the most common being a low water level in the boiler. If the top of the firebox (known as the crown sheet) is not covered with water, it will overheat and fail, resulting in a sudden catastrophic release of pressure. In the 19th century, locomotive boiler explosions were an all too common occurrence. One such horrific accident near Boston was reported in the *New York Tribune*, with the article reprinted in the August 28, 1875, issue of *The Railway Gazette*:

"Freight engine No. 1, standing in the Fitchburgh Railroad freight yard at Charlestown, blew up this afternoon with terrific violence. The engineer and fireman were blown to the top of a car in the rear of the tender, but strangely escaped serious injury. A switchman on the engine was, however, horribly scalded ... The violence of the explosion was so great as to blow a fragment weighing 200lb [91kg] through the wall of the freight house, 20ft [6m] distant. The men inside escaped injury. Rails were torn from the track beside the engine and bent as though made of lead. One rail was carried 15ft [5m] and forced through the wall of the freight depot ... One piece of the boiler, weighing 32lb [15kg], was blown into the air, and fell nearly a quarter of a mile [.4km] from the scene of the explosion, passing through the roof of the St John's Episcopal Church, on the corner of Bow and Richmond streets. The fragment fell into the main aisle, within 3ft [1m] of where a woman was engaged in washing the floor ..."

The incidence of such explosions was greatly reduced with improvements in locomotive design. Boiler failures also became less common with the introduction of stronger materials and more effective safety devices, along with better training of crews.

in the construction of the Bunker Hill Monument. It is somewhat ironic that the country's first railway used British-developed technology to build a monument celebrating American independence.

US engineers were well aware of the early railway successes in England, and organized investigative trips to study technical developments in the field. Railways were a young man's business; early American railway engineers were typically in their 20s and 30s. Horatio Allen, whose talent and expertise were brought to bear on several early US railway projects, was one of these. Allen was employed by the Delaware & Hudson (D&H) Canal Company, which was planning to connect anthracite coal fields in eastern Pennsylvania, near the Delaware River valley, with a port on the Hudson River. Allen

proposed using a railway line to move coal from the mines to the canal, and in 1828 the D&H sent him to Britain to learn about railways and to purchase locomotives and rails. Although little known today, at the time the D&H project was one of the largest industrial undertakings ever attempted and reportedly the first construction scheme to cost $1 million.

In May 1828, Allen returned from England with a supply of iron rails and four locomotives – one from George Stephenson, and three built by Foster, Rastrick & Company (FR & Co) of Stourbridge. Within three months, one of the FR & Co locomotives had been moved by water and land from the port of New York to the D&H's primitive railway line at Honesdale, Pennsylvania. On August 29, 1828, Allen operated the locomotive along the line, entertaining a

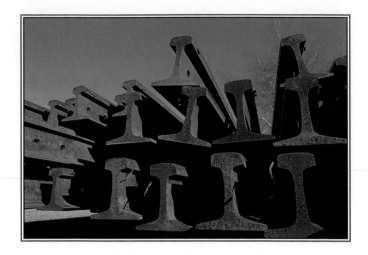

◄ The "T" style iron rail was developed by the Camden & Amboy's Robert Stevens. Its profile and construction was much stronger and more effective than the earlier strap iron rail. Today's rails use the same basic profile but are much heavier and made from steel.

large crowd of people. Named the *Stourbridge Lion* in honor of its place of manufacture, it was the first steam locomotive to run on an American line. This exciting event made history and provided valuable experience to Allen and his assistants, but it was deemed a failure by the D&H. The locomotive, which weighed a mere seven tons, proved damaging to the D&H's light-weight tracks. The combination of a rigid wheelbase and lack of a suspension system made these early British locomotives impractical for daily use on the line. As a result they were never used to haul coal, and three of the four never operated on the D&H at all.

The increasing practicality of steam locomotives soon put an end to public access to railroads

---

The famous *Stourbridge Lion* was displayed for many years before being eventually scrapped.

By the time of the D&H's pioneering steam loco-motive demonstration, several other railway projects had already begun. A number of these were originally conceived along the principles of the toll road, where a right of way would be provided and individuals would supply their own wagons, paying a fee for passage. Animal power was assumed to be the usual mode of transport, but the increasing practicality of steam loco-motives soon put an end to public access to railroads.

New York's competing ports did not sit idle follow-ing the success of the Erie Canal. Baltimore, the third

largest East Coast port in the 1820s, was concerned about its future. In 1826, Evans Thomas of Baltimore visited Britain's Stockton & Darlington Railway. On his return to Baltimore he, his brother Phillip E. Thomas, and other business partners proposed the building of a railway line west from Baltimore across the mountains to the Ohio River. The argument was simple: a railway to the interior would help Baltimore secure its share of inland traffic and enrich the city as well as the state of Maryland. The Baltimore & Ohio (B&O) Railroad was incorporated on February 28,

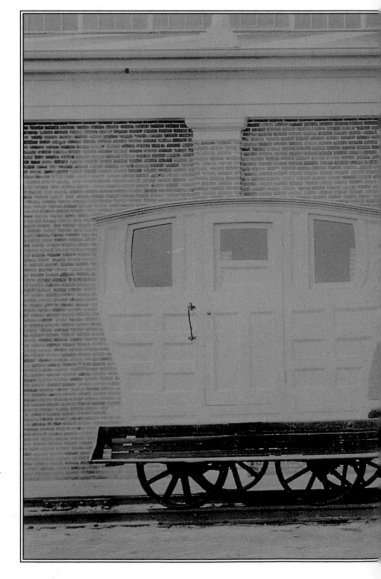

1827, and Phillip E. Thomas was its first president. Construction was initiated with a well-attended ceremony on Independence Day, 1828. Soon afterwards the B&O sent some of its top engineers – William G. McNeill, Ross Winans, and George Washington Whistler – to England to study the latest in railway practice. The B&O opened its line to Ellicott Mills, a few miles to the west, in May 1830. Regular passenger services were initiated in July. A year later the line had reached Frederick, Maryland. Initially, the B&O used horses to haul its trains, and its relay

station, approximately 9 miles (14.5km) from Baltimore, was where tired horse teams were exchanged for fresh ones. The B&O was also among the earliest American lines to investigate steam power.

Like Baltimore, Philadelphia was also looking to improve its westward transportation. It had recently lost its position as the nation's largest city to its rival, New York, and Philadelphians wanted to ensure their city's viability as a port. They sought to create a route across Pennsylvania to the Ohio River. Building an all-canal route across the Allegheny Mountains was deemed impractical and too costly. In 1828, after a few years of debate, the Commonwealth of Pennsylvania decided on a mixed-mode corridor embracing canals, railroads, and inclined planes – known as "portage railroads" – to traverse the Alleghenies and

▼ Early North American railways imported locomotives from Britain. This awkward-looking machine is the *Samson*, built by Timothy Hackworth in 1838 for a mining railway in Nova Scotia. It was one of the first steam locomotives to operate in Canada.

connect the major cities of Philadelphia and Pittsburgh. On these portage railway lines, trains were hauled up and down extremely steep grades using cables powered by large stationary steam engines.

After several years of intensive labor, the Main Line of Public Works entered operation in spring 1834. It was a complex system, following an awkward route that entailed several changes. To begin with, 82 miles (131.2km) of railroad ran west from Philadelphia. At Columbia, Pennsylvania, passengers and freight were transferred to canal boats for a 172-mile (276.8km) journey to Holidaysburg. Here a series of inclined planes carried traffic for 36 miles (58km) over the spine of the mountains to Johnstown, where the canal to Pittsburgh resumed for another 104 miles (167km). Although hailed as a vast improvement over earlier transport across Pennsylvania – and it was – the system faced significant problems. It was closed during the winter when snow and ice clogged the canals, and during dry periods when there was not enough water in the canals to accommodate boats. So, only a few

years after the completion of the first Main Line network, Pennsylvanians were already considering the advantages of a through railroad across the mountains.

FIRST STEAM PASSENGER TRAINS

Like other eastern ports, the city of Charleston, South Carolina, wanted better access to the West. Its solution was to build the South Carolina Railroad across the state to Hamburg (near Augusta, Georgia); this opened in 1830. Like other early lines, the South Carolina Railroad at first relied on horsepower, but Horatio Allen, who left the D&H after his unsuccessful attempt to introduce steam power, went to work for the new railway and found greater success with steam trains there. Allen brought steam power into revenue service on January 15, 1831, using the domestically built locomotive *Best Friend of Charleston*. This made the South Carolina Railroad the first in the country to use steam power on a regular basis for passenger service.

Allen's early steam-powered trains had mixed success. Initially, the first locomotive performed well, and Allen ordered a second from the same manufacturer, the West Point Foundry of New York. However, shortly before the second engine was delivered, the *Best Friend* suffered the country's first

▼ Robert Stevens imported a Stephenson-built locomotive named *John Bull* from England for his pioneering Camden & Amboy. Once in the United States, it was equipped with guiding pilot wheels to improve its tracking ability on lightly built American tracks.

WORKING ON THE RAILROAD
THE WHYTE CLASSIFICATION SYSTEM

North American steam locomotives are identified by the arrangement and number of their wheels, using a system devised by Fredrick M. Whyte and adopted around 1900. Wheels are denoted by their location: leading wheels at the front, followed by driving wheels, and trailing wheels at the rear. Each type of wheel is separated by a dash, and the absence of wheels in a category is indicated by a zero. Each numerical wheel arrangement usually has a common name as well. For example, a Mogul type is a 2-6-0, with two leading wheels, six driving wheels, and no trailing wheels. A Pacific type, or 4-6-2, has four leading wheels, six driving wheels, and two trailing wheels. A few common wheel arrangements, such as the 4-8-4, were assigned more than one name. Normally the 4-8-4 is known as a Northern type, after the Northern Pacific, which was the first to use it. However, some railroads devised their own names; for example, the New York Central called this type the Niagara.

For more complicated types such as tank locomotives, articulateds, and Duplexes, having more than one set of driving wheels and running gear, each set of drivers is counted separately, but the first and last categories are still reserved for leading wheels and trailing wheels respectively. The common Mallet type has two sets of six driving wheels, but no leading or trailing wheels, and thus is designated as an 0-6-6-0. Forney-type tanks, with a rigid frame incorporating both locomotive and tender, are denoted by the letter "T" following the wheel counts, as in the 2-4-4T. In the side views below, the < represents the front of the locomotive, an "o" represents an axle carrying two nonpowered wheels (used at the front for guiding, or at the back for supporting the firebox), and an "O" is a pair of driving wheels.

WHEEL ARRANGEMENT	CLASSIFICATION	WHYTE NAME
<ooOO	4-4-0	American
<oOOo	2-4-2	Columbia
<ooOOo	4-4-2	Atlantic
<oOOO	2-6-0	Mogul
<oOOOo	2-6-2	Prairie
<ooOOO	4-6-0	Ten Wheeler
<ooOOOo	4-6-2	Pacific
<ooOOOoo	4-6-4	Hudson
<oOOOO	2-8-0	Consolidation
<oOOOOo	2-8-2	Mikado
<oOOOOoo	2-8-4	Berkshire
<ooOOOO	4-8-0	Mastodon or Twelve Wheeler
<ooOOOOo	4-8-2	Mountain
<ooOOOOoo	4-8-4	Northern
<oOOOOO	2-10-0	Decapod
<oOOOOOo	2-10-2	Santa Fe
<oOOOOOoo	2-10-4	Texas
<ooOOOOOo	4-10-2	Southern Pacific
<ooOOOOOOo	4-12-2	Union Pacific
<OOO OOO	0-6-6-0	Mallet
<oOOO OOOo	2-6-6-2	Mallet
<oOOO OOOoo	2-6-6-6	Allegheny
<oOOOO OOOOoo	2-8-8-4	Yellowstone
<ooOO OOoo	4-4-4-4	Duplex
<ooOOO OOOoo	4-6-6-4	Challenger
<ooOOOO OOOOoo	4-8-8-4	Big Boy

fatal locomotive boiler explosion. This catastrophe, costing the life of a fireman, was blamed on the ignorance of a railroad employee who was said to have disabled the safety valve. Whatever the cause, the event made the public nervous of this form of transport, and for some time after the South Carolina Railroad was required to operate a buffer car between the locomotive and passenger carriages.

Despite the damage caused by the explosion, the *Best Friend* was rebuilt and returned to service. As passengers overcame their fears, the railroad thrived.

Col John Stevens' writings and demonstrations ultimately led to the opening of a railroad line across New Jersey. While his original charter came to nothing, another line was chartered in 1830, called the Camden & Amboy. This was designed to run from a point on Raritan Bay, across from Manhattan, to Camden, New Jersey, which sat opposite from Philadelphia on the Delaware River. Robert L. Stevens, one of the Colonel's sons, was the line's first president, as well as its chief mechanical officer. Today, one would be astounded at the idea of a top railroad official being seen in the workshops, or drawing up inventions, yet such versatility was common at that time. Robert Stevens personally made a trip to England to procure a Stephenson locomotive. This originally carried Stevens' name, but was later appropriately named *John Bull*, alluding to the mythical character still used to symbolize Britain. Among Stevens' most significant contributions to railroading was the introduction of the "T" style of rail, which was quite different from the typical imported British rail of the day. Early British railways used a heavy cast-iron type of rail, described as a "fish belly" because of its appearance – thicker in the middle than at the ends. Fish belly rails were relatively expensive to manufacture and very costly for American lines to import from Britain. As a result, some early US lines preferred to employ primitive wooden rails with a layer of iron strapping nailed to the head, known as "strap iron rails." These were relatively inexpensive, but not very strong; they were prone to causing accidents and were impractical for use with heavier locomotives. Stevens' all-iron T-rail offered an attractive compromise – rugged, strong, and economical to produce domestically. Today, the T-rail is preferred by railways worldwide, although it is now produced to much heavier standards and is made of steel rather than iron.

While New York State was largely content with its famed Erie Canal, it was also home to one of the earliest railways, the Mohawk & Hudson, a 17-mile (27km) line that connected Albany and Schenectady. This line was built to bypass a particularly circuitous section of the Erie Canal and served to trim a whole

▼ Power is transmitted from the cylinders to the wheels by the crosshead, seen at the far left. This connects to the main rod, which in turn is connected to side rods that link the driving wheels. Steam escapes from a safety valve when the engine is at rest.

▲ Locomotive construction quickly evolved into a big business. For more than a century the Baldwin Locomotive Works was the foremost builder of locomotives in North America. This view of Baldwin's erecting shop dates from 1892.

day off the travel time between New York and Buffalo. The line's chief engineer, John B. Jervis, had worked with Horatio Allen on the D&H and was instrumental in introducing steam power to the Mohawk & Hudson at a very early date.

During their formative periods, the first US railways had essentially three different approaches to acquiring locomotives: some were bought directly from British manufacturers, others were built in the United States from British prototypes, and yet others were made using domestic designs. Each philosophy had its advantages and disadvantages.

By the time American railways started to purchase locomotives, there was already a well-established industry building them in Britain, and several manufacturers, including the Stephensons, could provide engines to proven designs. After the Rainhill Trials of 1829, these early locomotives were based on the design of Robert Stephenson's successful *Rocket*. Among the more popular types of British imports into the United States in the 1830s were the "Planet" and "Samson" types. The Planet employed a single set of guide wheels and a single set of powered "drivers" on a rigid base, while the Samson powered both sets of two wheels, which were coupled together. Using the Whyte system of steam locomotive classification, in which each grouping of wheels – leading, driving, and trailing – is counted in that order, the Planet type featured a 2-2-0 wheel arrangement, and the Samson a 0-4-0 arrangement.

LOCOMOTIVE CLASSIFICATIONS

The Whyte system (p.19) was adopted after 1900 and is generally used in England and North America to describe steam locomotive wheel arrangements. Most standard arrangements were also given specific names in North America, although in several situations they have more than one name. While the Whyte system does take into account multiple groupings of driving wheels, and arrangements such as tank locomotives (where the tender and locomotive form a single unit), it does not account for pivoting wheel sets, or articulation. Other descriptive

21

▲ The *DeWitt Clinton* was the Mohawk & Hudson's first locomotive. It was designed by the railroad's engineer, John B. Jervis, and built in 1831 by the West Point Foundry in New York City, making it among the first engines made in the United States.

terms have specific meanings in locomotive parlance. For example, when driving wheels are discussed, they are often referred to by citing the number coupled together. Thus a "four-coupled locomotive" would describe the 0-4-0 Samson type, but it would also describe the 4-4-0 "American" type. "Inside connected" means that the drive rods, which transfer power from the cylinders to the wheels, are located between the wheels. Inside cylinders are located inside the frame of the locomotive, while outside cylinders are located outside the frame. In the early years of production, most locomotives were inside connected with inside cylinders. While British makers preferred this construction into the early 20th century, from the 1840s US practice was more often to use outside cylinders connected by outside drivers. Valve gear describes the arrangement of links, rods, and eccentrics (off-centre rotating wheels) regulating valve motion, which the locomotive engineer uses to control the direction and power of the locomotive. Like the cylinders and connecting rods, the valve gear may be placed either inside or outside the locomotive. Until after the turn of the century, most American locomotives used inside valve gear, of which the Stephenson-designed valve gear remained the most common type.

The Camden & Amboy's famous *John Bull*, imported in 1831, was in many ways a typical British locomotive of the period. It was built by Robert

order to correct for this deficiency, the railroad's master mechanic, Isaac Dripps, fashioned a set of leading guide wheels along with a pilot at the front end, to help guide the locomotive through curves and minimize the chances of derailment. Many authorities on railway history believe that this was the first such adaptation of a locomotive in the United States. The pilot and leading wheels would become a standard feature of American locomotives, and one of their distinguishing characteristics.

It is generally believed that the Philadelphia watchmaker Matthias Baldwin came to inspect the *John Bull* shortly after its arrival in the United States, and it inspired him to build his own locomotive. Baldwin's famous *Old Ironsides* was clearly an imita-

The pilot and leading wheels would become standard on American locomotives, and one of their distinguishing characteristics

tion of the Stephenson design. Baldwin was soon the leading manufacturer of American locomotives, and while his company improved and developed a variety of different steam locomotive designs over its long and productive history, nearly all of these types are direct descendants of early British examples.

Like the *John Bull*, other British imports often proved inadequate for service on American lines. Their perceived flaws were as much a result of the difference in track construction between Britain and the United States than any real design deficiency. British railways were well financed compared with US lines and as a result were better engineered. The track and right of way were also designed to a much higher standard than in the United States. While British railways enjoyed relatively level profiles, with numerous cuts and fills to even the grade, and fairly gentle curves, early American lines were characterized by relatively light construction and a dearth of complicated engineering. Track was rough, and often featured an undulating profile and sharp curves. British locomotives of the period had a relatively long, inflexible wheelbase and no guide wheels –

Stephenson, who by this time had completed an estimated 50 locomotives, making him one of the most experienced and best-respected locomotive builders of his time. As noted, the *John Bull* had four coupled drivers, which were inside connected with a pair of inside cylinders. The locomotive frame was slightly more than 17ft (5.18m) long, and the engine used a conventional horizontal fire-tube boiler of the type found on many British locomotives. The boiler lagging (outside protective insulation) was made of wooden slats, and there was a low, circular, domed firebox. The driving wheels had wooden spokes and iron-strapped rims, much like wagon wheels of the day.

Shortly after the *John Bull* entered service on the Camden & Amboy, it became clear that it did not track well, losing adhesion and slipping on the rails; this was a common problem with British imports. In

▲ In 1830, Peter Cooper, an aspiring New York businessman, built a small demonstration locomotive to convince the Baltimore & Ohio of the advantages of domestically constructed steam engines. Today we call this machine the *Tom Thumb*.

qualities that made them ill suited for these conditions. They wore track down quickly and performed poorly, suffering frequent derailments. US builders quickly took to modifying British designs by incorporating guide wheels, such as those fitted to the *John Bull* by Isaac Dripps. Within a decade, American-made locomotives had taken on a rather different appearance than their British cousins.

Despite these modifications, most early US locomotives copied the essential engineering of British designs, adapting them with pilot wheels and, later, distinctive trappings such as headlights, bells, and ornate wooden cabs. Nearly all successful American steam locomotives are descendants of Robert Stephenson's 1829 *Rocket*. They employ a fire-tube boiler, use a forced draft from exhaust steam, and feature a pair of double-acting reciprocating cylinders placed at the front of the locomotive. These

cylinders power one or more sets of driving wheels with a direct connection in the form of drive rods, rather than complex links involving gears and levers.

In these fledgling years, some railway lines preferred British imports, because they believed that American machine shops had neither the ingenuity nor the machinery to build an effective locomotive. It was thought that, without British engineering talent, such an achievement would not be feasible in the United States. This theory was quickly proved invalid as American manufacturers readily demonstrated their proficiency in locomotive construction.

Not all builders in the United States based their locomotives solely on British-inspired technology, however. There were a few early homegrown locomotive designs that developed independently. South Carolina Railroad's *Best Friend*, built by the West Point Foundry, was one example, and the company went on to build a number of locomotives based on the designs and specifications of American engineers. Unlike the vertical-boilered *Best Friend*, later West Point products used horizontal boilers. Among the most unusual locomotives of this period was a double-ended locomotive built for the South Carolina Railroad in 1831. Designed by Horatio Allen, this unique machine was named *South Carolina*. It was the world's first articulated locomotive – essentially two locomotives sharing a common firebox. Like so many early innovations, the *South Carolina* was novel but impractical and saw little real service.

EARLY EXPERIMENTATION

Perhaps the most intriguing and lasting example of early American locomotive ingenuity was a series of engines designed for the Baltimore & Ohio Railroad. Although the company had expressed serious interest in locomotive operation from its earliest days, it began service with horses. Like other early lines, it had purchased a British import, but this unfortunate locomotive sank while being transported to the United States. Its next experience with steam was the work of New York inventor and businessman Peter Cooper, who in 1830 demonstrated a small one-ton vertical-boiler locomotive on the B&O. Today this pioneering locomotive is known by the nickname *Tom Thumb*, although it did not initially carry this title. Cooper anticipated building a small fleet of engines for service on the B&O, but instead ended up passing on his ideas to Phineas Davis.

Inspired by Cooper's success and the historic Rainhill Trials in Britain, the Baltimore & Ohio staged a similar competition, but specified that locomotives must embrace American technology. The winning machine, named the *York*, was largely the work of Phineas Davis. At the B&O's prompting, Davis improved upon the vertical-boiler locomotive design with the help of the railroad's assistant master of machinery, Ross Winans, and built another machine called the *Atlantic*. This contraption is described in detail by locomotive chronicler Angus Sinclair in his 1907 treatise on the history of steam locomotives. Davis' unusual design featured a vertical boiler with a fan driven by exhaust steam to promote combustion. A pair of vertical cylinders transmitted power to the driving wheels using spur-and-pinion driving shafts connected to gears. All wheels were powered, so the full weight of the locomotive aided in traction. The *Atlantic*'s vertical cylinder motion and connecting shafts resembled the legs of a common grasshopper, giving this new type its name.

Although unusual, the "Grasshopper" was a sound design. Its short wheelbase, relatively small driving wheels (just 3ft, or 1m, in diameter), and good traction made it ideally suited for the B&O's fairly primitive track structure. Although later displaced from mainline service by more advanced designs, some of the railroad's Grasshoppers remained in service right up to the early 1890s, working in yards and shops, and on lines with tight curves not easily served by locomotives with longer wheelbases. Their 60-year service life is enviable by any standard and a lasting credit to their builders.

Davis made a number of Grasshoppers for the B&O. In 1833, the Baltimore & Ohio was the first American railroad to open company locomotive shops, and many Grasshoppers were constructed there. After Davis was killed during a trial run of a Grasshopper, Ross Winans took over his locomotive business. For the next 25 years, Winans refined and expanded upon Davis' and Cooper's ideas, developing a distinctive line of US locomotives.

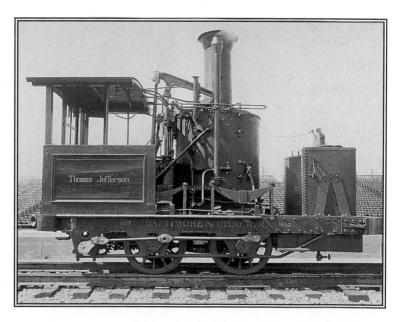

▶ Peter Cooper's designs led the B&O to build a fleet of Grasshopper locomotives. Unlike most locomotives based on British designs, these engines, featuring vertical boilers, were largely the product of American ingenuity.

2

THE RAILWAYS EXPAND

The early railroad networks grew rapidly, becoming catalysts for westward settlements and the growth of urban centers. New and more powerful locomotives were developed, along with passenger innovations such as sleeping and dining cars.

The enormous success of the first railways led to a building boom during the mid–1830s, when existing systems were lengthened and many new lines chartered. The pioneering Baltimore & Ohio reached the Potomac River at Harper's Ferry, Virginia, in 1834, and by 1850 it extended to Cumberland, Maryland, where its westward progress

◄ **The power of the locomotive quickly captured the imagination of Americans, who embraced its power to settle and develop the nation. Johnny Krause photographed this Maine Central locomotive as it rolled along near Pittsfield, Maine.**

was temporarily halted by the formidable physical barrier of the Allegheny Mountains. Soon, however, a line was built up and over the mountains, climbing a continuous 17-mile (27.3km) grade to the summit at Altamont, Maryland. This was among the steepest westbound grades built by that time, and an even steeper grade was located eastbound on the same line. The Cranberry Grade, between Rowlesburg and Terra Alta, would gain a reputation as one of the toughest climbs in the eastern United States and a proving ground for locomotives. Many new steam locomotives were put through their paces there, and

▲ Early railway cars were adaptations of traditional horse-drawn carriages. In Britain, railway cars are still known as carriages. This car, displayed at the B&O Museum in Baltimore, Maryland, is a replica of one used by the railroad in the 1830s.

of New York. By 1835 the Boston & Worcester had connected its namesake cities, using a fairly straight and level route. Worcester was the jumping-off point for the Western. There was considerable skepticism at the time that a railroad could be operated across such rough terrain. The modern observer can view the gently rolling Berkshire Hills and wonder what the controversy was about. Yet these hills presented a powerful obstacle to early railroad builders. Nearly all adhesion railroads (as opposed to inclined planes) had followed a near water level profile, avoiding any steep grades. Many engineers in Britain and the United States were ignorant of the laws of physics, especially friction, and did not believe that a locomotive could climb a grade, thinking erroneously that wheels of iron on iron tracks would lose traction and slip when trying to ascend any serious grade. Some early British locomotives were built with gears to mesh with a central cog rack, instead of relying on natural adhesion. Some of the earliest American lines crossed mountains using steeply graded inclined planes, or portage railways (p.14), such as those incorporated into Pennsylvania's Main Line of Public Works. On these lines, trains were hauled up and down using cables powered by large stationary steam engines.

The Western hired George Washington Whistler, one of the foremost railway engineers of his day, to survey the Massachusetts line. He had worked on a number of early railways, including the B&O, and concluded that an adhesion railway was feasible. He laid out a line following the west branch of the Westfield River, ascending the Berkshires, and crossing the summit near the present town of Washington, Massachusetts. Unlike some early railroads built to inferior specifications, Whistler's Western represented state-of-the-art engineering for the time. The line

even today new diesels are frequently assigned to the "West End" for trials.

However, true mountain railroading had been around for a decade by the time the B&O conquered the Alleghenies. The world's first railway to use an adhesion grade to cross a mountain range was the Western Railroad of Massachusetts. In the 1830s Boston, concerned that its port was losing business, looked for a transport link with the Erie Canal near Albany to attract some of the traffic moving west out

was designed to accommodate two main tracks, in preparation for the eventuality of double track operation. He designed massive stone bridges to carry the tracks over the Westfield River, which the Western crossed many times, and blasted deep rock cuts to keep the grade as even as possible. The line was open to traffic all the way to Albany in 1841. Considering the relatively primitive construction methods employed, it is impressive how quickly the work was completed. Most of Whistler's original line has remained in service to the present day, more than 160 years after it was built. Several examples of his stone-arched bridges still stand.

The speed of railroad building in the United States reached fever pitch in the 1840s and 1850s as thousands of rail miles were laid down. By 1850 there were some 9,000 railway route miles (14,483km), and by

▼ The maps below show the enormous growth of US railway network in just one decade, from 1850 to 1860. American railroad building stressed east-west routes and effectively altered the flow of traffic from a more traditional north-south pattern.

1860 this figure had more than tripled. These early lines soon began coalescing into systems, and railroad networks developed by connecting smaller lines together. By the early 1850s some lines were several hundred miles long. The four most significant routes to develop were the eastern trunk lines, major east-west corridors that connected principal eastern cities with interior points. The trunk lines were the Baltimore & Ohio, the Pennsylvania Railroad, the Erie, and the New York Central. Between the 1850s and 1880s, a Canadian system called the Grand Trunk was assembled and established links with the US rail network.

EXPANSION TO THE WEST

Having reached Cumberland in 1842, the B&O kept building westward, reaching its chartered destination of Wheeling, Virginia (later West Virginia), in June, 1852. Both of these points were significant terminals and established traffic corridors. The former connected the B&O with the National Road, while the latter gave the B&O access to the Ohio River. Within just a few years of reaching the Ohio, the

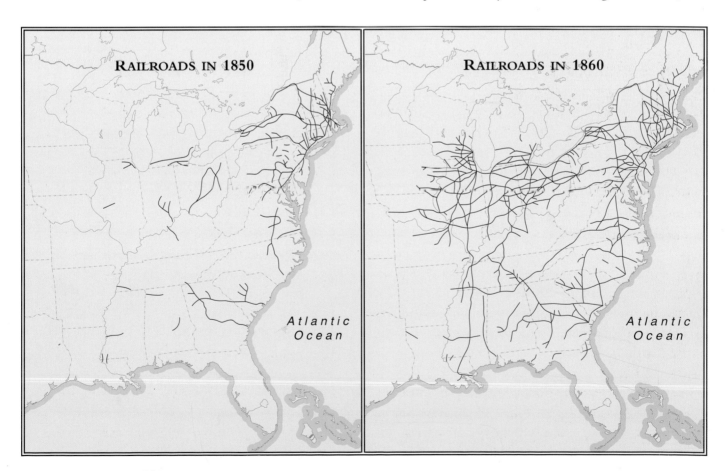

RAILROADS IN 1850

Atlantic Ocean

RAILROADS IN 1860

Atlantic Ocean

B&O had completed an all-rail route to St Louis, Missouri, on the Mississippi River.

The B&O had considered building through Pennsylvania to reach the Ohio at Pittsburgh but was refused a charter. Pennsylvania had its own railroad ambitions, and in 1846 the Pennsylvania Railroad (PRR) was created to construct an all-rail route westward across the state to replace the original awkward arrangement of railroads, canals, and portage railways. Unlike other lines chiefly run by entrepreneurs, the PRR was built and run by engineers. The company's chief engineer and first president was John Edgar Thompson. This talented man surveyed the railroad's route over the Alleghenies and planned the famous Horseshoe Curve west of Altoona, Pennsylvania, as a

Early railroad infrastructure demonstrates man's power over nature and the impressive capabilities of engineering in the 1840s

means of gaining elevation while maintaining a steady grade. Under Thompson's sound guidance, the PRR completed its mainline across the state, connecting Philadelphia and Pittsburgh, and assembled and built a large number of lines that brought the PRR to a variety of cities across the mid-Atlantic and mid-western states. With its connections the PRR reached St Louis in 1856 and Chicago in 1858. Although the PRR was a latecomer to railroading, it rapidly developed as one of the most powerful American railroad enterprises and became among the most influential companies in the world.

The New York & Lake Erie Railway began in 1832. This line, often known simply as "the Erie," was planned as a route connecting New York City and Lake Erie by way of the sparsely populated southern area of New York State. The Erie was unusual because it was built to a markedly different standard than

other lines. It used a 6ft (1.8m) track gauge, significantly wider than the Stephenson Standard gauge used by many early lines, and enjoyed a much larger loading gauge than many railroads. The Erie's magnificent structures are symbolic of its large-scale approach to railroading. The great Starrucca Viaduct

▶ The Baltimore & Ohio built west to the Ohio River at Wheeling, Virginia (later West Virginia), crossing the Alleghenies on a series of difficult grades. Here, a heavy B&O coal train ascends the Cranberry Grade, at Salt Lick Curve near Terra Alta, West Virginia.

at Lanesboro, Pennsylvania (a few miles east of Bing-hamton, New York), is a classic tall, stone-built arched bridge that spans an entire valley. Like so much of the early railroad infrastructure, this majestic viaduct demonstrates man's power over nature and reflects the impressive capabilities of engineering in the

1840s. At the time, the Erie's broad-gauge locomotives were considered gigantic compared with the types used on many standard-gauge lines, but today even the Erie's locomotives would seem small.

In 1851 the Erie reached the Lake Erie port of Dunkirk, its first western terminus. The railroad built

TRAVELERS' TALES
AN EARLY RIDE ON WHISTLER'S WESTERN

In the late 1830s, Englishman George Combe made a detailed diary of his experiences on several railway journeys in the United States. He had the privilege to ride George Washington Whistler's Western Railroad of Massachusetts shortly after a portion of that line opened for traffic, and his account of this journey was published in *Notes on the United States of North America during a Phrenological Visit in 1838–40.* Combe's writings were reprinted in August Mencken's railway treatise *The Railroad Passenger Car:* "On October 29 [1839] we left Springfield and started for Worcester by the railroad, which has been opened since we traveled to Springfield a month ago. Yesterday a stray horse had its legs and head cut off on this railroad by the engine, and the night before a carter had left a cart with stones standing on the track, which a train loaded with merchandise had run into in the dark and been smashed to pieces. We hoped to be more fortunate and were so; but although we encountered no danger, our patience was sufficiently tried. About 10 miles [16km] from Springfield we came to a dead stop and the whole train stood motionless for three hours, enlivened only by occasional walks in the sunshine and visits to a cake store, the whole stock of eatables in which was in time consumed, the price of them having risen from hour to hour in proportion to the demand.

"The cause of our detention was the non-arrival of the train from Worcester, which, from there being a single track of rails, could pass our train here and nowhere else. We heard nothing of its fate and expected it to arrive every minute till four o'clock, when at last an express on horseback came up and announced that it had broken down but that it was now cleared off the rails and that we might advance. Again I admire the patience and good humor of the American passengers which never forsook them in all this tedious detention.

This 1886 engraving titled "The Modern Ship of the Plains" attempts to portray the experience of traveling aboard a long-distance train. In reality, early railway cars were far more cramped than illustrated here, but just as spartan.

"At 6:00 p.m. we arrived at Worcester, but here found ourselves in another fix. The afternoon train from Boston does not arrive until 7:00 p.m. and we could not proceed to the city until it appeared. It was now dark, and for another hour and a half the passengers sat with exemplary patience in the cars. At half past seven we started again and arrived in Boston about 10 o'clock, with pretty good appetites, as we had breakfasted at half past seven in the morning and been allowed no meal since that hour. The car was seated for 56 passengers and contained at least 30. There was no aperture for ventilation and when night came on, the company insisted on shutting every window to keep out the cold. A few who, like us, preferred cool air to suffocation congregated at one end where we opened two windows for our relief."

So ends Combe's account of a most frustrating journey. Thankfully, delays such as those he experienced were largely eliminated by the advent of the telegraph, which aided in the dispatching of trains. The construction of a second track, and eventually the installation of line-side signals, also significantly improved railway operations.

▲ A mile east of Middlefield, Massachusetts, a Boston & Albany train climbs westward through the Berkshires along the banks of the Westfield River. This was George W. Whistler's Western Railroad of Massachusetts, the first true mountain railroad.

a multitude of branch lines and secondary main routes to reach a variety of traffic sources, and eventually extended its mainline all the way to Chicago. Nevertheless, it was always the weakest of the trunk lines, since its main route served primarily rural areas, bypassing most of the largest cities along the way.

The first New York Central Railroad was put together by Erastus Corning in 1853 by combining a

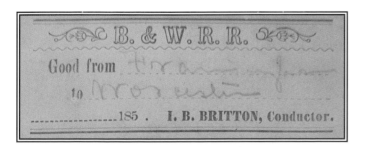

▲ A ticket issued by the Boston & Worcester Railroad. The Boston & Worcester merged with the Western Railroad of Massachusetts in 1867 to form the Boston & Albany. In 1900, the Boston & Albany was leased by the New York Central.

chain of 10 short railroads that connected end to end between Albany and Buffalo. The earliest and easternmost of these lines was New York's pioneering line, the Mohawk & Hudson. The original New York Central route competed directly with the Erie Canal. In 1867 Cornelius Vanderbilt, a successful businessman who had built his fortune in the steamboat trade and had recently branched out into the railroad business, seized control of the New York Central. Two years later he combined it with two other lines under his control, the New York & Hudson River Railroad and the New York & Harlem. The line was efficiently operated using spartan-looking locomotives known colloquially as "Black Crooks," and the railroad generated handsome profits. Vanderbilt was one of the first of a new breed of businessmen, the railroad

▲ The Western Railroad of Massachusetts ascended the east slope of Washington Mountain by following the west branch of the Westfield River, which it crossed many times on magnificent stone arched bridges such as this one near Middlefield.

tycoon – a type characterized by ruthless business practices, empire building, and the accumulation of a huge personal fortune.

In just a decade Vanderbilt had pieced together his railroad empire by buying, building, and leasing other lines. Before he died in 1877, the New York Central operated two routes to Chicago. One was the Michigan Central, which ran through Detroit and southwestern Ontario, Canada. The other was the Lake Shore route, which skirted the southern shores of Lake Erie in Ohio and Indiana. Blessed with a very low-grade profile, which reduced construction and operation costs significantly, the New York Central was known popularly as the Water Level Route. Apart from its favorable geography, the

New York Central had a second advantage over the other trunk lines. It passed through many important, established cities on its way west. Albany, Schenectady, Utica, Syracuse, Rochester, and Buffalo were all served directly by the New York Central. This made it an ideal passenger and freight carrier. Ultimately, like the PRR, the New York Central became one of America's greatest railroads. It remained under the control of the Vanderbilts long after the death of founder Cornelius, and the railroad became a symbol of the family's wealth and power. At its height, very few railway companies were more powerful than the New York Central.

The creation of trunk lines that linked east and west fundamentally changed the way freight and

► One of the most famous railroad bridges in the United States is the Erie Railroad's spectacular Starrucca Viaduct in Pennsylvania. Built in the 1840s, today it still handles heavy freight, such as this Conrail "double stack" intermodal container train.

▲ The engine type known as the 4-4-0 American (featuring four guiding wheels, four driving wheels, and no trailing wheels) was the most common and most versatile locomotive in North America during the 19th century.

passengers moved across the country. Importantly, the railroads encouraged travel and settlement, thus creating their own market. The ability to move people and goods over land relatively cheaply and quickly stimulated industrial development and fueled the economic growth of every area that the railroad served. A trip that would have taken days on horseback could now be accomplished in a few hours. Waterborne traffic – which preceded and competed with the railroads – was seasonal: canals and rivers typically froze in the winter and suffered from dry spells in the summer. Railroads, in contrast, could operate year round. For the passenger, improved transportation altered travel patterns, by making the distances effectively shorter, and ultimately reducing

the bulk of commerce flowed north and south. Even traffic to the interior moved this way, along the Mississippi and Ohio Rivers. Railroads shifted this north-south flow to an east-west pattern that has held ever since. While a few major railroads such as the Illinois Central were built on a north-south axis, most lines reached westward toward the American frontier.

Before the railroads arrived, most major settlements were dependent on water transportation, and

A trip that in 1820 would have taken days by stagecoach could by the 1880s be accomplished in just a few hours

as a result most traditional settlements were based around ports. The vast majority of the American population lived little more than one day's journey on foot from the Atlantic coastline, and the few cities that were further inland (such as Albany, New York) typically had excellent water transportation. Transportation was the key to prosperity; farmers shipped their harvests to market, industry sold its products, and the military moved troops and munitions. With the development of practical railroad transport to the vast fertile lands west of the Appalachians, people

▼ Railroad freight enabled heavy industry to develop throughout the United States. Here, a 2-8-0 Consolidation No. 98 engine belonging to the New York & New England Railroad leads a typical freight train.

the cost of travel. People were now able to travel over much greater distances and more frequently than before. In 1820 a trip from New York to Boston would have taken five days by stagecoach. By the 1850s the same trip took less than a day, while by the 1880s it could be achieved in only a few hours. Today, this is comparable to the difference between driving from New York to San Francisco and flying. Before the advent of the railroad, most transport followed the eastern seaboard or inland waterways. As a result

could suddenly earn a comfortable living many miles from the ocean and major rivers. Consequently, a mass migration westward began during the 1840s and 1850s. While the American frontier had attracted settlers for decades, the railroads helped open up what was then known as the "Northwest," now called the Midwest – the states of Ohio, Indiana, Illinois, Michigan, and Wisconsin. This area was the scene of intensive railroad building in the decade prior to the American Civil War. A complex of branch lines serving as feeders to the various trunk routes radiated across the flatlands of the Midwest. Little towns sprung up everywhere. Never had so much land been settled so quickly. Many people

Whole cities developed in a few short years where previously only a few European settlers or native tribes had lived

abandoned their traditional homes in New England and New York to make a better life for themselves farming the fertile valleys of Ohio. Why try to eke out an existence tilling the rocky hills of Vermont when all of the lush, level land of Indiana and Illinois beckoned? Immigrants from Ireland, Scandinavia, Germany, and other European countries also headed west from the port cities of the East and soon began to swell the numbers of newcomers.

Whole cities developed in a few short years where previously little more than a few European settlers or migratory native tribes had lived. For example, Chicago, a village founded in 1803 and incorporated in 1837, did not boom until after its establishment as a railroad center. Its strategic position at the bottom of Lake Michigan made it a natural jumping-off point for further travel westward. By the 1850s it had become the western terminus of choice for the big eastern railways. It was

▶ Wilson Eddy of the Boston & Albany designed and built some of the most distinctive American-type locomotives, known as "Eddy Clocks" for their precision performance. This is the *Mamoras*, in front of a B&A roundhouse at Worcester, Massachusetts.

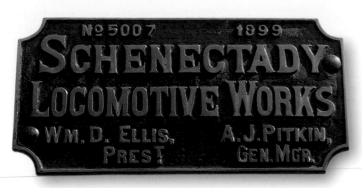

▲ Locomotive manufacturers attached distinctive metal builders plates that included the date of construction. The Schenectady Locomotive Works, one of the foremost makers, later became part of the American Locomotive Company.

specialized skills to service them. Rolling stock – passenger and freight cars – also needed attention. In the earliest days railroad shops were small, modest facilities because the first railways had only a few locomotives and a handful of cars. Some maintenance was done outdoors or in small sheds. As railroad traffic swelled, companies needed more locomotives, more cars, bigger yards, and more extensive shops. In the 19th century, locomotives usually traveled about 100 miles (161km) a day. Many lines assigned operating crews their own locomotives, and crews would usually run just over one division – an established

the place where East met West, a position it has held ever since. By 1860, nearly a dozen different lines converged on Chicago. As railroad traffic grew, Chicago became the site for numerous switching yards, shops, and passenger terminals, in addition to being one of the primary grain shipping points for farmers, and the site of the largest stockyards in the country. Every year hundreds of thousands of range animals from all over the far West were shipped by rail to the Chicago stockyards, where they were slaughtered and packaged for consumption in the big eastern cities. As Chicago grew, tracks radiated out in every direction and the city became known as the railroad capital of the United States. It is still the most heavily used railroad terminal city in North America. At one time, Chicago was typified by its ever present, telltale smoke, the sound of a switch engine, and box cars seen moving from yard to yard; there was always a train departing, or another rolling in from some faraway place. In the heyday of the passenger train, one could ride from Chicago to almost any major city in North America without changing trains. Other railroad hubs developed, too: For example, Buffalo, New York, became the terminus of many eastern lines and a major grain terminal, and Niagara Falls formed a primary interchange with Canada.

Many smaller cities and towns grew as railroad centers. Steam locomotives required lots of routine maintenance and needed small armies of men with

length of line between two major stations. These stations, where locomotives and their crews were exchanged, were known as "division points." Here railroads located their shops, yards, passenger terminals, offices, and other major facilities. In the early years these may have been situated in a large city, but as more extensive facilities were required, needing more land, railroads often located them away from established population centers.

The sites that were selected for major railroad facilities quickly became large towns, even if nothing had existed there before. The base of a steep grade was a favorite place for shops and yards. Most lines assigned different types of locomotives for graded territory than for level routes. Graded lines required powerful locomotives with high tractive effort and small wheels. Level lines needed faster, lighter locomotives that featured taller driving wheels, designed for speed and lower fuel consumption.

▼ Maine Central No. 147 was typical of later-built 4-4-0 American types. The colorful, ornate trappings that characterized earlier machines have given way to a more utilitarian style, yet the locomotive retains a classic, handsome, and well-balanced look.

The Western Railroad of Massachusetts located its shops and yards at West Springfield on broad, level ground directly across from the long-established city of Springfield. The steepest grades were to the west, and 25 miles (40.2km) down the tracks was Chester, which sat right at the foot of the steepest part of the grade. This was the location of a helper base, where extra locomotives were kept to help heavy freight and passenger trains over the mountains. A small shop and roundhouse were needed for storage and maintenance, as well as fueling facilities to keep the locomotives ready. On the B&O, shops and yards were located at Baltimore, at Brunswick, Maryland (near Harpers Ferry), and at the foot of its Allegheny grades in Cumberland. The Pennsylvania Railroad's most important shops and yards were located at the base of its Allegheny grade at Altoona.

Shop towns were guaranteed high employment and relative prosperity when the railroad was doing well. As a result there was fierce competition between rival communities to be selected as the site of major facilities. Important junctions were also prime spots for yards. Looking at a population map of the United States today, one can still easily tell where railroad junctions and shops once sat. Especially in the West, population closely followed the railroad. This is one of the major differences between railroads in the United States and Canada, and those in Europe. In North America, with the exception of a few long-established cities on the eastern seaboard, the railroads distributed the population and often created the towns they served. European railroads, on the other hand, were built to connect existing population centers.

AMERICAN BUILDERS

The market for locomotives expanded as the railroads grew, and by the 1850s a host of locomotive builders had entered the business. Although Philadelphia-based Baldwin was the most prolific and most familiar producer, it was by no means the only significant one. Thomas Rogers of Paterson, New Jersey, founded the Rogers Locomotive and Machine Works in 1835. Richard Norris and Sons was another Philadelphia-based manufacturer that

◄ The *Thatcher Perkins* was built by the Baltimore & Ohio at its Mount Clare shops in 1863. With all the resplendent trappings of a locomotive from that period, it is now a prized display at the B&O Museum in Baltimore, Maryland.

▲ The *William Crooks* epitomizes the Victorian-era American-type steam locomotive. It features a large "balloon" smoke stack, a broad wooden "cow catcher," a highly polished boiler plate, ornate ironwork, and a large headlight.

began building locomotives about 1845. Norris was in the business for only a few decades, yet made a great number of locomotives in that short time. New England, one of the country's first heavily industrialized areas and the location of many early lines, was home to numerous skilled locomotive builders. One of the earliest was the Locks and Canal Company of Lowell, Massachusetts, later known as the Lowell Machine Company. This firm was making locomotives in the 1830s. Other well-respected New England makers included the Hinkley Locomotive Company of Boston, the Mason Machine Works of Taunton, Massachusetts, and the Manchester Locomotive Works of Manchester, New Hampshire. Locomotives built in New England were characterized by conservative, but high quality designs and reliability.

Locomotive manufacturers often situated their plants near major railroad terminals, and sometimes near each other, too. For example, as well as Rogers, there were two other significant makers in Paterson, New Jersey: the Cooke Locomotive and Machine Company, and the Grant Locomotive Works. Brooks Locomotive arrived on the scene after the Civil War, setting up shop at the Erie's original western terminus city of Dunkirk, New York. Brooks was known for its many fine locomotives. Another prolific producer was the Schenectady Locomotive Works, which supplied engines for the New York Central and many other lines.

There were a few Canadian locomotive manufacturers that primarily supplied Canadian lines. One of the first was the Canadian Locomotive Company of Kingston, Ontario. Founded in 1850, it built thousands of steam locomotives over the course of a century.

From the start, locomotive types were designated by wheel arrangement, and were not exclusive to or necessarily characteristic of an individual builder (although in the earlier years some builders preferred and promoted certain arrangements over others). It was the style and performance that characterized the different builders. Some makers were noted for high

▲ Locomotives were greatly admired for their power and speed. As state-of-the-art machines, they were treated with respect and lovingly tended by their crews. Most were highly decorated and beautifully maintained.

quality and innovation, others for reliability and distinctive designs. Because locomotive manufacturing did not require any specialized machinery in the early days, any heavy machine shop could build a locomotive, and many did. Numerous small builders around the country made locomotives.

During the 19th century, many railroads built their own locomotives at company shops, and some of the most innovative designs were the work of railroad master mechanics. While a few of the large builders offered standard types, it was a more common practice for the railroads to work with the builders in adapting a locomotive design. As a result, motive power usually was custom-built to fit a specific railroad's needs, rather than fulfilling the existing design parameters of the locomotive builder.

Regardless of manufacturer, an individual railroad's locomotive fleet would typically display common characteristics specific to that line, such as a style of cab construction, a boiler type, or certain valve gear. Some lines tended to make regular purchases from one builder, while others regularly sampled locomotives from a variety of different producers.

North American locomotive building practice was typified by a conservative approach that favored simplicity and economy. While there was much experimentation, large-scale innovation was slow, and once a successful design was settled upon, railroads were inclined to stay with it, even when the prospect of newer, better technology offered increased productivity or performance. There was some of the "if it ain't broken, don't fix it" mentality, and complex machinery and complicated gadgetry were largely avoided in favor of basic designs.

American lines were at first characterized by lightly built tracks, with hill-and-dale profiles featuring steep grades, sharp curves, and few cuts and fills. In the early years, locomotives needed to be flexible yet powerful, but not particularly fast. For ease of maintenance, locomotives with outside cylinders and outside-connected rods were favored over earlier inside-cylinder and inside-connected types, as in Britain. There were a few exceptions to this, and some lines continued with inside-connected locomotives until the mid-1850s.

One of the first popular wheel arrangements of an American design was the 4-2-0. This was the work of John B. Jervis, who produced the design for his Mohawk & Hudson line after encountering difficulties with British imports. With a four-wheel guiding truck, this locomotive provided the flexibility needed to negotiate American tracks. However, its single set of drivers did not give the type sufficient power, and it soon fell out of favor.

THE "AMERICAN" TYPE

The preferred locomotive wheel arrangement of the 19th century, and perhaps the most commonly used design of all time, was the 4-4-0, known as the "American Standard" type. H. R. Campbell (affiliated with the Baldwin company) first built the type in 1836, but the innovation that made the 4-4-0 a real success was the adaptation of its suspension system a couple of years later by Philadelphia builder Eastwick & Harrison, which introduced an equalizing beam on the drive wheels. This gave the locomotive three-point suspension, allowing it the flexibility to negotiate rough track with ease. By using an additional set of drivers, the 4-4-0 developed significantly more power than the 4-2-0 while retaining the benefit of the leading truck. The combination of a flexible wheelbase and the high tractive effort made this locomotive a real winner. However, it took a few years to catch on, and the 4-4-0 American did not become a dominant type until

the 1840s. By the 1850s it was the most numerous form, and would remain so for several decades.

The 4-4-0 was well suited to all types of traffic, and many locomotives were assigned both freight and passenger runs. Some lines had a tendency to specialize their fleets, and 4-4-0s with low drivers would work freight, where smaller wheels were

▼ The Baltimore & Ohio's *Memnon*, built in 1848, features an 0-8-0 wheel arrangement for heavy freight service. The locomotive places all of its weight on the drivers for greater adhesion, but lacks guide wheels and therefore cannot travel very fast.

▲ The 2-6-0 Mogul type was considered a large, powerful loco-motive when it was developed in the 1860s. Yet this example, built by Baldwin in 1875, is dwarfed by a much later machine behind it. Locomotives were growing to meet new demands.

better suited for moving heavy tonnage. High-driver 4-4-0s were given passenger assignments where they could sprint along at speed on the mainline. More than 120 years after the type was invented, some were still in regular use. Three examples on the Canadian Pacific worked on light lines in Quebec and New Brunswick until the early 1960s.

The early 4-4-0s retained the characteristics of the more primitive machines they replaced. They had short boilers, low drivers, and narrowly spaced leading wheels, and lacked superficial trappings such as cabs and bells. They were tiny compared with later locomotives, weighing a mere 12–15 tons (24,000–30,000lb, or 10,886–13,608kg). By the 1850s the 4-4-0 was refined into the handsome, well-

were intended to be more than just utilitarian motive power – they were designed as things of beauty. The boiler plate would be made of highly polished iron, cabs of glossy, varnished hardwood, while driving wheels were colorfully and intricately painted. Bells, whistles, and other items were of brass, polished to a high sheen. Painted murals adorned tenders, cabs, and the sides of headlights. Many railroads named their locomotives as well as numbering them for identification.

Crews were often assigned to a specific locomotive, and were expected to look after it. The culture of the railroad fostered this attitude: a locomotive engineer was the man with the power of steam in his hand; his engine was a symbol of power and its upkeep was his personal pride. Before leaving on his run, he made sure that his locomotive was in top working order and that it was clean and looking

▼ This curious-looking 4-6-0 locomotive was built by the B&O for heavy freight service, using an early "Camelback" design, where the locomotive engineer rode astride the boiler while the fireman stood on a platform behind.

proportioned locomotive for which this wheel arrangement is most famous. Cylinders were brought down to a level plane, and centered over the leading truck. The boilers were lengthened, and cabs, headlights, bells, and decorative trimming added. By this time the average weight of the locomotive had doubled; 4-4-0s often weighed 25 tons (25,400kg).

The classic American Standard was a Victorian-era machine that exhibited all the ornate decoration and charm associated with the period. Locomotives

▲ The logical extension of the 2-6-0 was the development of the 2-8-0 Consolidation. This type, featuring eight driving wheels, offered improved power yet retained good tracking ability, and became widely used for freight service by the late 19th century.

sharp. The most handsome locomotives were those reserved for special service, such as for company directors. Passenger locomotives were kept in particularly good trim, but even lowly switch engines received their share of attention.

Many railroads ordered specialized locomotives using a variety of different wheel arrangements. The 4-4-0 was excellent for general purposes, but it was not always the ideal choice. Mountain lines in particular were perpetually in need of engines with greater

pulling power. In this regard, famed railroad chronicler Angus Sinclair wrote: "M. W. Baldwin had been building locomotives only five or six years when he began to be impressed with the necessity for securing greater adhesion to meet the growing demand for more powerful locomotives." Baldwin went on to build high tractive-effort types, including comparatively big engines using a "flexible beam" design.

The pioneering mountain line, the Western Railroad of Massachusetts, ordered some of the world's first 0-8-0s – heavy locomotives with small wheels that placed the entire weight of the engine on the drivers. This gave the new machines great adhesion. Western's 0-8-0s employed an unusual design by Ross Winans, who had close links with Whistler,

having worked with him on the B&O. These machines featured a vertical boiler and a geared drive and had evolved from the very early Grasshopper types used on the B&O. They were known as "Mud Diggers" because of their propensity to stir up the dirt and rocks between the ties. While not particularly successful, the Mud Diggers led Winans to build a more practical, high tractive-effort locomotive. This design, another 0-8-0, was descriptively called a "Camel" for its awkward, hump-backed appearance.

► The Civil War was one of the first major conflicts where the railroad played a significant role in the movement of troops and munitions. This period etching depicts Civil War troops and an American type locomotive. Note the men riding atop the car.

In the years leading up to the Civil War, Winans sold a number of his Camels for eastern mountain service. The natural extension of the 4-4-0 type was the 4-6-0,

◄ The Western & Atlantic's *General* was the Confederate-held locomotive famously captured by Union raiders during the Civil War. It is a typical 4-4-0 American type locomotive of the day, and a classic example of Victorian engineering and aesthetics.

which essentially added another set of drivers to the wheel arrangement. With these extra drivers and a correspondingly larger boiler, the 4-6-0 could generate 25–30 percent more power than a typical 4-4-0. This type was originally intended as a heavy freight locomotive and was invariably assigned to routes with steep grades. These mountain-climbing "Ten Wheelers" were awe-inspiring because of their sheer size, compared with the typical 4-4-0 of the period. Like other "big" early locomotives, they seem pretty small today. In later years, the Ten Wheeler was developed as a dual-service locomotive, and some were even built for express passenger use.

In the early 1860s, another "big" locomotive type emerged – the 2-6-0. This new type used a recently developed two-wheel guide truck, known as "Pony

Mountain-climbing "Ten Wheelers" were awe-inspiring because of their sheer size, compared with the typical 4-4-0

wheels" or a "Pony truck," and had the advantage of bearing more weight on the drivers than a Ten Wheeler, while still employing a practical guide truck. In their day, these locomotives were also considered huge, and were known as "Moguls" because of their bulk.

A few years after the Mogul was introduced, an even larger engine type was developed. Coal lines in eastern Pennsylvania were faced with tough operating conditions, pulling heavily laden coal trains up long, steep grades. This required plenty of power, and of course power was expensive. Following Winans' lead, a variety of 0-8-0s was designed. The 0-8-0 was capable of high tractive effort because all its weight rested on the drivers. Unfortunately, it lacked guide wheels, caused considerable wear on the track (requiring more frequent maintenance), and was not well suited for speed. In 1866 the Lehigh & Mahoning line

▲ Many railways
in the South were
destroyed during the Civil War and
required considerable rebuilding before they were
again able to function normally. Here a track gang is seen
laying tracks near Atlanta, Georgia, in the late 19th century.

ordered a new type, the 2-8-0, which had most of the pulling power of an 0-8-0 but enjoyed the smooth tracking ability of a 2-6-0. By the time this line received the new locomotives, it had been absorbed into the Lehigh Valley system. In recognition of that merger (a consolidation of the two companies), the new locomotive type became known as the "Consolidation." The power of the Consolidation, combined with its weight being distributed evenly over four pairs of drivers, made it a great freight hauler, and during the late 19th century it became one the most popular locomotive types in the United States.

Without the benefit of experience, the early railroads struggled to run their lines efficiently. There were no proper signaling systems or communications networks to assist in scheduling or dispatching trains. Braking systems were crude, and there were hardly any safety features. Initially, few lines featured double track; a more common arrangement was a single line with periodic passing sidings, to enable trains moving in opposite directions to pass one another. The inability to communicate over distances was a serious problem. Trains had to adhere to strict timetables to guarantee safe operations. If one train broke down, or ran late, the whole scheduling system fell apart. From time to time there were horrific accidents where trains collided or careered off tracks, but more often there were simply long delays.

THE TELEGRAPH ARRIVES

During the 1850s and 1860s, railroad technology and operations matured. The railroads introduced a variety of new devices and practices that we have come to associate with the classic era of railroading. Primary among these was the telegraph, adapted to railroad use in the early 1850s. This was extremely advantageous, since it allowed stations to communicate with each other, even over great distances, thus allowing more effective and safer movement of trains. Because of the railroads' close involvement with early telegraph companies, telegraph lines typically followed the tracks. Heavy eastern trunk lines were flanked by imposing rows of multiple-tier

TRAVELERS' TALES
JOURNEY ON THE PACIFIC RAILROAD

In 1884 *The Pacific Tourist,* an illustrated guidebook for westward travelers, described the compelling ride on the Pacific Railroad (the common name for the Union Pacific, Central Pacific, and connecting lines in those times). The publication's evocative account no doubt enticed many new travelers onto this highly scenic route:

"On the second day out from Omaha the traveler is fast ascending the high plains and the summits of the Rocky Mountains. The little villages of prairie dogs interest and amuse everyone. Then come in sight the distant summits of Long's Peak and the Colorado Mountains. Without scarcely asking the cause, the tourist is full of glow and enthusiasm . . . Ah! It is this keen, beautiful, refreshing, oxygenated, invigorating, toning, beautiful, enlivening mountain air which is giving him the glow of nature, and quickening him into greater appreciation of this grand impressive country. The plains themselves are a sight . . . the vastness of wide-extending, uninhabited, lifeless, uplifted solitude. If ever one feels belittled, 'tis on the plains, when each individual seems but a little mite, amid this majesty of loneliness. But the traveler finds with the Pullman car life – amid his enjoyments of reading, playing, conversation, making agreeable acquaintances, and with constant glances from the car window – enough to give him full and happy use of his time . . .

"You soon ascend the Rocky Mountains at Sherman, and view there the vast mountain range, the "Backbone of the Continent," and again descend, and thunder amid the cliffs of Echo and Weber Canons [sic] . . . It is impossible to tell of the pleasure and joys of the palace [car] ride you will have – five days . . . It will make you so well accustomed to car life, you feel, when you drop upon the wharf of San Francisco, that you had left genuine comfort behind, and even the hotel, with its cosy parlor and cheerful fire, has not its full recompense.

The completion of the first transcontinental route spurred an intense railroad building boom in the West. This Nevada Northern locomotive is pictured against the spectacular, and challenging, terrain that typifies the western United States.

"Palace car life has every day its fresh and novel sights. No railroad has greater variety and contrasts of scenery than the Pacific Railroad. The great plains of Nebraska and Wyoming are no less impressive than the great Humboldt Desert. The rock majesties of Echo and Weber are no more wonderful than the curiosities of the Great Salt Lake and the City Desert. And where could one drop down and finish his tour more grandly and beautifully than from the vast ice-towering summits of the Sierra into the golden grain fields of California, its gardens, groves, and cottage blossoms?"

▲ This 1891 view of a market along the tracks at Wall Street in Atlanta, Georgia, shows a typical 4-4-0 American locomotive and some wooden box cars. Railroad yards were distribution centers where goods were delivered from around the country.

telegraph poles, enhancing their grand appearance and function as major avenues of commerce.

By the 1860s railway journeys were significantly longer than when the railroads began. Naturally, this led to a demand for more comfortable passenger facilities. George Pullman was among the first to build and operate sleeping cars. He entered the business in 1858, and within a few decades his sleepers were running on trains all across the North American continent. As the best-known and longest-lived of the sleeping car companies, the name Pullman became synonymous with this increasingly popular mode of travel.

The dining car was another important innovation for rail travelers. This new feature allowed passengers the luxury of eating in relative comfort while the train was moving, and eliminated the need to halt for meal stops en route. These stops were notoriously unpleasant, with harried travelers given just 15–30 minutes to disembark, fight one another for attention from busy restaurant staff, and hastily consume whatever sustenance they were able to secure. Over the years, the railroads refined the serving of refreshments on trains into a art, with attractively decorated dining cars offering meals that one would previously have expected only at fine restaurants. The railroads learned that they could profit handsomely from the privilege of offering a food service, since they had both a captive audience and no competition.

The American Civil War began on April 12, 1861, and concluded just under four years later, with railroads having played a crucial role. The war was a complex and vicious conflict involving fundamental differences in ideology and lifestyle between the northern and southern states. One of the underlying issues was directly related to the development of the railroads, and that issue was the power of the new industrial economy versus a more traditional agrarian society. Once the war had started, the railroads quickly demonstrated their usefulness in moving vast numbers of troops and munitions with unprecedented speed. Never had armies been deployed so far afield so quickly. The American Civil War experience changed the whole idea of how a war could be waged.

CIVIL WAR STRUGGLES

The Union forces (those of the northern states) had a much more extensive and better developed railway network than the Confederate forces of the southern states. The entire south boasted just one-third of the country's total railway mileage. More important than the sheer number of miles, however, was the fact that the railway lines in the north were linked together, while the southern railways were still operating as separate, independent lines, many connecting only principal terminal cities. Serious gauge incompatibility problems and a lack of through connections only added to the Confederacy's troubles. These difficulties often made it impossible to run through trains, and negated some of the advantages of rapid railway transport. Southern railways also suffered from a lack of heavy industry. Before the war, they had acquired most of their locomotives, rails, and other vital equipment from northern companies. Once war broke out, they were cut off from these sources and quickly found themselves critically short of supplies.

Much of the Civil War was fought on southern soil, and the railways there were often military targets and subject to attack. During the war much of the southern rail system was destroyed. Bridges were blown up, tracks sabotaged, and locomotives and cars wrecked. Depots, roundhouses, and shops were burned to the ground. By comparison, the northern network escaped largely unscathed. The only northern rail system that received significant damage during the war was the B&O, whose lines ran right through areas of intense fighting. By the end of the war most lines in the southern states had been destroyed and needed to be completely rebuilt.

One of the most famous episodes in Civil War railroading has become known as "The Great Train Chase." This event has been the subject of several Hollywood movies, including the silent film star Buster Keaton's 1927 production, *The General*. The story tells how a group of Union raiders, led by James J. Andrews, slipped into Confederate territory

▼ President Abraham Lincoln is pictured wearing his trademark stovepipe hat at a Union army camp during the Civil War. Lincoln was instrumental in getting the first transcontinental rail link underway by supporting the Pacific Railroad Act of 1862.

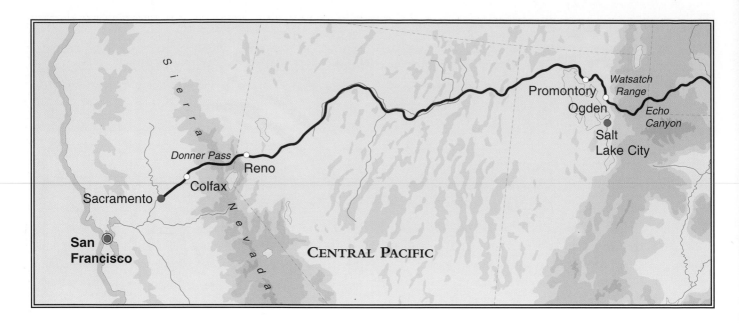

▲ The first transcontinental line was a joint effort by two great railroads. The Central Pacific started in Sacramento, California, and worked eastward over the Sierras, while the Union Pacific began in Omaha, Nebraska, and built west across the plains.

and captured a Western & Atlantic locomotive called the *General* (pp.50–51) at Big Shanty, Georgia. As they raced northward toward Union-controlled territory, they sabotaged the railway line by cutting telegraph cables and destroying tracks. They were hotly pursued by Confederate forces on another engine and caught before they could reach safety. The *General* was recovered and Andrews and others of his party were tried and executed. Although the event was of little strategic importance, it symbolically demonstrates the vital role of the railway during the war and the value of a single locomotive.

A number of key figures in the Civil War also played important roles in the development of the railroad. Before he was elected president, Abraham Lincoln had represented the interests of several railroads in his position as a lawyer. His knowledge and interest in railroads helped him during the height of the war to make the influential decision in 1862 to support the Pacific Railroad Act and other legislation that enabled the construction of the first transcontinental railroad. Other men who earned their reputations during the war went on to become great railroad builders. General William Jackson

Palmer had worked for the Pennsylvania Railroad's John Edgar Thompson before embarking on his military career. After the war he returned to railroading and became one of the great western railroad builders, first constructing the Kansas Pacific line to Denver, then establishing the Denver & Rio Grande, the most influential and extensive narrow-gauge line in the US.

The engineer Theodore D. Judah may have been the single most important person involved in getting the first transcontinental railroad underway. In the 1850s Judah moved to Sacramento to build California's first railway. He had come from the east, where he had engineered several lines. Once in Sacramento he dreamed of building a railroad over the Sierra Nevada Mountains – those towering peaks that walled off California from points east. In his spare time, he and his wife Anna carefully surveyed a route over the Sierras that would involve a minimum of tunneling yet rose from just above sea level to an elevation of more than 7,000ft (2,133m) at Donner Pass, on the spine of the Sierras. But Judah did more than just devise a viable route. He also drew up the charter for the Central Pacific Railroad, actively sought investors, and traveled to Washington D.C. on several occasions to lobby Congress and the President for support. Judah was more than just an engineer; he was a visionary. Yet he was often abrasive and unyielding, and was eventually forced out of the project by those holding the purse strings. Sadly, he

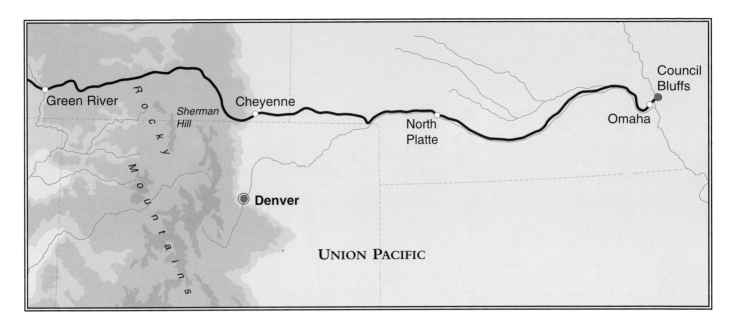

did not live to see his dream realized. He died in 1863, just as work on the transcontinental railroad began. Judah never got to ride over Donner Pass in a train; but thanks to him, many others did.

The building of the first transcontinental route was a monumental effort. The Pacific Railroad Act of 1862, which initiated the project, established that two railroads would build toward one another – Judah's Central Pacific from west to east, and the Union Pacific from east to west. The Act provided Federal land and money to the railroads, but only after sections of track were completed and approved. Despite this guarantee of Federal assistance, the railroads at first had great difficulty in raising money, and for the first few years, progress was almost imperceptible. Most railroads enjoyed the benefits of considerable on-line traffic as they constructed their lines. As a result, even though a railroad might take years to complete a route, it had the ability to earn revenue along the way. However, the vast tract of land that the Pacific Railroad was building across was not likely to attract much traffic until the entire line was finished. This posed a real financial problem, and despite Federal grants, investors were reluctant to fund the project.

The Civil War was crucial to getting the Pacific Railroad Act passed because a Pacific railroad was seen as a way of keeping western states in the Union fold. Yet the war hindered the actual construction of the line. There were shortages of labor and materials

such as rails and locomotives. In the early years, the Central Pacific was better organized than the Union Pacific but faced greater obstacles. While the Union Pacific could start westward across open plains, the Central Pacific was faced with the wall of the Sierras and the barren Nevada desert beyond. In 1863 the Central Pacific held a gala public celebration at Sacramento to mark the beginning of construction from the West, but more than two years later the railroad had built only 35 miles (56.3km) of track and had not yet surmounted the toughest climb. When the war was finally concluded, the building began in earnest.

WORKING TO LINK THE NATION

Union Pacific's eastern terminus was established at Omaha, Nebraska, on the Missouri River – despite the fact that this frontier outpost did not yet even have a rail connection to the east. Although it was remote, the logic behind using Omaha as a terminal was simple: it sat at the eastern end of the broad Platte River Valley, long considered one of the best routes west. A few years later the terminus was moved to Council Bluffs, directly across the river from Omaha in Iowa. Soon the Union Pacific gangs were building westward at a furious pace, and the race was on. The railroads were paid handsomely by the mile, and both railroads wanted to build as much track as possible to secure the largest grants. By 1866 the Union Pacific had reached North Platte in western Nebraska, and

▲ Laying tracks was slow, labor-intensive work. To keep the gradient as even as possible, cuts and fills were necessary to compensate for the natural roll of the land. This track gang is pictured in 1898 on the Prescott & Eastern Railroad in Arizona.

by 1867 the Central Pacific had reached the summit of the mighty Sierra Nevada at Donner Pass.

While the Union Pacific employed gangs of Civil War veterans and Irish immigrants, the Central Pacific embraced a novel labor solution and hired some 14,000 Chinese laborers, many of whom emigrated from China specifically to build the line. Central Pacific construction boss Charlie Crocker, one of the so called "Big Four" who financed the Central Pacific and would control the destiny of California's railroads for decades to come, preferred Chinese labor over traditional European rail gangs. Donner Summit posed a serious engineering challenge to the Central Pacific workers because several long tunnels had to be blasted out of the rock. Heavy snowfall, for which Donner is famous, delayed work and forced the company to take alternative action to keep the railroad moving eastward. Locomotives, men, and equipment were hauled on sleds over the mountains, so that crews could begin working on the eastern slope and start pushing across the Nevada desert while the summit tunnels were being completed.

The Union Pacific had other difficulties. Its crews were notoriously wild, and were known as "Hell on Wheels." Wherever they set up camp, a host of gambling halls and brothels soon followed. Additionally, several tribes of native Americans lived on the plains across which the crews were building. Some tribes proved helpful to the railroad builders, but others were understandably hostile. They were already fighting to maintain their lifestyle and culture and the coming of the railroad threatened to completely destroy their way of life. The tribes had relied on the buffalo for food and clothing, and worshipped it as a spiritual icon; now the buffalo was being slaughtered by hunters. There were some instances of native American attacks on railroad crews, but these did not seriously delay the Union Pacific's westward progress once the armies of Civil War veterans had arrived to work on the track.

SUCCESS AT LAST

Finally, after years of planning, surveying, track laying, and untold political shenanigans, the Central Pacific and Union Pacific rail gangs met at a lonely, windswept spot north of the Great Salt Lake called Promontory, Utah. Here on May 10, 1869, a little more than four years after the Civil War had ended, the railroads staged the single most famous event in the history of American railroading: the Golden Spike Ceremony. Two 4-4-0 American Standard locomotives – one representing each line – were posed pilot to pilot, as dignitaries made speeches and struggled (unsuccessfully) to hammer a specially inscribed golden spike into the ties. Photographs were taken, champagne was consumed, and a telegraph operator on the scene relayed the word "Done!" to the world, and people all across the United States celebrated. It is said that the world shrank that day, and in many respects it did. The overland journey that had taken months by wagon could now be accomplished in just a week. Perhaps no trip had ever been shortened so much, so quickly.

However, the Golden Spike Ceremony was only the beginning of the railroad story in the American West. Four men, who came to be known as "The Big Four," had been principally responsible for building the Central Pacific: Leland Stanford, Colis P. Huntington, Charles Crocker, and Mark Hopkins. They had defied those who deemed the task impossible and went on to build a transportation empire. Soon after the completion of the transcontinental railroad, they took control of a fledgling railway company called the Southern Pacific. Before long, the Central Pacific, the Southern Pacific, and a host of other companies, subsidiaries, and consortiums under their direction had laid tracks from the woods of Oregon to the bayous of Louisiana. The Big Four were hugely influential in the growth of California and western railroads, and made untold fortunes, crushing anyone and everyone who stood in their way.

The men behind the Union Pacific also achieved notoriety. Shortly after the transcontinental route was opened, it was revealed that the Union Pacific's owners had bribed politicians and squandered the public's and railroad's money. In their haste and greed, they had rushed to completion a line of extremely poor quality, while funneling funds into their own pockets. As they grew rich, the railroad suffered, and it emerged in such poor shape that it needed a great deal more work before it could begin to serve in the capacity for which it was intended.

The Union Pacific/Central Pacific was the first transcontinental route, but by no means the last. Soon there were a variety of proposals for new lines across the West. A new era of railroad building had begun.

▼ **The famous Golden Spike Ceremony at Promontory, Utah, on May 10, 1869, was the culmination of a decade of planning, political wrangling, and hard work. Here the rails of the Central Pacific and Union Pacific were formally joined, linking east and west.**

DAWN OF
THE GOLDEN AGE

As rail became the dominant mode of transportation in North America, fierce competition between the railroads led to a vast growth in track mileage. Technical advances also greatly improved efficiency and safety.

The last three decades of the 19th century were one of the most dynamic periods in the history of North American railroads. There was an exceptional amount of building, especially in the West, and during this time Canada was spanned by its own transcontinental line, the Canadian Pacific Railway. Railroads had evolved into big businesses

◄ **In the golden age at the end of the 1800s, North American railroads reached their influential peak. In this evocative image, Chicago & North Western 4-6-0 No. 1385 steams toward Baraboo, Wisconsin, on a frigid February morning.**

and were played as pawns in complex financial schemes, as the new empires of railroad moguls rose and fell with the turbulent economic tides of the period. Traffic was robust and growing. A variety of important inventions and innovations allowed trains to grow in size and length. Passenger trains were getting faster and more comfortable, while freight trains grew heavier and much longer. Locomotive technology progressed as engines were made not just bigger and more powerful, but also more efficient.

The railroad had established a predominant role in travel and North American life, and it enjoyed a

▲ Northern Pacific 4-6-0 No. 328 was a typical early 20th-century locomotive. Significantly larger than the 4-4-0 Americans built in the mid-1800s, it was a powerful and versatile machine capable of working both freight and passenger trains.

near monopoly on transportation. Most goods and passengers were now carried by rail, and the individual railroad companies fought desperately for their share of the market, resulting in bitter rate wars, colorful advertising campaigns, and Byzantine financial struggles. It was this period in North American railroading that became known as the "golden age."

TRANSCONTINENTAL VISIONS

The Central Pacific/Union Pacific route was merely the first of many rail links across the continent. By the time the last spike was put in place at Promontory, Utah, there were already several other lines looking westward. The Santa Fe Railroad, founded in 1859,

had acquired a substantial Federal land grant in 1863. It built across Kansas, reaching Colorado in 1872, and California in 1887, but not before becoming involved in a serious tussle with the Denver & Rio Grande. Quite early on, transcontinental railroad planners had discussed establishing a railroad via a northern route in addition to those being built on central and southern routes. In 1864, an Act was passed authorizing a line traversing the north; this was the genesis of the Northern Pacific Railroad, one of the most troubled of the transcontinental lines. While the first transcontinental railroad went from concept to completed route in less than 10 years, the Northern Pacific took nearly two decades to reach its goal.

▶ By the turn of the 19th century, the steam locomotive had become an ubiquitous symbol of progress. Examples could be found all across North America, hauling everything from pigs to pig iron. The days of fast passenger trains and fast freight were born.

Financier Jay Cooke originally backed the railroad, and construction began in 1870. By 1873, the tracks had reached the budding town of Bismarck, North Dakota, but that year Jay Cooke's financial empire collapsed, halting the Northern Pacific dead in its tracks. Today, Jay Cooke seems like an obscure figure, but, in his time, he was as well known to the general public as Microsoft's Bill Gates is to us. When Jay Cooke's empire crashed, he precipitated the worst financial depression known until that time. This not only stalled the Northern Pacific, but also forced many lines to stop building for a few years, until the

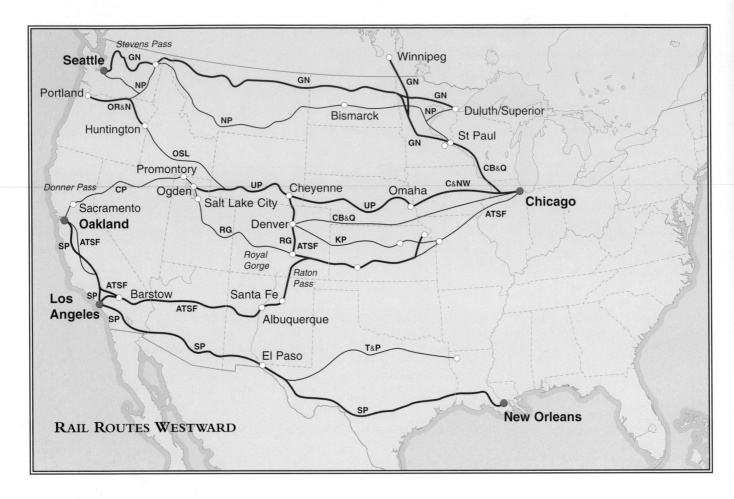

▲ Railroads with routes westward in the 1890s included the Central Pacific (CP), Union Pacific (UP), Southern Pacific (SP), Atchison, Topeka, and Santa Fe (ATSF), Northern Pacific (NP), Great Northern (GN), Denver & Rio Grande (RG), Denver Pacific (DP), Chicago & North Western (C&NW), Chicago, Burlington & Quincy (CB&Q), Kansas Pacific (KP), Texas & Pacific (TP), and Oregon Railways Navigation Company (OR&N).

economy returned to good health. The fortunes of the Northern Pacific were then directed by Henry Villard, a German-born businessman whose love for the Pacific Northwest greatly influenced railroad construction. He saw to it that the Northern Pacific reached the Pacific Ocean, but lost control of the railroad just as the last spike was being set in place in 1883.

The "Big Four," who constructed the Central Pacific, used their power and railroad-building skills to lay tracks all over California, and were soon creating a second transcontinental route to the East, called the Southern Pacific. This route passed over the Tehachapi Mountains, where the railroad employed a circular track arrangement, whereby the tracks actually cross over the top of one another in order to gain elevation in the confines of a narrow cleft in the terrain. This is the internationally famous Tehachapi Loop, one of the most photographed sections of track in the world.

Across the wide plains and prairies, a myriad of mainlines and branches were built to serve the areas' developing agricultural communities. The Chicago & North Western, the Milwaukee Road, and the Rock Island are some of the best known of these "Granger" lines. One of the most extensive, most efficiently run, and most influential of the Granger railroads was the Chicago, Burlington & Quincy – a line known as simply the Burlington and referred to affectionately as the "Q." By 1900, the Burlington had assembled a 7,600-mile (12,200km) system that connected Chicago with Montana, Wyoming, and Colorado; with affiliated lines, it also reached from Denver to Texas. The power of the Q lay in its well-connected western mainlines and its extensive branch-line network, which mirrored the rapid growth of agriculture in Illinois, Iowa, Missouri, and Nebraska.

General William Jackson Palmer, the man behind the construction of the Kansas Pacific, effectively brought railroading to Denver, Colorado. In the early 1860s, the residents of this village, set on the edge of the plains at the foot of the Colorado Front Range, were aghast when they discovered that the fabled transcontinental railroad was bypassing Denver in favor of the more northerly route through Wyoming. The completion of Palmer's Kansas Pacific from the east, and also the Denver Pacific from the north, was small consolation for having missed the prize as a prime station on the main east–west artery of the nation.

PALMER'S DENVER & RIO GRANDE

While Denver did not enjoy a premier position on the primary east–west line, Palmer did have other plans for it. He envisioned building a railroad empire that would connect Denver with Salt Lake City, and

also reach southward to Santa Fe and, ultimately, Mexico City. He called his line the Denver & Rio Grande. The Kansas Pacific was uninterested in his ambitions, so Palmer set out on his own. While he was drawing up plans for his railway, Palmer got married and took his honeymoon in Britain. One of his associates advised that, while there, he inspect a small slate hauling railway in North Wales called the Festiniog. This line used narrow-gauge tracks just 2ft (610mm) wide and had recently introduced steam locomotives to augment its gravity-powered and animal-hauled trains.

Palmer was convinced that the advantages of narrow-gauge railways would greatly suit his new line, so he chose 3ft (904mm) gauge instead of the standard

▼ The Welsh 2ft (610mm) gauge Festiniog Railway, seen here at Tan Y Bwlch, was a model for the Denver & Rio Grande line, which used 3ft (904mm) gauge tracks instead of the standard 4ft 8¹/₂in (1,435mm) gauge used on most US lines.

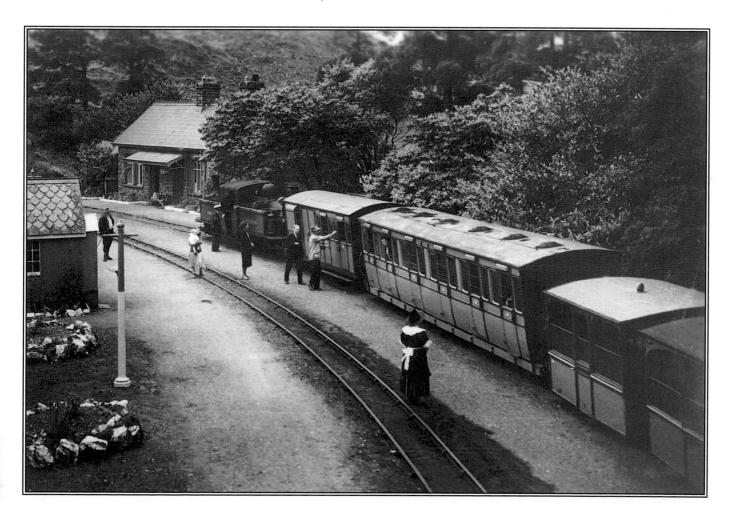

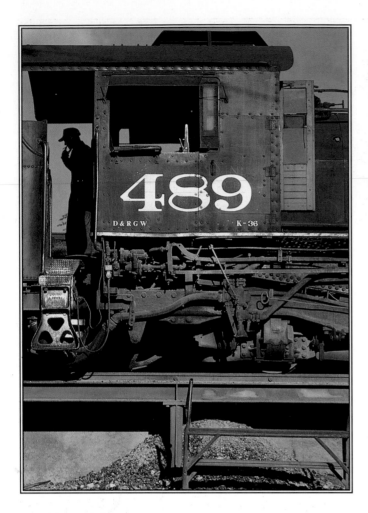

▲ Palmer's narrow-gauge Denver & Rio Grande reached deep into the mountains of Colorado, New Mexico, and Utah. The railroad spurred mining booms, since prospectors at last had an economical method of transporting machinery, men, and ore.

▶ In the 1870s and 1880s, there was an ardent narrow-gauge movement in the United States. Since narrow gauge was cheaper to build than standard gauge, it allowed the construction of many new lines, such as the East Broad Top, seen here.

(4ft 8½in/1,435mm). Narrow gauge was significantly cheaper to build, as the smaller right–of–way required fewer materials, and, more importantly, could negotiate sharper curves and steeper grades more easily than standard-gauge lines. This was especially advantageous in the mountains. Operations cost less, too. Locomotives and cars were smaller and lighter, they cost less to build, and they needed less fuel to operate. The disadvantage was a lack of compatibility with other lines. At the time, Palmer was dreaming up his north–south

narrow-gauge empire, so he did not see this as an immediate problem.

The Denver & Rio Grande became one of the very first, and ultimately the most extensive, narrow-gauge railways in North America. On October 28, 1871 – only two years and a few months after the completion of the first transcontinental line – a diminutive Baldwin 2-4-0 chugged southward from Denver. It ran 76 miles (122km) over the summit of the Lake Divide and down to Colorado Springs, which Palmer had visions of becoming a mountain utopia. Lake Divide is today known as Palmer Lake, Colorado, and in the center of Colorado Springs, a statue of Palmer stands in his honor. After reaching Colorado Springs, Palmer pushed his line further south to Pueblo, but the financial crash of 1873 slowed his progress. Finally, when funds became

available again, Palmer faced a more serious concern: the incursion into his territory by the Santa Fe. The two lines first vied for control of Raton Pass, a vital cleft in the mountains ideally suited for a railroad building south or west. At Raton, the Santa Fe beat the Rio Grande, but the rivalry did not end here.

Soon, the Leadville, Colorado, mining boom attracted both lines to build west into the mountains, and the narrow pass known as the Royal Gorge of the Arkansas River became the site of a vicious skirmish in a very real shooting war between the two lines. It was a complex battle and went well beyond the bounds of a mere legal wrangling, as both lines employed private militias; shots were exchanged and workers killed on more than one occasion. For a short time, the Santa Fe seized financial control of the Rio Grande, but then Palmer regained his charge. Finally, a settlement was negotiated in 1880, which changed the map of western railroading and scaled back Palmer's ambitions. The Santa Fe relinquished its plans to build to Leadville, and the Rio Grande agreed to abandon its southward push, instead developing an extensive

▼ The Silverton Railway was one of several narrow-gauge mountain railroads that met the Denver & Rio Grande at Silverton, Colorado. Here, passengers are being transferred to horse-drawn wagons at Red Mountain Town.

▲ In Maine, 2ft (610mm) gauge lines were constructed into the timberlands. The Wiscasset, Waterville & Farmington was one such line. Its diminutive locomotive, No. 7, built by Baldwin, was typical of Maine narrow-gauge tank locomotives.

narrow-gauge empire in Colorado, Utah, and northern New Mexico. Under Palmer's direction, it undertook a period of frantic expansion, building lines in a variety of directions and precipitating a mining boom in Colorado. The arrival of the narrow gauge was effectively a license to start prospecting. Silver and other precious minerals were the initial commodities mined.

Narrow-gauge lines were built all over the United States, providing access to places that had previously proved uneconomical

---

Later, during World War II, some narrow-gauge lines were used to haul uranium for the Manhattan Project.

The popularity of the narrow gauge really took off in the 1870s and 1880s – and not just in the Rockies. Narrow-gauge railways were built all over the United States, as the cheaper construction costs suddenly allowed railroads to reach places that had previously proved uneconomical. In Pennsylvania, lines such as the East Broad Top tapped into mineral traffic ignored

by the standard-gauge lines. In Maine, a host of 2ft (610mm) gauge railroads developed to reach timber traffic, while narrow-gauge lines in California and Nevada exploited mineral and timber resources.

There were other, more ambitious, narrow-gauge plans that went beyond merely mines and timber. The narrow-gauge movement became one of the most controversial issues in the contemporary railroad press. One of the most extensive systems planned was the Grand Narrow Gauge Trunk, designed to connect Ohio with Texas, and ultimately reach Mexico City. Other lines had a more modest scope, such as the Boston, Revere Beach & Lynn, a suburban passenger railway serving the North Shore of Massachusetts.

The interest in narrow-gauge railways logically led to a significant trade in narrow-gauge locomotives and railway cars. While most narrow-gauge locomotives were essentially smaller versions of the machines

TRAVELERS' TALES
NO TIME LIKE TRAIN TIME

One of the railroads' contributions to modern life was the introduction of standard time zones. Before time zones were established in North America, every community had their own "solar time," which was not ideal for the practical operation of railways. To minimize confusion among employees, railroads set a common company time, usually based on the solar time at a principal city or at the company headquarters. This was then used as a standard in the dispatching and scheduling of trains.

August Mencken, in his book *The Railroad Passenger Car*, relates an episode from T.S. Hudson's *A Scamper through America*, describing a trip on the Baltimore & Ohio after the railroad had agreed upon its own offi-cial timekeeping, but before the introduction of standard national time zones:

"We left Washington for the West in the forenoon, taking parlor-car tickets for Cumberland and sleeper tickets thence to Cincinnati for night traveling. A great source of inconvenience in traveling is what appears to be the foolish arrangement of clocks. An attempt is made by every large place to use solar time, hence trains are made to run as nearly as possible to the time of the sun. In the 40 hours' ride now commenced, we had three times – Washington, Vincennes, and St Louis. It became indispensable to carry with our watches a reconciliation card with little dials showing the hour at a dozen different places when noon at New York."

used on standard-gauge lines – the 4-4-0 and 4-6-0 being popular types – other more unusual locomotives were developed for narrow-gauge use. Robert Fairlie, one of the most vocal British proponents of narrow-gauge railways, had designed a clever double-ended articulated locomotive that was essentially two locomotives back to back on a single frame. One of

---

Transcontinental interchange traffic was lost as cargo had to be loaded from standard- to narrow-gauge cars, and then back again

---

the most important features of the Fairlie was that its driving wheels were on a pivoting bogie. Its design's intention was to place the majority of weight on the driving wheels, while remaining sufficiently flexible to negotiate lightly built tracks.

Although quite popular in Europe and around the world, this type never caught on in the US (only one Fairlie locomotive was operated there) but it did inspire another type of articulated locomotive: the single-ended Mason Bogie, developed by William Mason, one of New England's foremost locomotive builders. This locomotive used the principle of placing drivers on a pivoting bogie, but with just one engine in a more conventional format. The Mason Bogie enjoyed some popularity in North America on both narrow- and standard-gauge lines. The Denver, South Park & Pacific (a Rio Grande competitor and the second most extensive narrow-gauge system in Colorado) and the Boston, Revere Beach & Lynn both operated small fleets of Mason Bogies.

One of the most outspoken opponents to the narrow-gauge movement was a locomotive specialist named Matthias Forney, best known for his 1876 text *Catechism of the Locomotive*, who designed a locomotive combined with its tender on a single frame. Like Fairlie's locomotive, Forney's was intended to place the majority of its weight on driving wheels, yet, because the weight of its tender was carried separately, the locomotive would not lose traction as its fuel and water were depleted – a problem associated with many "tank" designs. Forney intended his locomotive for standard-gauge applications, but the design turned out to be well suited to narrow-gauge lines and was one of the most popular types on the Maine 2ft (610mm) gauge routes.

Heavier narrow-gauge types included the 2-8-0, and most of them resembled their standard-gauge cousins. After the turn of the 19th century, a new breed of powerful narrow-gauge locomotives was developed for use on the Rio Grande's steeply graded lines. These were an adaptation of the recently introduced 2-8-2 Mikado type, discussed at greater length toward the end of this chapter.

The narrow-gauge movement was relatively short-lived, but in just two decades some 18,000 miles (29,000km) of narrow-gauge railway had been constructed in the United States. The economies of narrow-gauge operation proved to be somewhat less advantageous than hoped for, and the inconvenience caused by the inability to interchange cars easily with standard-gauge lines forced many narrow-

gauge railways to reconsider their track width. Gradually, there was a move to convert narrow-gauge tracks to the standard width. Even portions of Palmer's pioneering Rio Grande had to make this concession. Once it reached Salt Lake City, the Rio Grande found that it was losing a good deal of transcontinental interchange traffic because cargo needed to be reloaded from standard- to narrow-gauge cars, and then back again. By the late 1880s, the Denver & Rio Grande had undertaken the construction of a standard-gauge mainline and was adding a third rail to other routes, including its original line south of Denver and the line through the Royal Gorge. However, many of the Rio Grande's

▼ These narrow-gauge tracks at Rockhill Furnace, Pennsylvania, display an antiquated "stub" switch, which required that the rails be moved to select a route. More modern switches used moveable points between the rails to make a route selection.

▲ The Erie Railroad was one of several broad-gauge lines in the United States. While most railroad tracks were built to a standard width of 4ft 8¹/₂in (1,435mm), the Erie's were 6ft (1,829mm). In the 1880s, all broad-gauge lines were forced to convert.

lawlessness of the American West. In the 1870s and 1880s, there were hundreds of train robberies, typically committed by stopping a train on a remote section of track and looting the riches on board.

During the decade following the American Civil War, railroad mileage in the United States roughly doubled. While western lines received most of the attention, other lines were constructed and networks assembled all around the country. In the South, efforts focused on repairing railways badly damaged during the Civil War, usually with the backing of northern lines or investment bankers. The Illinois Central and Louisville & Nashville were two of the largest railways in the South, and had expanded their reach and improved their properties after the war. Among the new lines established were the Seaboard Air Line, Atlantic Coast Line, Norfolk & Western, and the Southern Railway System.

Despite the proliferation of narrow-gauge lines during the 1870s and 1880s, there was a parallel effort to eliminate gauge incompatibilities among older railroads built to broad gauge. Most of those railroads were rebuilt to the 4ft 8¹/₂in (1,435mm) standard at this time. Even the Erie Railroad, with its legendary 6ft (1,829mm) gauge, was forced to comply. The benefits of having a uniform gauge were obvious, but changing a railroad's gauge was far more complicated

---

Railroads attracted the shrewdest businessmen – financial buccaneers, empire builders, manipulators, and conmen

---

than simply adjusting the track width. Locomotives and rolling stock also had to be regauged, rebuilt, or replaced – a costly undertaking that often had to be implemented gradually. By 1890, virtually all the broad-gauge lines had been rebuilt.

Railroads were the largest businesses of their day, and, not suprisingly, their tremendous revenue-generating capacities attracted the shrewdest businessmen of the times – financial buccaneers, empire builders, manipulators, and confidence men alike. The ethics of the business world then were much more

secondary lines were never converted and remained narrow gauge throughout their existence.

While some companies were quick to convert, others survived for decades in narrow-gauge form. Some lines, such as Pennsylvania's East Broad Top, developed mechanisms interchanging freight cars by lifting them up and exchanging standard-gauge tracks with narrow-gauge ones. A few narrow-gauge systems survived into the 1960s, although most were either converted or abandoned (see Chapter 8). The image of diminutive narrow-gauge trains working their way over the Rocky Mountains remains one of the most romantic visions of the period.

Western railroad building had captured the imagination of the popular press, as Americans focused their attention on the development of the frontier. Western railroading conveyed images of 4-4-0s with their tall balloon smokestacks rolling west across the Great Plains, chasing herds of buffalo. A new style of bandit emerged: the train robber. Despite their brutality, train robbers were often popular characters. Jesse James was probably the best known of this new style of outlaw, whose lifestyle reflected the wild

lax than they are today, and there were fewer rules, regulations, and laws regarding the nature of financial transactions. Men often vied for control of railways – not in order to direct the destiny of the company for the greater good, but simply to maximize their own fortunes. If they happened to provide a better service, reach new territories, open new routes, and run better, faster, and more comfortable trains as a result of their financial machinations, that was all well and good. However, if they made their millions through dealings that damaged railway lines, reduced service, and put the companies into bankruptcy at the expense of the passengers, shippers, employees, and stockholders, the public had little recourse.

RISE OF THE RAILWAY TYCOON

Perhaps one of the most infamous rail barons was the legendary Jay Gould. From the late 1860s until his death in 1892, he variously controlled the destinies of the Erie Railroad, the Wabash, and the Union Pacific, as well as New York's elevated railways and the largest telegraph monopoly, Western Union. While he reaped an enormous personal fortune,

from this empire, many felt he did so at the expense of the properties he controlled.

The actions of Gould, the Vanderbilts, Forbes, and others led to a series of vicious rate wars, especially on Eastern trunk lines where competition was fierce. This often led to bouts of railroad building by companies directly into their competitors' territory. The New York Central and the Erie both built lines into Pennsylvania's coal country. The Pennsylvania built routes to a variety of major points on the New York Central. The Granger railroads built lines all over the Midwest in an effort to reach the most lucrative traffic sources. In the most extreme cases, redundant railroads were built directly parallel to existing lines, typically without regard to potential traffic volume. In some places, one could find two, or even three, sets of adjcent, independently owned tracks, each accommodating only a few trains a day.

▼ Elevated railways were a new breed of railway that ran above street level on steel viaducts, to relieve traffic congestion on city streets and to speed urban passenger travel. New York and Chicago built the most extensive elevated railway systems.

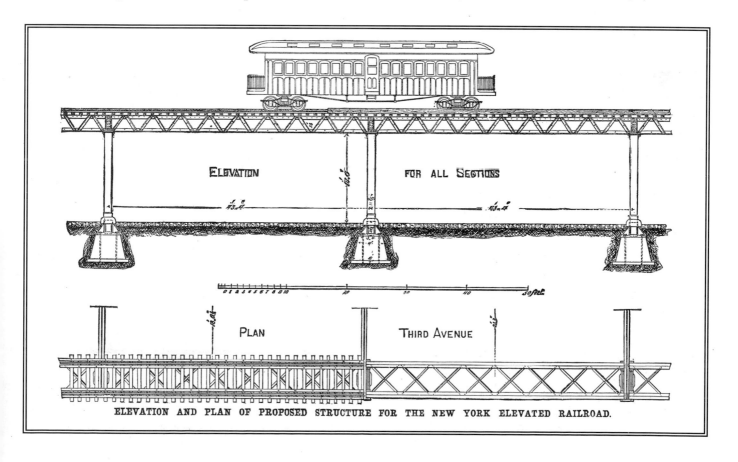

ELEVATION AND PLAN OF PROPOSED STRUCTURE FOR THE NEW YORK ELEVATED RAILROAD.

▲ The Pennsylvania Railroad's logo incorporated a keystone, the symbol of the Commonwealth of Pennsylvania. Today the design is still used by other Pennsylvania-based companies such as H. J. Heinz, famous for its ketchup.

A line known as the Nickel Plate Road was built parallel to the New York Central between Buffalo and Chicago to compete for traffic. West of Buffalo, the tracks of the two routes were set side by side, and their respective trains could race each other for miles. However, whereas the New York Central's Lake Shore & Michigan Southern line was a soundly built, multiple-track line, designed with a level profile characterized by high fills and cuts, the Nickel Plate was a single-track line that followed a tangent but on a hill-and-dale profile and used tall, spindly trestles. To protect its traffic, the New York Central sought control of this line, although it did continue to run it as a separate entity. The story behind the name of the Nickel Plate Road is that Vanderbilt, head of the Central, asked if the tracks were "nickel-plated" to justify the high price he was forced to pay to gain control.

▶ An Alco Brooks-built 2-8-0 Consolidation type locomotive leads a long freight on the Nickel Plate Road in the 1920s. The boxcars behind the locomotive are typical of the era; they have wooden bodies with large brake wheels at the tops of the cars.

In the 1880s, the competitive situation got out of control when Pennsylvania Railroad interests built a completely new mainline parallel to the New York Central's main artery – its New York City to Buffalo route. This new line was called the New York, West Shore & Buffalo, because it followed the west shore of the Hudson from the New Jersey shore opposite Manhattan to the Albany area. From there it headed

▶ A workman emerges from the coal smoke in the Nevada Northern's locomotive shop at Ely, Nevada. A town blessed with railroad shops and yards was assured growth and prosperity, and railroads often drove the economy in developing areas.

west, and (like the Nickel Plate line further west) in many places it ran adjacent to the New York Central. Unlike the Nickel Plate, however, the West Shore

---

TRAVELERS' TALES
A NOVICE PASSENGER'S TICKET TROUBLES

Early American railways were a potpourri of different companies, each operating their own trains. This made things confusing for the novice traveler, especially since some trains used a number of different lines. "Coupon tickets" valid for travel over several different railways were introduced to simplify passengers' paperwork and save them the inconvenience of having to purchase individual tickets for each line traveled on. However, not everyone was clear on this system, as illustrated by a humorous tale relayed by Horace Porter, vice president of the Pullman Palace-Car Company, in an essay published in the late 1880s:

"A United States Senator-elect had come by sea from the Pacific Coast who had never seen a railroad till he reached the Atlantic seaboard. With a curiosity to test the workings of the new means of transportation of which he had heard so much, he bought a coupon ticket and set out for a railway journey. He entered a car, took a seat next to the door, and was just beginning to get the 'hang of the school house' when the conductor (who was then not uniformed) came in, cried: 'Tickets!' and reached out his hand toward the Senator. 'What do you want of me?' said the latter. 'I want your ticket,' answered the conductor. Now it occurred to the Senator that this might be a very neat job on the part of an Eastern ticket-sharp, but it was a little too thin to fool a Pacific Coaster, and he said: 'Don't you think I've got sense enough to know that if I parted with my ticket right at the start I wouldn't

have anything to show for my money during the rest of the way? No sir, I'm going to hold on to this till I get to the end of the trip.' The conductor, whose impatience was now rising to fever heat, said: 'I don't want to take your ticket, I only want to look at it.'

"The Senator thought, after some reflection, that he would risk letting the man have a peep at it, anyhow, and held it up before him, keeping it, however, at a safe distance. The conductor, with the customary abruptness, jerked it out of his hand, tore off the first coupon, and was about to return the ticket, when the Pacific Coaster sprang up, threw himself upon his muscle, and delivered a well-directed blow of his fist upon the conductor's right eye, which landed him sprawling on one of the opposite seats. The other passengers were at once on their feet, and rushed up to know the cause of the disturbance. The Senator, still standing with his arms in a pugnacious attitude, said: 'Maybe I've never ridden on a railroad before, but I'm not going to let any sharper get away with me like that.'

"'What's he done?' cried the passengers.

"'Why,' said the Senator, 'I paid 17 dollars and a half for a ticket to take me through to Cincinnati, and before we're five miles out, that fellow slips up and says he wants to see it, and when I get it out, he grabs hold of it and goes to tearing it up right before my eyes.'

"Ample explanations were soon made, and the new passenger was duly initiated into the mysteries of the coupon system."

route was a heavily engineered double-track line. The New York Central duly responded by financing the beginning of a new super mainline across the southern tier of Pennsylvania to compete directly with the Pennsylvania Railroad (PRR). The results of such competition would have devastated both companies, as a new round of rate wars could have forced them both into bankruptcy.

At this time, the iron-willed J. P. Morgan entered the fray to stop the insane duplication of infrastructure between the PRR and the New York Central. Morgan had recently established himself as a formidable financier, and he was on his way to becoming one of the most powerful bankers in the world. He invited the principal men of the New

York Central and the PRR for a cruise on his luxurious yacht, the *Corsair*, where he dictated a settlement that both parties could accept and that would solve the railroading crisis. In the end, the

---

Strikes, rate wars, poor service, and inadequate safety practices contributed to a growing discontent with the railroads

---

New York Central bought the West Shore Line and ceased construction on its South Penn route. The West Shore soon proved a valuable asset and was integrated into the Central system. The South Penn right-of-way was partially incorporated into the Pennsylvania Turnpike in 1940.

During the 1870s and 1880s, the railroads were faced with another series of conflicts. In the previous decade, the first serious labor organizations had gained

▼ In a classic period scene, an 0-6-0 switcher moves freight cars in Worcester, Massachusetts, circa 1900. It was standard practice for brakemen to ride on the tops of cars in order to set handbrakes. Here, a brakeman stands on the first car behind the locomotive.

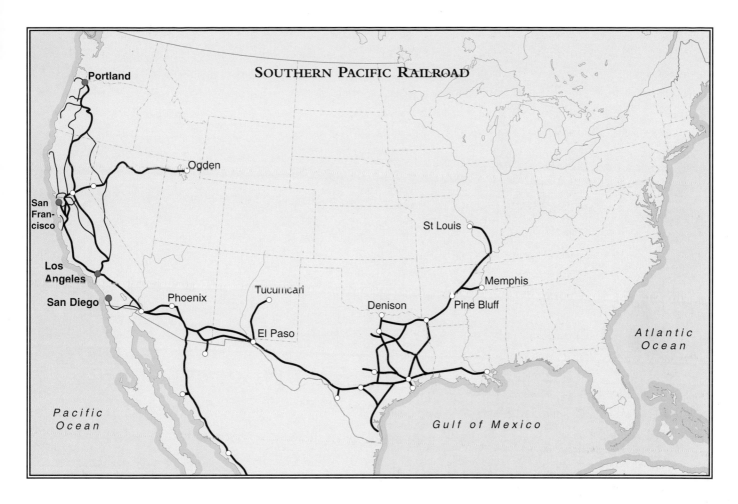

SOUTHERN PACIFIC RAILROAD

▲ The Southern Pacific bought, built, and controlled lines all over the West and South. When E. H. Harriman took control of the railroad in 1901, he described its comprehensive system as an empire. This route map dates from around 1945.

a hold on railroad employees. Brotherhoods representing the different crafts had formed, with locomotive engineers and firemen among the first to organize. As the railroads grew busier (and trains longer), working conditions became more harried and dangerous. In response, railroad men began to demand increased wages and more favorable working conditions. Profit-conscious railroad management was often unreceptive to the rights and needs of its employees. This resulted in strikes, the most serious of which occurred in 1877. By today's standards, these strikes were more akin to a small revolution than a labor action. Hundreds of men were involved and, in some cases, there was terrible violence, resulting in the destruction of railway equipment and the intervention of armed soldiers firing against the strikers.

Meanwhile, the rate wars on eastern trunk lines resulted in railroads hauling freight and passengers at a loss, in an effort to undercut their competition. By contrast, other lines that held near monopolies on transportation routes charged exorbitant rates to gouge the wallets of small shippers and ordinary travelers. This situation was particularly acute with farmers in the West, who were dependent on railroads to ship their produce, but did not have the financial clout to fight the rising prices.

FINANCIAL FIASCOS

While some railroads were extremely profitable, others were essentially pyramid schemes. Small investors were often ruined by fraudulent or poorly planned railroad enterprises, and could easily be duped by incompetent or unethical men selling stock for plausible-sounding but impractical projects. On other occasions, the manipulations of rail barons such as Gould left people with stock barely worth the paper on which it was printed.

All of these actions – strikes, rate wars, and stock manipulations – combined with poor service, late passenger trains, inadequate railroad stations, disastrous train wrecks, lost freight, maimed employees from poor safety practices, and other annoyances, contributed to a growing discontent with North America's railroads. The distaste for railroad abuses resulted in a negative image and, by the 1880s and 1890s, the railroads were forced to take action to improve their public image. Technological advancements allowed them to improve their services by offering faster, safer, and more comfortable passenger

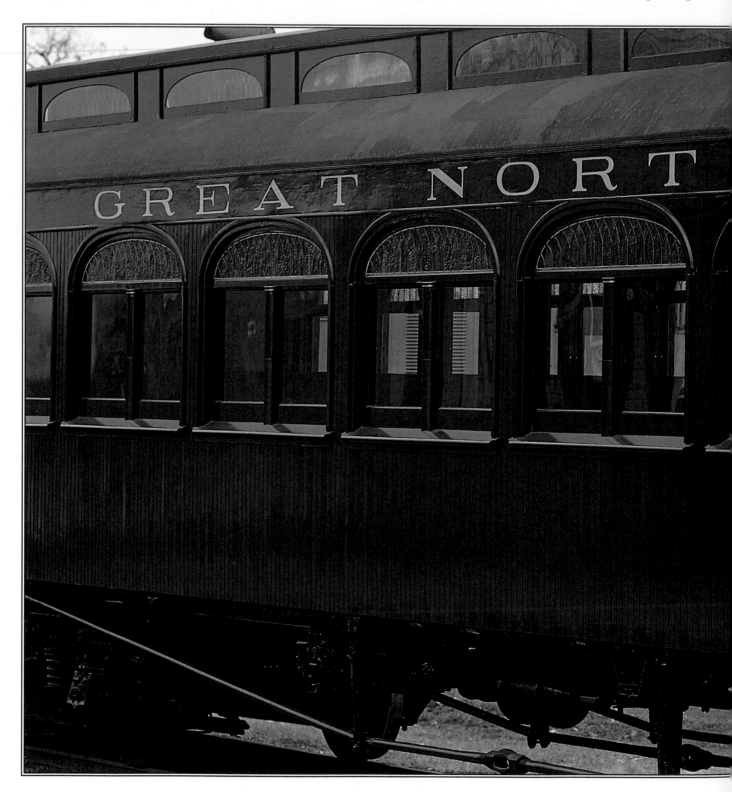

trains. Some used their excess profits to build ever more opulent railroad depots, replacing bleak older facilities with glorious new ones. A short article from the August 28, 1875 issue of the *Railway Gazette* illustrates this point: "The new depot of the New York, New Haven & Hartford road [at New Haven,

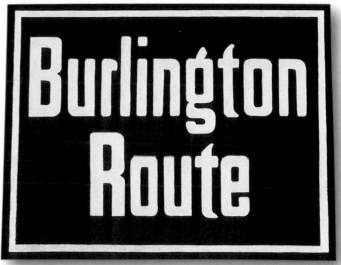

▲ The Chicago, Burlington & Quincy, better known as the Burlington Route, was among the best-run Midwestern "Granger" roads. Its lines connected Chicago with the Twin Cities, Omaha, Denver, and Kansas City, among other points.

Connecticut] is a delightful contrast to the old, dark underground black hole into which passengers were thrust in former times."

Railroads began advertising, using decorative posters promoting romantic visions of rail travel. They published sumptuous literature proclaiming the wonders of their routes and the splendid qualities of their newest trains. Many hired authors to write colorful histories of their lines, which made heroes out of their founders and emphasized the important role the companies had played in American history. The effect of all this positive publicity was to get the public to forget the disgusting abuses of power in which the railroads had been engaged.

The myths that the railroads perpetuated during this time have since become intertwined with history, and so the stories and fables of the "golden age" of railroads have remained popular over the years, alongside the less glowing accounts of the activities of railroad owners, operators, and officers. Today, we

◄ James J. Hill's Great Northern connected the Twin Cities with Seattle, Washington. This handsome wooden passenger car dates from the time when Hill and Harriman vied for control of the West. Notice the stained-glass windows and clerestory roof.

TRAVELERS' TALES
A RAILWAY THROUGH THE HOUSE

The October 30, 1884 issue of *Railway Age* reported the following incident:"At St Louis a few nights ago, a special train on the Missouri Pacific, running between St Louis and Kirkwood, encountered an obstruction in the shape of a house on the track, which it completely demolished, besides damaging the engine . . . It appears that an ingenious house mover, having a contract to move a building [across the Missouri Pacific], consulted the timetables and chose an hour late at night, when he was certain there would be no regular trains to interfere with his work, to cross the railroad tracks. To guard against any possible danger, however, he employed a flagman to stay on guard and flag any train that might happen along. Having done this, he told the occupants of the house to go quietly to bed and he proceeded with his moving. At about 11:20 p.m., when he had just fairly gotten the building on the track, the special came along, and [with] the flagman having deserted his post [the train] dashed into the building with the result above stated. Strange to say, none of the occupants were injured, although the house was a complete wreck."

Although such a bizarre enterprise is certainly not to be encouraged, here is something to remember: when around a railway line, one should always expect a train in either direction on any track. Had the unfortunate house mover heeded this rule, he may have taken the precaution of contacting the railway before making his ill-fated decision.

embrace the romantic visions of the railroad, while acknowledging the failings, abuses, and corruption of their owners. Unfortunately, the antipathy and hostility toward railroad management resulted in stifling legislation a generation after the worst abuses had occurred. The introduction of these new laws greatly limited the railroads' ability to compete effectively, and certainly contributed to their demise as a first-class American transportation network. Many people felt that the railroads' owners had deservedly brought this ruin upon themselves. However, the rich men who benefited from the abusive nature of the railroads had already made their millions and sold out, and therefore suffered little from the vindictive nature of public attitudes and subsequent regulation. In many cases, it did not matter anyway – most of the worst offenders were dead by the time the new legislation took effect. In the end, the public suffered most – from a poorer, less efficient network.

Although many of the early transcontinental lines enjoyed Federal land grants and financial support, not all benefited from such governmental assistance. The Great Northern was the second northern transcontinental route in the United States. It was built by railroad legend James J. Hill, a man known for his shrewd business practices, cunning strategies, and personal stamina. Hill was not the type of boss to sit around the boardroom leaving all the work to his minions. He was respected for his great understanding of railroading, and his willingness to work hard. While hated by his enemies, he was admired by many of his employees, who knew that he was working every bit as hard as they were.

HILL'S GREAT NORTHERN
Hill constructed the Great Northern using mostly private funds, and it was one of the best-built and most financially sound of the transcontinental routes. This was partly due to Hill's careful development of on-line traffic as the railroad pushed west. Unlike other lines that were forced to survive on Federal

▶ The pride of the Southern Pacific was its famous *Daylight* passenger trains, boasted to be "the most beautiful trains in the world." Here, the Southern Pacific's streamlined 4-8-4 No. 4449 leads an historic *Daylight* through Emeryville, California.

money for income while the railroad was under construction, the Great Northern built a strong network of branch lines to feed traffic to its main stem as it crossed the plains. The Great Northern also worked hard to promote settlement along its lines by encouraging immigration, a common strategy for traffic building in the West. As a result, when the Great Northern finally reached Seattle, Washington,

in 1893, it was already carrying ample traffic to pay for itself and was much stronger than both the Northern Pacific and Union Pacific lines, which had reached the Northwest earlier.

Both the Union Pacific and the Northern Pacific succumbed to the financial depression of 1893, which proved a pivotal event in western railroading. After the depression, the Northern Pacific came

under the control of Hill, while Edward Henry Harriman acquired the Union Pacific. These two men would vie for supremacy in the West for the next two decades. They battled for the control of crucial lines such as the Burlington, in an attempt to assemble great railroad empires. Harriman, who had made his start with the Illinois Central, would also ultimately helm the Union Pacific and the Southern Pacific, while Hill controlled the Great Northern, the Northern Pacific, and the Burlington. Both men

▲ One of the Pennsylvania Railroad's 4-4-0 American types – a class D13 built at Altoona, Pennsylvania, in 1891 – hauls the company paycar at Thorndale, Pennsylvania. A railroad tradition, the paycar would make its rounds every week to distribute cash wages to employees.

were visionary in their outlook, and invested heavily and wisely in their railroads, making numerous improvements to infrastructure and equipment.

Harriman is noted for his extensive rebuilding of the Union Pacific. He straightened out curves,

relocated the line over tough grades, and added a second mainline track across Nebraska. His improvements to the Southern Pacific were equally impressive. He relocated many miles of the original Central Pacific route across Nevada and Utah, including the building of a tremendously long series of trestles across the Great Salt Lake in 1903. This bypassed the original line via Promontory – a route that remained in place for another four decades as a secondary line – and provided a much shorter desert crossing. He initiated many other improvements that would be carried out after his untimely

---

While Canada would boast three continuous transcontinental lines, the US never had a true coast-to-coast route under one owner

---

death in 1909. Among Hill's achievements were the building of a lower Cascades crossing over Stevens Pass in Washington and the railroad's eventual electrification using a state-of-the-art three-phase alternating current system.

Despite the progressive managements of Hill and Harriman, both railway systems were deemed anti-competitive and were broken up by the government. However, the men's visions were well founded and, decades after they were broken up, both systems would re-emerge. Today, they form the basis of the two largest transportation companies in the West: the Burlington Northern Santa Fe and a greatly expanded Union Pacific, respectively.

Hill and Harriman were not alone in their empire building. Jay Gould's son, George, had his own ambitions, and in the decade following the turn of the century, George Gould attempted to piece together a true American transcontinental rail network. He purchased and controlled a variety of railroads, including the Western Maryland, the Missouri

▲ The development of the Janney automatic knuckle coupler was one of the great safety improvements forced upon the railroads. In the early days, the companies preferred dangerous link and pin couplers, which were cheaper than automatic couplers.

◄ Automatic block signals kept trains a safe distance from one another. These lower quadrant semaphores on the Southern Pacific indicate that the track is clear in both directions. A sunset silhouette of semaphores was the SP's symbol of safety.

Pacific, and the Rio Grande, and initiated the construction of one of the last major western lines, the Western Pacific – effectively an extension of the Rio Grande from Salt Lake City to Oakland, California. Although more visionary than his father, Gould was less adept as a businessman, and his scheme collapsed before he could put the pieces together. While Canada would eventually boast not just one, but three, continuous transcontinental lines, the United States has still not managed to assemble a true coast-to-coast railroad under one ownership.

Between the end of the Civil War and the turn of the century, a number of technological advances had

▲ Many railroads built new stations between 1880 and 1910 using elaborate architectural styles to replace original wooden, utilitarian structures. This Greek revival style station was built by the Pennsylvania Railroad at Richmond, Indiana.

were moving together. This required the man on the ground to have agile hands as well as fast feet. Failure to move quickly could easily result in a lost finger or crushed hands; railroaders of the period were routinely maimed in this fashion. A more serious accident would result if the man coupling the cars lost his footing, or did not get the pin in place quickly enough. Then he was easily crushed between the moving cars. While railroads were callous and unsympathetic to the plight of their workers, the gung-ho attitudes of the men did not help matters. Early attempts at introducing safer working practices were dismissed as unmanly. Survival of the fittest was the rule, and many men were killed and wounded every year while coupling cars.

John H. White Jr., the author of many books on 19th-century railroad practice, estimated that 38 to 40 percent of all railroad employee injuries during

---

Dangling ropes were erected ahead of low overhead clearances; when the brakeman felt a tickle he knew he had to hit the deck

---

great impact on the operation of trains. The introduction of automatic knuckle couplers, air brakes, improved draft gears, better lubricants and wheel bearings, and advanced signal systems made railroading significantly safer for both passengers and employees. These improvements also allowed railroads to operate longer, heavier, and significantly faster trains, and on closer headways than ever before, thus vastly improving the efficiency and capacity of most railroad lines. What may seem surprising is that, despite the many benefits of such new inventions, most railroads were extremely resistant to adopt them. It was only safety legislation introduced by state and Federal government that forced the implementation of such crucial inventions as the automatic coupler and the automatic air brake.

Traditionally, railroads used link and pin couplers. There was a multitude of different designs, but all had the same significant weakness — they were extremely dangerous to work with. To couple cars effectively, the couplers had to be guided together by hand and an iron pin dropped between them as the freight cars

this period were caused by coupling errors. While automatic couplers had been patented in the late 1860s, railroads were reluctant to implement their use because they were much more expensive than, and incompatible with, link and pin couplers. As in the case of changing gauges, a massive investment was required to change from one style of coupler to another. The preferred automatic coupler was the Janney knuckle coupler, which was self-locking. Massachusetts led the way with legislation in 1880, but it took 20 years before all cars for intercity services were equipped with knuckle couplers.

The introduction of automatic braking systems followed a similar pattern. Traditionally, trains were stopped using engine brakes. As consists grew longer and heavier, brakes were added to freight and passenger cars. These needed to be applied manually, typically with a large iron wheel that would be used to tighten them down. One of the principal responsibilities of the brakeman was to go from car to car setting and releasing brakes as required. On passenger trains, this was fairly easy, as the trains were short, and a brakeman could walk (or run) from car to car when he received the appropriate whistle signal from the locomotive engineer.

The operation of freight trains presented a more difficult situation altogether. Trains were longer, and brakemen had to walk on top of the cars to set brakes. At least two or more brakemen were assigned to each run, and long trains might have four or more brakemen. They could sometimes take shelter in the relative comfort of the locomotive – or, in later years, the caboose tacked on the rear of the train. Often, however, they were forced to ride up on the cars, regardless of the weather, waiting for the whistle that sent them jumping from car to car, turning down brake wheels as fast as they could. Failure to set the brakes quickly could result in a collision, so it was important to get the job done as rapidly as possible. This task was very hazardous, and thousands of men lost their lives when they slipped off moving cars, were struck by overhead bridges and tunnels, or died from exposure. Some safety features were implemented to aid the brakeman in his task. He was often armed with a small wooden pole to give him leverage when turning the brake wheels. Many freight cars had catwalks installed on them for better footing, while warning devices – called "tell tails" and comprised of dangling ropes – were erected ahead of low overhead clearances; when the brakeman felt a tickle from the rope, he knew he had to hit the deck immediately.

▶ **The publishing of detailed scheduling information, embellished with enticing illustrations, encouraged people to ride trains. Today, old train timetables are valuable collector's items.**

◄ Massachusetts-based photographer Bill Bullard caught a New Haven switcher crew in a classic pose around 1905. Most freight trains required six or more men. A typical crew comprised a locomotive engineer, fireman, conductor, and three brakemen.

A variety of automatic braking systems offered to improve the way in which trains were brought to a stop. The most popular of these was George Westinghouse's airbrake system. His original invention dated to 1869, but he introduced a far better version in 1873. The later airbrake was designed to be "fail safe," meaning that, in the event of a brake system failure, the brakes would be applied automatically. This was particularly advantageous if a train broke in two pieces on the roll, an event all too common in freight railroading. Some lines were quick to adopt

---

Not only did the airbrake improve safety and reduce the number of injuries, but it also allowed trains to run longer and faster

---

the airbrake for passenger runs, and by the mid-1880s steeply graded western lines, such as the Central Pacific, embraced the airbrake for freight, too. However, most railroads were ambivalent to the advantages of airbrakes, and resisted them because of their expense. Railroad managers at the time found it hard to envision any savings from such an investment. Ultimately, legislation forced the railroads to adopt the airbrake, and they were much better off because of it.

Not only did the airbrake improve safety and reduce the number of terrible injuries to brakemen, but it also allowed trains to safely run longer and faster than ever before by enabling them to stop much more easily and quickly. Other innovations such as a much stronger draft gear (the components that hold couplers to the cars, and which bear the pulling and braking forces of the train in motion), superior lubrication, and better bearings made the practical operation of much longer consists possible. It was now becoming easier to start, accelerate, control, and stop trains.

▲ The Wootten firebox was designed with a very broad grate to accommodate slow-burning anthracite coal, and required a "Camelback" arrangement. The engineer rode astride the boiler and the fireman behind. Reading No. 1187 is an 0-4-0 Camelback.

All the improvements in auxiliary technology provided a demand for much more powerful loco-motives. A number of innovations came about in the last decades of the 19th century that permitted the growth of locomotive size and power. Steel was known to be much stronger than iron, but traditional technologies meant it was vastly more expensive to produce. However, this changed with the advent of cheap steel-making processes in the 1860s, which enabled railroads to employ steel components. This resulted in stronger rails, stronger

bridges, and better boilers, all of which helped pave the way for bigger locomotives.

For many years, the size of the locomotive was effectively limited by the capacity of its firebox and boiler, and by the maximum weight that bridges on the railroad line could accommodate. Efforts to build more powerful locomotives usually resulted in the addition of more driving and guiding wheels, to help distribute the greater weight of a bigger boiler. Often, the building of large locomotives resulted in engines that could not maintain sufficient steam

▶ More driving wheels gave a locomotive greater tractive effort, while distributing the weight of the engine over more wheels, permitting a heavier, more powerful engine. The 4-8-0 Mastodon was considered a big locomotive in 1895.

power to fully take advantage of their size. Further-more, the inability to significantly increase the weight on drivers did not permit necessary adhesion.

In the early 1880s, the Central Pacific's master mechanic A. J. Stevens designed a fleet of big loco-motives using the 4-8-0 wheel arrangement. These long-boiler machines, descriptively known as "Mastodons," were designed for service over Donner Pass, where heavy grades and heavy tonnage demanded lots of power. While not the first of their type, they were among the most successful examples of large locomotives from the period. They had

to his railroad duties – encouraged A. J. Stevens to build an even bigger locomotive.

Stanford wanted his railroad to operate the world's largest locomotive, and he got his wish. So, despite Stevens' better judgement, he fulfilled his boss's request and built a gigantic engine with a 4-10-0 wheel arrangement named *El Gobernador*. (It was the product of the Central Pacific's Sacramento Shops, one of the few locomotive works on the West Coast.) But, as so often happens when politicians interfere with engineering, the locomotive was a spectacular failure. It was too big for its firebox and could not deliver sustained power. It was useless for

The most flamboyant member of the "Big Four," Leland Stanford, encouraged Stevens to build an even bigger locomotive

service on Donner Pass, but found work as a helper engine in the Tehachapi Mountains for a few years before it was eventually cut up for scrap.

The traditional location for the firebox was between the frame of the locomotive. With small 4-4-0s weighing just 12 to 15 tons (10.9 to 13.6 tonnes), this was perfectly adequate; however, this placement proved constraining as locomotives grew. By the 1890s, 4-4-0s weighing 50 to 60 tons (44.4–54.4 tonnes) were common for passenger service, and even heavier 4-6-0s, 2-8-0s, and 4-8-0s were used for freight. A bigger firebox was necessary to obtain greater power from the locomotive. One solution was to build the firebox above the locomotive frame. This was popular with the Eastern anthracite railroads, which began using locomotives with a broad firebox grate, better suited for slow-burning anthracite coal, in the 1880s. Many of these locomotives placed the engineer's cab over the boiler, while leaving the fireman alone at the end of

ample steaming power and tractive effort to replace several 4-4-0s on freights. Stevens' long-boiler machines were so successful that the most flamboyant member of the "Big Four," the Central Pacific's Leland Stanford – who variously served as Governor of California and as a senator, in addition

the locomotive. These odd-looking engines were commonly known as "Camelbacks" or "Mother Hubbards" because of their humpbacked appearance.

Despite these innovations, firebox size was still limited by the weight it placed on the drivers and space limitations imposed by the driving wheels. In the mid-1890s, the weight-bearing trailing truck was introduced to help support a greatly enlarged firebox. More firebox meant more power, and more power meant more speed. Initially, the 2-4-2 Columbia type was developed for express passenger service. While fast, this type suffered from poor tracking ability. Soon the 4-4-2 Atlantic type was introduced, and, by 1896, this had become one of the most popular new types of passenger locomotives. Its greater stability and ability to maintain sustained high horsepower at speed made it ideal for fast passenger service.

By the mid-1890s, many railroads were operating relatively fast trains, made possible by faster locomotives, innovations in coupler designs, automatic braking systems, and new automatic block signals that allowed for safer operations at higher speeds. One of the best-known high-speed passenger trains was the New York Central's *Empire State Express*. The Central proclaimed it as "the fastest train in the world," and to emphasize this point, the railroad's chief public relations man, George Daniels, staged a well-publicized stunt. A special 4-4-0 locomotive was built with a large boiler and extra tall driving wheels, 7ft (2.1m) high. It was numbered 999. On May 10, 1893 – exactly 24 years after the completion of the transcontinental railroad at Promontory – number 999 raced the *Empire State Express* across New York State. A few miles west of Batavia, New York, on a long stretch of open tangent track, the 999 was reported to have hit a top speed of 112½mph (181kph)! Soon, newspapers everywhere proclaimed the 999's speed record, and the world knew of the New York Central's accomplishment. While there is little doubt that the 999 went very fast that day, no

one knows for certain if it really hit 112½mph, as the methods used for determining speed were based on the less than accurate practice of timing the distance between mileposts with a pocket watch. In this case, publicity was more important than precision.

American locomotive manufacturers were some of the best and most prolific in the world. In addition to building engines for the domestic market, they supplied tens of thousands of locomotives for railways around the globe. Of the roughly 175,000 steam locomotives built in the United States, some 37,000 were shipped abroad. During lean times domestically, locomotive builders would survive on orders from overseas. The foreign market also gave

---

American locomotive makers were among the most prolific in the world, supplying tens of thousands around the globe

---

manufacturers the opportunity to experiment with different types of locomotives, before introducing them to relatively conservative American lines.

The advantages of a trailing truck were not immediately applied to heavy freight locomotives, as railroads were content to continue using 4-6-0s and 2-8-0s for most heavy freight assignments. In the late 1890s, Baldwin built a small fleet of 2-8-2s for export to Japan. Several years later, the type was developed for domestic freight service as essentially an expansion of the 2-8-0 Consolidation type. Because of the Japanese connection, the 2-8-2 became known as the Mikado type – *mikado* being the Japanese word for emperor. Ultimately, the Mikado became one of the most popular steam locomotive types of the 20th century.

While popular, the Mikado was by no means the largest. During the decades to come, the United States would develop the largest, heaviest, and most powerful locomotives in the world. The 2-8-2 was also developed into one of the best-known heavy narrow-gauge types. The Rio Grande operated a significant fleet of outside-frame 2-8-2s on its narrow-gauge lines in Colorado and New Mexico.

◄ **The 2-8-2 Mikado type became the most common type of steam locomotive in the 20th century. Duluth & Northern Minnesota Railway No. 14 was built by Baldwin in 1913, and represents a typical locomotive of the period.**

GRAND CENTRAL
TERMINAL

4

TRAINS IN THE GLORY YEARS

As the railroads achieved a new level of sophistication, traveling became a luxurious experience. New electric lines gave the steam railroads fresh competition, while impressive terminals were built to cope with expanding traffic.

By the 1890s, the North American railroad industry had matured, and the art of railway travel had been refined. The majority of the North American route structure was in place, leaving just a few more important lines to be opened, mostly in the West. While freight traffic had always remained the largest source of revenue for most

◀ **The magnificent statuary on the 42nd Street facade of Grand Central Terminal is the work of sculptor Jules Coutan. This elaborate station reflected the wealth of the New York Central Railroad, and the importance of New York as its prime terminal.**

North American lines, passenger traffic and revenues peaked. The railroads enjoyed their premier position as intercity carriers and competed with each other for market share. Competition from new electric interurban railways was just beginning and would soon add a whole new element to the railway network. If you planned to take a long overland trip, the railroad was your best possible option, and, if you intended to ship goods – be it a box of gifts or 10,000 tons of coal – again, the railroad was your best choice.

The locomotive business had also matured. Unable to compete, many of the early builders had

▲ **The massive balloon-arched train shed at the old Grand Central Depot was inspired by the shed at St Pancras Station in London. While the latter still stands, New York's shed was demolished to make way for the new Grand Central Terminal.**

exited the business, leaving Baldwin as the largest producer of locomotives. In 1901, most of the remaining locomotive builders joined forces by forming the American Locomotive Company, often known as "Alco." This allowed them to better compete with Baldwin. Among the components to Alco were the Schenectady Locomotive Works, Brooks Locomotive Works, Cooke Locomotive Works, and the Rhode Island Locomotive Works. A few years later, the Montreal Locomotive Works became Alco's Canadian subsidiary – an arrangement that survived well into the diesel-building era.

In their first five decades, North American railroads were largely content to operate one type of passenger train – one that ran from terminal to terminal, making all stops in between. Such trains would amble along at moderate speeds, making much better time than any other form of transportation available at that period, but not exactly pushing the limits of technology. They may have carried different classes of cars, each catering to the style of travel and the budgets desired by different categories of passengers. Advances in technology and the competition between different railroad networks helped bring about a marked improvement in passenger services.

FASTER, CLASSIER TRAINS

During the 1880s, new trains running on significantly faster schedules than ordinary trains and limited to serving larger towns were introduced. These carried fancy names followed by superlatives indicating they were a better service to distinguish them from ordinary, common trains. Thus the "limited," "express," "special," and "flyer" were born. These trains used a higher quality of passenger equipment. They featured the very finest sleeping cars, parlor cars, and diners. Usually, a specific set of equipment was assigned to one of these fine trains and was often painted accordingly. The large eastern trunk lines set the standard, and soon railways all across the continent were adding new, faster, deluxe trains. The *Florida Special* debuted in January 1887, as a seasonal express, connecting New York City (by way of ferries across New York Harbor) and the "Sunshine State." This train originated on the Pennsylvania Railroad and traveled over several different lines to reach its destination.

LUXURY LIMITED SERVICES

In 1887, the Pennsylvania Railroad debuted its all-Pullman *Pennsylvania Limited* service to Chicago. This train was one of the first to use Pullman's patented vestibule cars. A vestibule was an enclosed compartment at each end of the car that served two important functions: it protected passengers traveling from car to car from the wind and the rain, and, more importantly, added a significant measure of safety in the event of a collision by protecting against telescoping. (Early wooden, open-ended cars would often compact during violent crashes, sliding directly over one another, like a collapsible telescope. The result was a terrible loss of life among the occupants of the telescoped cars.) Initially, four separate consists were required for the *Pennsylvania Limited*. In 1898,

▼ In this dynamic image of steam locomotive power, Grand Trunk 0-6-0 No. 7470 catches the sun on a beautiful, clear autumn morning, as it rolls past an automatic block signal at North Conway, New Hampshire.

▲ This old wooden coach from James J. Hill's Great Northern Railway, with its elegantly arched windows embellished with leaded glass, dates from 1900. Decorative touches such as these were typical on major passenger cars in the Victorian era.

the Pennsylvania Railroad revamped the cars for this luxury train and painted them in distinctive colors. The lower portion of the cars was green, the band along the length of the windows was bright yellow, and above the windows was a subdued red. The yellow window band was most striking, and the train became known as the "Yellow Kid." In its day, it was one of the most familiar names in railroading.

STYLISH NEW CARS

During the 1880s and 1890s, heavyweight wooden cars designed for long-distance trains had evolved into lush, elegant rooms adorned with the ornate styles of the period. They were made of hardwoods, featured detailed decorations and gold striping, and were covered with layer upon layer of heavy varnish

that made them glisten. As a result, passenger trains – especially the important named trains – became known to railroaders as "Varnish," distinguishing them from the common, tawdry, dusty freight trains. The interiors of these passenger cars featured tall, full Empire or groin arch style ceilings; rich tapestry-covered upholstery with complex repetitive patterns; arched windows with heavy draperies; and often decorative stained-glass end windows. Rich, somber colors prevailed, and the cars resembled Victorian sitting rooms and parlors. The most elaborate cars for public use were the parlor cars and diners on the best known named trains. Parlor cars were lounges where passengers could relax, take in the passing scenery, and socialize with each other. Many trains carried club cars, often called "Smoking Cars," which were typically the sole domains of adult male passengers. Here, men could drink hard liquor, smoke cigars, and discuss a host of unsavory subjects such as the machinations of business, hunting trips, and affairs with women.

TRAVELERS' TALES
MISS WOODS AND THE SOUTHERN PACIFIC

In the golden age of American railroading, railroaders who took it upon themselves to get the job done were greatly admired. This was an age of rugged individualism and self-determination. Such is the tale of a woman telegrapher on the Southern Pacific route over Donner Pass related by Southern Pacific chroniclers Neill C. Wilson and Frank J. Taylor in their popular history *Southern Pacific, the Roaring Story of a Fighting Railroad.*

About 1900, the Southern Pacific's "Miss Woods" – whose first name seems to have been forgotten – was a telegrapher at the depot in Truckee, California, at the base of the steepest part of the ascent over Donner Summit. This is a place known for exceptionally heavy snowfall – the stuff of which legends are made. Miss Woods was a tall, healthy, good-looking woman in her early 30s – proud of her job and resourceful. During the winter storms that often plague operations in the High Sierra, the Southern Pacific's Miss Woods all too often found herself cut off from the rest of the railroad. Snow would tear her telegraph lines down, and, during the height of a blizzard, it was impossible to find anyone with the wherewithal to get the lines back up again. This did not stop Miss Woods from getting the trains over the road.

Donner was the Southern Pacific's link between California and the East, and, in those days, the only practical way east from northern California. Therefore, it was crucial that trains made it over the mountains

The telegraph console at a railroad station was crucial to daily operations. The telegrapher, working from a desk such as the preserved example above, decoded messages from the dispatcher and gave them to the train crews.

with minimal delay. Without the aid of Southern Pacific dispatchers, the intrepid Miss Woods would direct the trains as she saw fit. She might hold a heavy westbound freight for the Overland and make an eastbound take the siding for a loaded train of perishable fruit. Back then, the Southern Pacific's Donner had just one mainline track, and Miss Woods knew as well as anyone how to make the most of that single track. Legend has it that, during the height of a storm, she would be out in the snow, wrapped tightly with a shawl around her ears, mittens on her hands, with a bright lantern in her hand, keeping the railroad moving.

Sleeping cars had developed into big business, and, by the turn of the century, Pullman dominated this trade, both building and operating sleeping cars. This became an extremely popular way to travel between cities, and most long-distance trains carried Pullman sleepers. On many routes, sleeping car passengers were afforded a through service, meaning that they did not have to change trains; instead, railroads passed sleeping cars from one train to another. Sleeping passengers might simply feel a bump in the night, as their car was taken off one train and coupled to another using a switch engine at a remote terminal or junction. By the 1920s, Pullman was accommodating an average of 100,000 passengers a night on trains all across North America. This totalled more than 35 million sleeper passengers a year.

Sleeping cars and diners went hand in hand. Being able to enjoy a meal as well augmented the luxury of

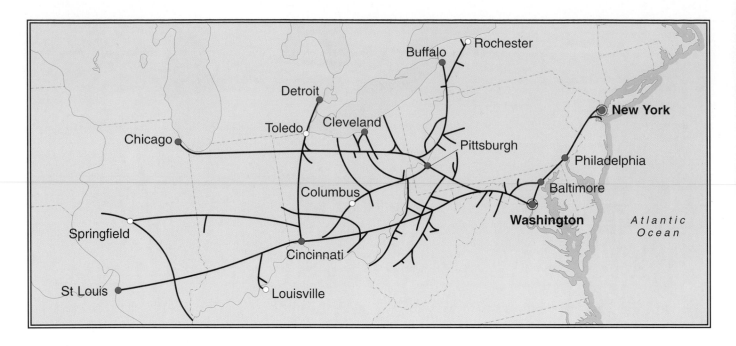

▲ The Baltimore & Ohio connected the port of Baltimore, Maryland, with the interior of the country. The line originally reached as far as Wheeling, Virginia (now West Virginia), and was later extended to St Louis, Chicago, and numerous other cities.

sleeping on the train. The art of a sublime, rolling culinary experience had been perfected by the 1890s, and railroads took great pride in the diversity and quality of their menus. Railroad diners were modeled after fine restaurants and featured fine china (usually to a pattern specific to the owning railroad), elegant environs, and well-mannered staff.

GOURMET FARE ONBOARD

Passengers traveling on the *North Western Limited* between Chicago and the Twin Cities had a delectable choice of dishes and appetizers that included: canapé caviar, bisque of pigeon à la notelière, lobster à la Newburg en casserole, prime roast beef, endive salad, a "home-made" plum pudding, and a selection of Waukesha Cream and Camembert cheeses. By comparison, the Santa Fe contracted its diner service to Fred Harvey. In an earlier era, Fred Harvey was legendary for having elevated the meal stop from an abysmal rushed experience to a decent, respectable meal at a reasonable price. The Santa Fe's dining car menu featured Harvey's name so that all passengers knew to expect quality and value. On it, bold letters

enthusiastically proclaimed: "It is the best in the world." Inside the menu, one would find a tenderloin steak for 80 cents; veal cutlet (plain or breaded), calf's liver and bacon, or broiled lake trout, all available for a very affordable 45 cents each. Some railroads featured local dishes. Many eastern lines offered Blue Point oysters on the half shell, while the Rio Grande featured Rocky Mountain trout.

The selection of fine food alone was often a sufficiently compelling reason to take the train. Railroads with inferior routes often made up for slower schedules by providing better service. An excellent example was the New York to Washington D.C. run. After 1910, the Pennsylvania Railroad had a direct route from downtown to downtown via the new Hudson tunnels, and offered frequent fast services. The B&O route, in contrast, was much slower, and still required a ferry ride to Jersey City from Manhattan to board their trains. The B&O captured a portion of the business despite the inconvenience in part because of its superlative diners, considered some of the best in the East. In those days, traveling often meant more than just getting where you were going as cheaply and as quickly as possible. How you traveled was as important as where you went. Traveling was meant to be enjoyed, savored, and remembered.

Fancy limited trains, such as the Santa Fe's deluxe *California Limited*, would feature observation cars

TRAVELERS' TALES
EXPENSIVE BREAKFAST ON THE PENN

The old adage goes, "Nothing is finer than dinner in the diner"; however, the price for that dinner was usually higher on board the train than it was in a regular restaurant. The dining car was a convenience and a luxury, not a necessity of travel.

One traveler writing in the May 1904 issue of *Railway and Locomotive Engineering* described her experience on a train of the great Pennsylvania Railroad: "... Being very anxious to see the Horse-shoe Curve, I traveled over the Pennsylvania to Chicago, on the finest train they run. The man who fashioned that horseshoe surely whistled the 'Anvil Chorus' when he had finished. It is a wonderful piece of engineering.

"It was very nice to travel on this limited train, but it had its drawbacks; unless limited to time, I would not care to do it again. My 'grumbling' is, however, confined to the meal business and overheated cars. The dining car service is, I believe, operated by the Pullman Company. I want to say most emphatically the 'dollar a meal' system ought to be abolished. Who wants to eat a dollar breakfast? Then comes luncheon and dinner; I am quite willing to pay a dollar for my dinner, but I am not willing to pay a dollar for each of these meals and be glared at by a waiter because, in his eyes, my tip is too small, and be given a finger bowl the water in which has been used by someone else. I am very certain the Pennsylvania Railroad would not tolerate this.

"Many lines for traveling northwest are offered one in Chicago; as I could go by one only, I chose the CB&Q, one of their finest trains – splendidly equipped cars, well lighted, but overheated. On my return I bought my ticket via the Chicago, Milwaukee and St Paul – I am not handing out bouquets, but if I were, I might select a few flowers to give the CB&Q, but the biggest, choicest bunch would be offered the 'St Paul.' It will be pleasant to remember that trip all my life: the roadbed is smooth, the cars are the very finest, the attendants – conductors, porters, waiter and the men in charge of the dining cars – most kindly and attentive. The food is excellent, abundant, and carefully served; the 'tips' it suited me to give were accepted in a nice manner, the men seemed pleased.

"Here I want to say that where railway companies operate their own dining, parlor, and sleeping cars, the service is the best, one's comfort the greatest, the employees act as if they wanted to please their 'road' by doing well by its patrons, and I think the traveling public recognizes this."

Nearly one hundred years later, this rail traveler's observations on quality of service could easily be applied to other modes of transportation offered today – a lesson, it seems, to be learned again and again.

---

with an open rear platform, where passengers could get a breath of fresh air and watch the tracks roll away. Open observation cars became popular in the early 20th century. One of the first trains to carry them on a regular basis was the Northern Pacific's *North Coast Limited*. These observation cars are best known as the platforms for political speeches made by hopeful candidates rolling from city to city on "whistle-stop" tours. What better way to conduct a campaign than from the back of a steam train?

Premier runs were carefully named to convey a sense of the specific railroad's character, speed, and quality, and the geography of the region. These trains – the pride of the railroad – were known as the company flagship. More than just transportation, they also served as an indicator of the company's prosperity, an advertising vehicle for the railroad's freight services, and a status symbol. Competing lines would work hard to present the finest flagship, and few expenses were spared. Their décor was elaborate, elegant, and even opulent, and the trains were given the best schedules possible. The line they traveled over would be known for the flagship's name.

On the transcontinental "Overland Route," the Southern Pacific, Union Pacific, and Chicago & North Western operated the *Overland Limited*. It ran directly from Chicago to Oakland, with a direct ferry connection across San Francisco Bay to San Francisco. The *Overland Limited* was known as the train of the rich and powerful, and was the very best way to reach San Francisco from the East Coast. What may surprise many people today is that there

was no through transcontinental train in the United States that offered a true coast-to-coast service. Passengers from the East had to make connections at Chicago, St Louis, or Kansas City. Perhaps the closest thing to a coast-to-coast train was the Southern Pacific's *Sunset Limited*, which operated between Los

▲ Most short-distance second-class passenger cars offered comfortable but fairly minimal accommodation. This all-steel coach, with an open observation deck at the rear, dates from the mid-1920s, and would have remained in daily service for 40 years.

Angeles and New Orleans along what the Southern Pacific dubbed its "Sunset Route."

Canada, by contrast, was served by a classy service that operated directly from Montreal to Vancouver, over the Canadian Pacific. The *Imperial Limited* was introduced in 1899 and touted as the only transcontinental train operated by one railroad management.

There was no through transcontinental train in the United States that offered a true coast-to-coast service

It provided a 100-hour service between its two terminals and was considered by many to be one of the finest trains in Canada. A railroad would often update its service by introducing a new, even fancier train to supplement (rather than supercede) an existing operation. Following World War I, the Canadian Pacific debuted its new *Trans-Canada Limited*, a first-class, all-Pullman sleeper train on the route of the *Imperial Limited*. This was advertised as "Canada's

◀ In this period postcard view, the Santa Fe's *California Limited* passes Joshua trees in southern California's Mojave Desert. The train is "double headed" – hauled by two locomotives. Larger engines eliminated the need for this practice.

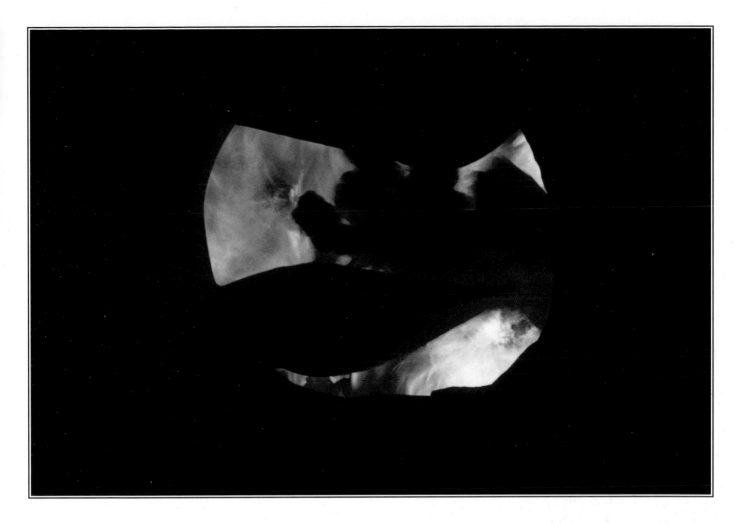

▲ The fireman was responsible for maintaining the fire on the locomotive. On a heavy run, he might shovel as much as two tons of coal an hour from the tender into the firebox. An efficient fireman would not keep the firebox doors open any longer than he had to.

Premier Train." Canada's Intercolonial Railway — a predecessor to the Canadian National Railway — operated the *Maritime Express*, which it expansively called "Canada's Famous Train" (billed as "one of the finest on the American continent"). This particular run connected Montreal and Halifax, Nova Scotia, by way of New Brunswick.

There was fierce competition on parallel railroads serving the same cities and vying for passenger business. High-quality service, speed, and status were all advertised in an effort to attract patronage. One of the most competitive routes in the United States was between New York City and Buffalo, where there were no fewer than seven different routes open to travelers (albeit two of

◄ Open-ended observation cars were typically parlor cars. Passengers could sit out on the open platform and enjoy the passing scenery — an appealing option on warm afternoons in the days before air conditioning was installed on trains.

them entirely under the control of the New York Central). Why would passengers use one line over another? Cost, convenience, and speedy schedules were all considerations. As described in Chapter 3, the New York Central had the quickest route and operated the fastest train with its famous *Empire State Express*. It was also blessed by virtue of its superior geographical location, with the only direct route between New York City and Buffalo. Initially, all other lines relied on ferry trips across the Hudson River to reach New York City.

Opposite Manhattan, in New Jersey, sat a line of great train terminals, each serving one or more lines. The Lehigh Valley offered its *Black Diamond Express*, which was introduced in 1896 on the 50th

▲ An artist's depiction of the Pennsylvania Railroad's famous *Broadway Limited* racing an airplane. By the mid-1930s, railroads were beginning to feel the sting of airline competition. Some, including the Pennsylvania, were actually involved in the air travel business before anti-trust action prohibited this.

anniversary of that route's opening. While the New York Central had its "Fastest Train in the World," the Lehigh Valley boasted the *Black Diamond* as the "Handsomest Train in the World." The name of the train was selected in a contest and reflected the primary commodity of the railroad – coal. Another competitor on the New York to Buffalo run was the Delaware, Lackawanna and Western – the Lackawanna for short – commonly known as the "Road of Anthracite," for its major commodity. The Lackawanna's magnificent Hoboken Terminal sat in view of Manhattan Island, as it still does today. Its flagship

Buffalo in her white dress and arriving as clean and pure as she left. Each promotion featured a catchy verse that followed a formulaic pattern. The most famous of these ditties is still remembered today:

> *Says Phoebe Snow*
> *About to go*
> *Upon a trip*
> *To Buffalo,*
> *"My gown stays white*
> *From morn till night*
> *Upon the Road of Anthracite."*

In this case, the advertising worked, and the *Phoebe Snow* was a great success. Despite its longer run, it attracted a fair share of the New York to Buffalo trade. The train is much better remembered than its predecessor, the *Lackawanna Limited*, and operated continuously for 60 years – albeit in later years with diesels, rather than anthracite-burning steam.

While the New York to Buffalo market was competitive, one of the fiercest rivalries in the US was on the New York to Chicago route. The best-known

---

With clean-burning anthracite instead of bituminous coal, passengers would not become covered in grime and soot

---

trains were the New York Central's *Twentieth Century Limited* and the Pennsylvania Railroad's *Broadway Limited*. Each was the corporate flagship and a source of great pride. When one company introduced a faster schedule, or an innovative improvement, the other was quick to match and exceed it. When the *Twentieth Century* debuted in 1902, its 20-hour schedule was considered exceptionally fast. As competition between the Pennsylvania Railroad and the Central heated up, however, the schedule was gradually tightened up to 18 hours and eventually to less than 17 hours. That meant lots of fast, non-stop running. The Central's *Twentieth Century* only made intermediate stops at a handful of places and used bypass routes around congested junctions in order to avoid delays.

train was known as the *Phoebe Snow*, personified by a mythical woman wearing a white dress. The railroad's gimmick was simple but compelling: its locomotives used clean-burning anthracite instead of the common – and much dirtier – bituminous coal. As a result, passengers would not become covered in nearly as much grime and soot during the course of their trip. A long-running series of advertisements portrayed the fictional "Phoebe Snow" riding to

▲ Interurban railways using electrically powered trolley cars gave the steam railroads their first real competition. Here, a trolley bound for Worcester, Massachusetts, is seen near the Central Massachusetts Railroad station at Holden.

In the heyday of these great trains, they received the highest priority. No train was permitted to foul up the line ahead of them. Pity the poor railroad official on duty the night the *Broadway* ran late over his division! For many years, both trains left their respective Chicago terminals at the same time. They would pause at suburban Englewood alongside one another, and then race eastward on parallel adjacent tracks for miles until the lines finally diverged. It was a race symbolic of the tight schedule of the two trains and also of the fierce competition between the New York Central and Pennsylvania railroads.

The *Twentieth Century Limited* took its name from the beginning of the new century in 1900, which, at that time, had a modern connotation in the same way that the term "millennium" would have 100 years later. This train was the vision of the Central's master showman and publicist, George H. Daniels,

who had made the *Empire State Express* a hit in the previous decade. The *Twentieth Century Limited* had several important distinctions that made it different from all other New York Central trains. It was entirely composed of sleeping cars, and carried no coaches. It made only a handful of stops and even bypassed major cites such as Rochester and Buffalo along the way. And, lastly, it was an "extra fare" train, meaning that there was a surcharge to ride it. Certainly, passage on the *Twentieth Century*, with famous personalities and celebrities aboard on many runs, was a lot more than just a train ride.

THE *BROADWAY LIMITED*

The Pennsylvania Railroad's *Broadway Limited* was not named for New York City's famous Broadway, but rather Pennsylvania's multiple-track mainline across New Jersey, known as the "Broad Way." Originally, this train was called the *Pennsylvania Special* and was not renamed until 1912. The train carried sleeping cars named for important people and places associated with the Pennsylvania route, including prominent figures of the American Revolution.

INTERURBAN COMPETITION

In 1888, Frank Sprague introduced the first successful electric streetcar system in Richmond, Virginia. The use of electric streetcars represented a vast improvement over horse-drawn trams, which were small, slow, and dirty. By contrast, electric streetcars were larger, could travel faster, and were clean, easy to heat in cold weather, and fairly comfortable to ride in. The concept caught on quickly, and soon cities all across North America, as well as around the world, were building electric streetcar lines. Small towns were not to be left out, and many little towns had "Toonerville" trolley lines. It did not take long for a whole new type of railway enterprise to develop: the interurban electric railway.

Interurban lines used electric traction and connected cities and towns. Compared to the mainline "steam" railroads, these lines were built to especially light standards. The tracks required very little grading, and permission was often granted by local authorities to build along the side of existing roads or even right down the middle of streets. Interurbans charged low fares and offered a cost-effective alternative to the steam railways for relatively short journeys. In just a few years, interurban lines were constructed all over North America. They were particularly popular in the East and Midwest, where the high population density guaranteed a solid traffic base. Often inter-urban railways utilized city streetcar tracks to enter larger cities, but the interurbans themselves rarely connected with one another. Some interurban lines were built to accommodate light freight traffic, thus offering communities that did not have a steam rail road the benefits of railroad freight.

▼ The Milwaukee Road was one of a few American railroads to electrify its mainline. Photographer Mel Patrick lit up the night with flashbulbs to effect this classic portrayal of Milwaukee's famous electrics, including one of its original 1915-era boxcabs.

◄ The Niagara, Ste Catherines & Toronto was a Canadian interurban railway. Typical of many electric railways established in North America, it featured miles of tracks running alongside the roads, and operated both freight and passenger services.

The old steam railroad companies were understandably displeased with the advent of the new interurbans, as these new lines attacked their traffic base, and typically hurt where the steam railroads were already weakest: on branch lines. Some railroads responded by matching interurban competition; others, such as the New Haven Railroad and the Southern Pacific, reacted by buying up competing interurbans. The Southern Pacific's Pacific Electric, which operated in the Los Angeles Basin, was the most extensive and one of the most comprehensive electric suburban rail networks. It was far more than just a country trolley and even operated its own sections of four-track mainline, had a subway and elevated in downtown Los Angeles, featured modern

---

The large eastern cities developed suburban commuter traffic, as people fled in search of greater space and comforts

---

automatic block signals, and carried a significant amount of freight. Eventually, the interurban was displaced by the motor bus, and especially by the advent of the private automobile.

By making transportation easier, the railroads facilitated travel and effected suburban growth. It was now possible to live outside a major downtown area and commute by using the railroad. And this is exactly what happened. The large eastern cities of Boston, New York, and Philadelphia developed significant suburban commuter traffic, as people fled the cities in search of the greater space and comforts offered in the country. In the Boston area, the Boston & Albany, Boston & Maine, and New Haven lines had all developed brisk commuter business by the 1880s. By 1900, Boston's magnificent new South Station had become the busiest railroad station in the world. This terminal, with its large cantilever train shed, served Boston & Albany and New Haven routes. In 1904, some 861 trains a day were using it, accommodating tens of thousands of passengers. South Station consolidated several older terminals,

▼ Proud of its Yankee heritage, New England's Boston & Maine Railroad used the colonial "minuteman" soldier, a potent symbol of the American Revolutionary War, to adorn its cars. The Boston & Maine also ran a train called the *Minute Man*.

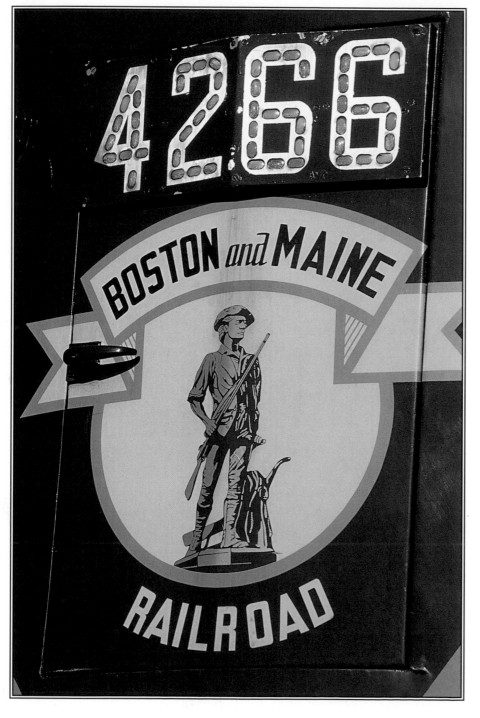

yet did not serve the Boston & Maine, whose trains terminated at its own North Station.

New York City was the largest city in the United States by the mid-19th century and, as a result, had some of the heaviest suburban traffic, as well as some of the most intensive long-distance passenger traffic. Yet, at the turn of the 20th century, New York City still lacked a through rail service on most of its routes because of its island status. Passengers had to take ferries to Manhattan Island from waterside railway terminals in New Jersey and on Long Island. The one through line to Grand Central Terminal that served both owner New York Central and tenant New Haven faced saturation point, as hundreds of trains were using the station daily.

GRAND CENTRAL

The New York Central had enlarged Grand Central in 1899, but realized that it would have to build a completely new terminal in order to keep pace with growing demand. The difficulty was quite simply finding available space to expand. Real estate in Manhattan was then – as it is today – a premium commodity. The New York Central planned to increase capacity by locating new tracks and facilities below ground. This was a difficult prospect in the days of steam – because of smoke – and it was impractical to consider operating large numbers of steam locomotives in underground tunnels. The public would not stand for it. As it was, locomotives serving Grand Central spent an absolute minimum time in the station's great arched train shed to avoid smoking it up.

TRAVELERS' TALES
ATTENTION: STOLEN STATION!

Many railway stations in the early years were substantial structures of above-average durability. Others were more diminutive in stature and strength. In its April 14, 1906 issue, the *Railway and Engineering Review* reported a most unusual story. One assumes that the station in question was a fairly minimal structure, probably little more than a light shelter:

"According to the *New York Herald*, two station buildings have been stolen from the Central Railroad of New Jersey, at Bayway, N.J. About a year ago, the wooden station building at that place disappeared mysteriously, and no trace of it has ever been found. The company then erected another, but one night a pack of thieves fell upon it and carried it off."

Talk about temporary facilities!

Of course, there were alternatives to steam. Electric streetcar and interurban lines were well established by 1900, and in 1896, the Baltimore & Ohio pioneered a short mainline electrification system in order to operate its new line through tunnels in downtown Baltimore. The New York Central was investigating the possibilities of electric operations when it suffered a terrible disaster in its two-mile (3.2km) Park Avenue Tunnel on the approach to Grand Central. This tunnel had long been an operating nightmare. In January 1902, a loaded passenger train had paused in the tunnel, waiting for permission to proceed toward Grand Central, and was struck from behind by another train that had overrun a "stop" signal obscured by heavy smoke in the tunnel. This catastrophe precipitated a public scandal, resulting in legislation mandating the development and adoption of electric operations in New York City. The New York Central wasted no time in complying, and began developing mainline electric traction immediately. Within a few years Grand Central was electrified.

EARLY ELECTRIC MAINLINES
The New Haven, tenant of the Central, embarked on an even more ambitious plan: it set out to electrify its entire mainline operations east of New York to Stamford, Connecticut (and later to New Haven), and pioneered one of the first heavy mainline electric railways in the world. Meanwhile, the New York

Central pushed forward its plans for its magnificent new Grand Central. This multilevel complex with two levels of tracks took years to design, involved two major architectural firms, and would not be completed until 1913. However, the final result was outstanding, and Grand Central Terminal (as it was

---

New York City's magnificent Grand Central Terminal remains the most famous railroad station in the United States

---

now known) took the title of the largest passenger station in the world. Today, preserved and restored to its original grandeur, it remains the most famous railroad station in the United States, although these days it serves only suburban trains.

While the New York Central was undertaking the planning and construction of Grand Central, its arch competitor, the Pennsylvania Railroad, was working on its own scheme. Pennsylvania's president, the visionary Alexander Cassatt, had recently visited the marvelous new Gare d'Orsay in Paris (where his sister, Mary Cassatt, was an aspiring, soon to be world-famous, artist). Here, he saw the latest in railway technology: clean, modern, electrically hauled trains that ran in underground tunnels. Unlike dirty, smoky steam trains that were relegated to drafty sheds, these electrics came right into the

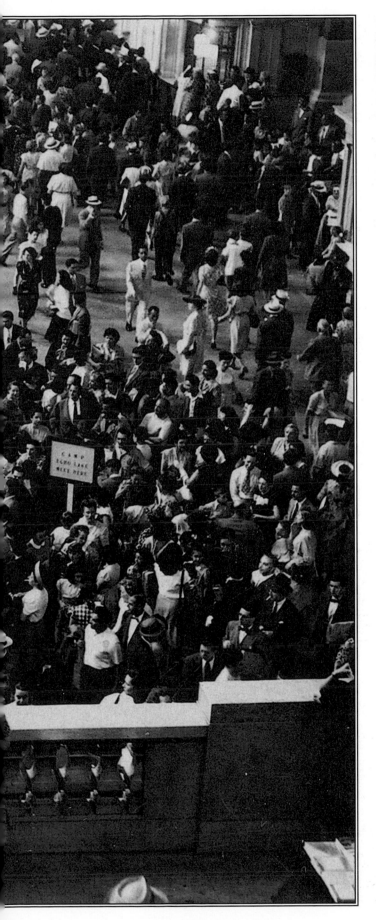

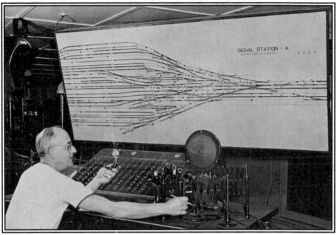

▲ This New York train director is pictured at work circa 1951. He is seated in Tower A of Grand Central Terminal, and his job is to control all movements of through trains on the upper level of the station; Grand Central is unusual in having two levels.

totally enclosed station! Inspired by this, Cassatt had his engineers draw up a grand plan to bring the Pennsylvania Railroad to New York City. Although the Pennsylvania had long served New York by way of its Exchange Place terminal in Jersey City, Cassatt found this arrangement, which required passengers

Pennsylvania Station – opened in 1910, three years before Grand Central – was hailed as an architectural wonder

to change to ferries, second rate. The Pennsylvania Railroad's plan involved digging tunnels below the Hudson River to give New York City direct access to the west. Another set of tunnels to the east would allow Pennsylvania's Long Island Rail Road subsidiary access to Manhattan as well, and ultimately provide the New Haven with a second New York terminal via a huge bridge across the Hell Gate estuary. The Long Island Rail Road was a very heavily traveled

◀ New York City's monumental Grand Central Terminal was designed to handle enormous crowds. For many years, it was the busiest railway station not only in the United States but in the world. Today, it has been restored to its original grandeur.

commuter railroad, and its passengers would greatly benefit from direct access to Manhattan.

As with the New York Central, the Pennsylvania Railroad's plans mandated electrification. Despite the ambitious nature of the Pennsylvania's undertaking, its terminal was opened three years prior to the New York Central's project in 1910. Pennsylvania Station itself was an architectural wonder, considered as one of the most impressive stations ever built. With the completion of the Hudson River

▲ **Pennsylvania Station, in New York, was one of the greatest railway stations ever conceived. Inspired by the Gare d'Orsay in Paris, Penn Station was part of the Pennsylvania Railroad's grandiose scheme to bring its trains directly into the city.**

tunnels, passengers could ride from New York City directly to Philadelphia, Baltimore, Washington, and beyond. Old John Stevens, who 100 years earlier had proposed the first railway line to connect New York and Philadelphia, would have been amazed by this new innovation. Never in his wildest dreams would he have imagined a direct connection between these two major cities.

ELECTRIC VERSUS STEAM

The advent of the New York electrification schemes led to a movement among American railroads to electrify their lines. Electric locomotives offered a number of distinct advantages over steam. In addition to their cleanliness, they were more powerful (particularly at low speeds), offered more rapid acceleration, and required far less maintenance. A single electric locomotive could replace several steam locomotives. Through the development of multiple-unit technology – invented by traction pioneer Frank Sprague – two or more electric locomotives could be controlled from a single throttle. This potentially reduced labor costs, as only a single locomotive crew would be required to move even the heaviest trains (provided all the locomotives were on the front of the train). Since electric locomotives and electrically powered cars were bi-directional, they could be reversed simply and easily, without the need for elaborate turning facilities.

One of the most obvious applications for electrification was suburban commuter railways, and the pioneering New York Central eventually electrified all of its New York City area trackage, with mainline electrification extending to Harmon on its Hudson Line, and North White Plains on its Harlem route. Many of the Long Island Rail Road's suburban routes were electrified. After its initial success with Penn Station in New York, the Pennsylvania Railroad went on to introduce suburban electrification on its heaviest Philadelphia lines. While this system

▼ Cars on the Erie-Lackawanna roll past a crossing. The Lackawanna electrified its suburban passenger lines from its terminal in Hoboken, New Jersey, in the early 1920s. Hoboken is located directly across from Manhattan.

► Electrically powered streetcars were once found in most American cities. While most streetcar lines were powered by overhead trolley wires, a few, such as the Capital Traction Co. in Washington D.C., were powered by a third rail in an underground conduit.

was very different than that used for Penn Station — it used high-voltage overhead wire, like the New Haven Railroad, instead of a low-voltage direct current third rail — it ultimately prevailed as the railroad's primary electric standard. In the 1920s, the Pennsylvania Railroad initiated one of the most ambitious railroad electrification schemes in the United States and set out to wire up its entire New York to Washington D.C. mainline operation. This proved to be an enormous undertaking and ultimately the most extensive mainline electrification in the United States.

The cost advantages of electric operations were especially evident on heavily traveled lines. As a result, other suburban passenger railways in the United States and Canada embarked on electrification programs. Another advantage was in providing pulling power at slow speeds and entirely smokeless

▼ The Long Island Rail Road's *Cannonball*, seen at Montauk Point, Long Island. The luxury of the open-end observation car was lost with the introduction of modern streamlined trains. Today, a few such observation cars remain, in private hands.

operation. Because of this, electrification was especially appealing for routes with numerous long tunnels, where smoke problems from locomotives had proven troublesome. A number of mountain railways installed electrification systems in order to ease heavily graded operations, such as the Great

Northern on its Cascade route (discussed in Chapter 3) and the Boston & Maine Hoosac Tunnel in the Berkshires of western Massachusetts. This 4³/₄ mile (7.6km) long bore had presented an operational nightmare since its completion in 1875. This long tunnel below Florida Mountain was right at the top of the Boston & Maine's Berkshire grades, which resulted in trains having to work up grade through the tunnel in both directions, filling it with thick smoke. Electric operations obviously eliminated the smoke problems and expanded the capacity of the whole railroad.

One of the most impressive electrification projects of the period was the extensive wiring of the Chicago, Milwaukee, St Paul & Pacific's Pacific Extension, completed in May 1909 – 40 years after the first transcontinental railroad. The Milwaukee Road, as the line was known, had been dissatisfied with the stranglehold the Hill and Harriman railroads had on transcontinental traffic, and extended its own line clear to the Pacific Coast. This was one of the last totally new transcontinental routes and ran roughly parallel to the Northern Pacific. To reach Seattle from the Twin Cities, the Milwaukee Road

crossed numerous summits in the Rocky Mountains of Montana, the Bitter Roots in Idaho, and the Washington Cascades. Difficult routes made for heavy operations that required lots of coal, which the railroad had to bring in, since it did not have the large online reserves that its competitor, the Northern Pacific, enjoyed. Soon after the route was completed, the Milwaukee Road decided to electrify two crucial segments – ultimately totaling 676 route miles (1,088km) – separated by a long, non-electrified gap.

When its first electric operations were initiated in 1915, the line was heralded as one of the most

▲ One of the Milwaukee Road's huge "Bi-Polar" electric locomotives, on display in Milwaukee, Wisconsin. These distinctive electrics operated between Othello and Seattle, Washington, on the railroad's innovative Pacific Extension line.

modern in the world, and it was felt at the time that many railroads would see the advantages of mainline electrification and follow the Milwaukee Road's example. The popular boy's adventure book series, *Tom Swift*, even featured an episode called "Tom Swift and his Electric Locomotive," inspired by the Milwaukee Road. It had launched a visionary motive power system and, while a few other lines experimented with mainline electrification, the extremely high costs of installation discouraged most American lines from making the investment. The Milwaukee Road remained an unusual but fascinating example

of American mainline electrification until the railroad's decision to discontinue electric operations in 1974. One type of new electric locomotive was the massive articulated "Bi-Polar," built by General Electric for the Milwaukee Road's service on the electric lines in Washington State. The railroad staged an event where one of its Bi-Polars was coupled to two

▲ A North Shore interurban electric train bound for Chicago negotiates the streets of Milwaukee, Wisconsin, only a few blocks from the site of the Bi-Polar shown on pages 124–125. The North Shore was among the United States' last interurbans.

large steam locomotives. The steam engines pulled in one direction, and the electric in the other. In this spectacular show of force, the electric prevailed.

As more people were traveling and more freight was being hauled, the railroads were always looking for even bigger and more powerful locomotives,

Electrification was not practical for most American railways, so locomotive builders sought more conventional solutions

while also seeking ways to make the engines more efficient. While electrification offered one solution, it was not a practical or feasible system for the vast majority of American railways to implement, so the locomotive builders sought more conventional motive power solutions.

Passenger trains were growing heavier, not just because of an increase in the length of consists, but also because the weight of the cars was increasing,

◄ "Doubleheading" – using two locomotives on one train – was a common technique used to haul a heavy train over the line expediently. Here on the B&O, a Q-class Mikado and a P-class Pacific lead a long passenger train at Hancock, Maryland.

▲ The first New York Central Pacific type poses at Worcester, Massachusetts. With four guiding wheels, six driving wheels, and a large firebox, the Pacific type was ideal for hauling a long passenger train at a respectable speed, making it very popular.

too. Traditionally, passenger car bodies had been made primarily of wood. Longer trains and safety concerns gradually resulted in a switch from all-wood cars to wooden ones with steel frames, and then finally all-steel cars. As in the case of electrification, New York City forced the issue of all-steel cars as the result of grisly crashes and terrible fires. Since the New York Central and the Pennsylvania Railroad, along with the New Haven, were some of largest operators of railway passenger cars, and sleepers on their trains connected with dozens of other lines, there was suddenly a large market for all-steel passenger cars, particularly sleepers. Pullman led the way and built the first all-steel sleeping car in 1907. In 1910, the company had completely switched from wood to steel construction. Soon steel cars were standard for interstate services throughout the United States. In fact, the US adopted all-steel equipment years before

many other countries. All-steel cars were significantly heavier than wooden ones, contributing to the need for more powerful passenger locomotives.

"DOUBLEHEADING"

The 4-4-2 Atlantic, which had been introduced in the 1890s, was ideal for relatively short, fast trains, since the type could sprint along with four or five wooden cars in tow without straining. As the trains grew longer and heavier, railroads found their new Atlantics just were not powerful enough for many assignments. To solve the problem, some railroads relied on the established solution of "doubleheading" – that is, using two locomotives to haul a single train. This was expensive, as two crews were required, and the use of two locomotives to haul a train was considered wasteful. For a short time, some railroads assigned heavy 4-6-0s to passenger service; on fast trains, others employed a new type, with a 2-6-2 wheel arrangement, called a "Prairie."

While the Prairie had lots of tractive effort, it did not ride well at speed. A better solution came with the introduction of the 4-6-2 type, a locomotive known as a "Pacific." This type was built by Baldwin for export in 1901 and quickly caught on for domestic use. With the introduction of all-steel cars, the Pacific had a marked advantage over the Atlantic, and by 1910 it had become the new standard passenger locomotive. The Pacific was characterized by tall drivers and a large firebox and boiler, which gave it plenty of power for acceleration and sustained speed. The average Pacific type could easily haul a loaded passenger train containing eight to 10 steel cars in level territory.

However, not all lines were blessed with such even profiles. The Chesapeake & Ohio, for example, had a mountainous route. In 1910, the Chesapeake & Ohio decided that it needed an even bigger locomotive to alleviate the need to doublehead its new Pacifics over steep Allegheny mountain grades. The new locomotive used a 4-8-2 wheel arrangement, thus employing one more set of driving wheels than the Pacific. This type enjoyed high tractive effort because of eight drivers, benefited from the greater stability of a four-wheel leading truck, and had additional power made possible by a large firebox

▼ A rare action photograph of the Boston & Albany's Mallet No. 1300 with a train at West Newton, Massachusetts, in 1926. While very powerful, articulated Mallets were not known for speed, and on the B&A they were supplanted by faster Berkshire types

▲ The Baltimore & Ohio's first Mallet, known as *Old Maud*, was built by Alco in 1904. A Mallet was an articulated locomotive that used two sets of cylinders: the rear set of high-pressure cylinders exhausted steam into the large, low-pressure cylinders located at the front, thus enhancing efficiency.

supported by a trailing truck. Initially used on mountain lines, the 4-8-2 became generally known as the "Mountain" type. While intended as a heavy passenger locomotive, it proved a solid freight hauler as well. The New York Central was one of the largest users of 4-8-2s, at first for fast freight service on its famous Water Level Route. Because of its low-grade line, the Central was not keen on calling its locomotives Mountains, so its 4-8-2s were always known as "Mohawks," after the river they ran alongside.

In addition to the development of new wheel arrangements, such as the 4-4-2 Atlantic and 4-6-2 Pacific, locomotive builders introduced other technologies to improve the performance and efficiency of the locomotive. Beginning in the 1880s, one popular method for achieving greater fuel efficiency was the use of a compound engine. In a compound engine, there are two sets of cylinders: high pressure and low pressure. On a simple steam engine (one that is not a compound), the exhaust steam is released directly, which wastes energy. On a compound, the high-pressure cylinders exhaust into the low-pressure cylinders, which make

double use of the steam, thereby generating more power and conserving fuel.

There were a variety of different compound arrangements. Two of the most popular were the cross compound and the Vauclain compound. The cross compound employed just two cylinders, with the high-pressure and low-pressure cylinders on opposite sides of the locomotive. Since a low-pressure cylinder was much larger then a high-pressure cylinder, the cross compound had an awkward, unbalanced appearance. The Vauclain compound, designed by Baldwin's Samuel Vauclain, used two sets of high-pressure and low-pressure cylinders, one of each located on both sides of the locomotive. This more balanced compound approach enjoyed the greater success in the United States.

MODERN COMPOUNDS

Vauclain compounds were often built as 4-4-2 Atlantics and 4-6-0 Ten Wheelers for fast passenger work. At the start of the 20th century, the Vauclain compound Atlantics were viewed as a model of efficiency and regarded as a thoroughly modern machine. They were typically assigned to the most prestigious runs. However, not all railroads were enthralled with compounding and stayed with simpler designs.

In 1904, another type of compound was introduced, the articulated Mallet compound, which used two separate sets of cylinders and running gear

type for heavy standard-gauge railroading. The very first American Mallet was a 0-6-6-0 that acquired the nickname *Old Maud*. After making a celebrity appearance at the 1904 Louisiana Purchase Exposition in St Louis, where the huge locomotive was deemed a monster by observers, it went into service as a helper west of Cumberland, Maryland, on the Sand Patch Grade.

The type was an immediate success and demonstrated the advantages of compounding and the use of a double locomotive. A couple of years later, Baldwin adapted the Mallet type for road service on the Great Northern, where the type was used for hauling freight over Stevens Pass in the Washington Cascades. By 1910, many lines were using Mallets with various wheel arrangements in heavy freight service. One of

below a single boiler. The low-pressure engine was in the front of the locomotive and the high-pressure engine in the back. Anatole Mallet designed this type in Europe for narrow-gauge mountain railways. The Baltimore & Ohio worked with Alco to develop the

▼ The Southern Pacific adapted the Mallet to cab-ahead operation, which allowed it to work its difficult Donner Pass crossing. The SP later acquired a large fleet of simple articulated cab-ahead locomotives, lacking the compound cylinder arrangement.

▲ Soldiers leave Worcester, Massachusetts, by train, presumably to take part in World War I. The railroads were unfortunately not prepared for their war duties.

the most popular types was the 2-6-6-2, which enjoyed high tractive effort, good tracking ability, a reasonably large firebox, and a flexible wheelbase.

THE SANTA FE'S MALLETS

Two interesting Mallet types were the Southern Pacific's cab-aheads and the Santa Fe's passenger articulateds. The Southern Pacific's heavy grades in the California Sierra demanded lots of power to move freight trains. As a result, the railroad often assigned five or six locomotives to a single train. When the Mallet was introduced, the Southern Pacific recognized that this new type of motive power would be well suited for its mountain lines and bought two to try them out. It quickly learned that the big engines produced excessive smoke when operating through the numerous snowsheds and tunnels over Donner Pass, and actually risked asphyxiating crews.

The Great Northern had experienced similar difficulties and experimented with elongated smokestacks and oxygen masks for crews, before finally choosing to electrify its Stevens Pass crossing.

The Southern Pacific Railroad adopted a more novel approach and turned the locomotives around, running them "cab ahead," with the smokebox (normally at the front of the engine) facing the tender. What permitted this unusual arrangement was the Southern Pacific's choice of fuel – oil. There was very little coal along the railroad's lines, but oil was plentiful. By the turn of the century, many Southern Pacific locomotives were converted to oil operation. Thus the Southern Pacific's cab-aheads were oil burners, and the fireman did not require direct access to the tender, as he would have with a typical coal-burning locomotive. Although the Southern Pacific's first Mallets were built as freight locomotives, later examples had larger driving wheels, and were intended for use on passenger services.

Meanwhile, the Santa Fe – which had been enamored with earlier compound designs – spent a few years developing Mallets with tall drivers for express passenger services. A few locomotives were even built with flexible boilers. Unlike the Southern Pacific's cab-ahead concept, the Santa Fe's fast passenger Mallet did not enjoy lasting success, and most were either retired or converted into other designs after a few years. The Santa Fe also built some of the largest Mallet types – massive 2-10-10-2s. The Virginian, a Pocahontas region coal-hauling line known for its big locomotives, also used this wheel arrangement, and its massive Mallets were some of the most powerful locomotives ever produced. The Virginian, along with the Erie, also experimented by taking the Mallet concept one step further, constructing "Tri-plexes," which used three sets of cylinders and running gear. The Santa Fe actually drew up plans for even more ridiculous machines with four and five sets of running gear, but had the sense to leave them in the realm of the hypothetical.

The compound era came to a close with the advent of superheating, which was introduced in the United States on a wide scale after 1910. Super-heating equipment employed extra tubes with which to recirculate steam back through the fire tubes of a locomotive, thus "superheating" it. Raising the temperature of the steam gave it more expansion power and greatly improved the efficiency of the locomotive, more than the compounding method.

WARTIME PRESSURES

Most locomotives could easily be converted to superheating without requiring extensive rebuilding. One of the flaws with compounds had been that they demanded significantly more maintenance than simple locomotives. This disadvantage meant that many railroads had actually abandoned compounds a decade before superheating became practical.

As World War I spread in Europe after 1914, traffic on American lines grew enormously, to carry increased loads of food and supplies for the combatants. Just prior to the United States' entry into the war in 1917, the railroads were literally bogged down with freight and passenger demands. Eastern lines, in particular, became saturated, and the efficiency of normal operations eventually collapsed, resulting in

serious delays at a time of grave national crisis. Finally, the situation became intolerable and all of the railroads were placed under Federal control.

The United States Railroad Administration (USRA) controlled American lines for the duration of the war, effectively renting them from their owners. It did not return the railroads to private ownership until 1920. The USRA attempted to rectify the traffic flow situation by pooling railroad resources and minimizing the negative effects of competition. For example, across the Nevada desert, the Southern Pacific and Western Pacific operated

---

The government controlled American lines for the duration of the war, and did not return them to private ownership until 1920

---

parallel single-track lines. The USRA established a "paired track" arrangement that used one line for eastbound traffic and the other for westbound traffic. This greatly improved the flow of both railroads, and practically eliminated delays caused by trains having to negotiate meetings on single track.

The USRA also drafted standard locomotive and car designs, a policy that ran contrary to typical American railroad practice. Normally, each railroad would order equipment specifically designed for its individual needs. Generally speaking, the USRA designs were well balanced and designed for operation over many lines. After the USRA relinquished control, some of the improvements it had implemented were retained, including the Southern Pacific–Western Pacific paired track; however, the concept of a standardized national locomotive fleet did not catch on. While some railroads adopted the USRA designs, and even used them for the basis of more advanced locomotives, most returned to the time-honored practice of drafting their own custom-tailored designs. The railroads' failure to accommodate wartime traffic did not sit lightly with management, which took corrective action. The next time there was a crisis – during World War II – the railroads would be far better prepared.

5

CANADA – FOUNDED BY RAIL

Canada's development as a nation is inextricably linked to transcontinental railway networks. After a slow start, construction was swift, and the result, unlike US links, truly connected east to west.

The British colonies that make up present-day Canada were quick to adopt the railway, yet slow to develop them. The building of its railways became imperative once the new Dominion of Canada was established on July 1, 1867. Quite simply, the existence of Canada was fundamentally related to the development of its railways.

◄ A Canadian Pacific Railway 4-6-0 races an approaching blizzard near East Lyndon, Maine, on January 28, 1958. The Canadian Pacific's transcontinental line skirted the top of Maine on its way from Montreal, Quebec, to St John, New Brunswick.

The early history of the country and its railways were often the same story. Perhaps no other nation's existence has been as closely tied to rail development as Canada's: without the railway, the Canadian confederation might never have come into being.

In the 1830s, Canada consisted of a few sparsely populated British colonies, separated by vast stretches of wilderness but loosely linked by rivers and rough roads. In the pre-rail era, people and freight moved along the waterways, which were open from April to November. Agriculture, fishing, and fur trading largely drove the colonies'

▲ Like their American counterparts, Canadian railways relied on imported British locomotives in their early years. The *Albion*, pictured here, was built in 1854 by Rayne and Burn of Newcastle. For many years it worked on a mine railway in Nova Scotia.

economies; there was virtually no heavy industry. The first British and American railways clearly demonstrated the advantages of rail transport, and entrepreneurs in Canada realized the importance of building their own lines – but it took a few years before any progress was made.

In 1832, just seven years after the opening of the Stockton & Darlington in England, Canada initiated the building of its first railway line, called the Champlain & St Lawrence. It caused great excitement in Montreal when it opened on July 21, 1836. Just 14½ miles (23.3km) long, it connected St John, Quebec, with the Lachine Rapids, a few miles from Montreal on the St Lawrence River. It initially operated with a Stephenson locomotive named *Dorchester* imported from Britain. This pioneering

machine was a wood burner with two pairs of 40-inch (102mm) driving wheels. Like other locomotives of the period, it did not carry most of the trappings we now associate with steam locomotives. It had neither bell, nor whistle, nor did it have a cab to protect its crew. The Champlain & St Lawrence was a spectacular success and attracted numerous excursionists in its first few years of operation. Visiting English novelist Charles Dickens rode the line on a visit to Montreal.

INITIAL PROGRESS

Despite the success of the Champlain & St Lawrence, Canada did not enjoy the benefits of the railway building boom in the 1830s and 1840s that its southern neighbor did. In 1850, there was about 9,000 miles (14,500km) of railway line in the United States; by contrast, Canada had completed less than 100 miles (160km). However, during the following decade, Canada would begin to catch up, constructing some 2,000 miles (3,200km) of railway.

In the winter, ice flows clog the St Lawrence River, making it impassable and effectively landlocking the inland port of Montreal. In the mid-1840s, railway entrepreneurs looked to free Montreal of this unhappy seasonal handicap by connecting it with an ocean port on the east coast of the United States. The cities of Boston, Massachusetts, and Portland, Maine, vied for the privilege, but ultimately Portland won out. Its desire for an inland railway connection reflected the same economic yearning as experienced by other eastern seaboard cities. Like Boston, New York, and Baltimore, Portland needed connections to expand its traffic base by giving it access to the interior. On July 4, 1846, construction on the Maine portion of the railway began. Seven years later, the railway was opened to Montreal,

although it still required substantial work to ready the line for regular traffic.

Unlike most New England railroads, the Atlantic & St Lawrence was built to broad gauge: its rails were 5ft 6ins (1.68m) apart, making it one of the widest gauges in North America. Among the reasons the railway's promoters selected this non-standard gauge was to employ the greater freight capacity of broad-gauge cars, but also to alleviate concerns that the American military might try to use the line for a Canadian invasion. Since the line was conceived as a

▼ In a composite picture representing competing technology, a Canadian National train races a bi-plane to Montreal. The airplane was in its formative stage of development, while the locomotive was highly refined, established technology.

TRAVELERS' TALES
THE THRILL OF THE SLEEPER

The Grand Truck Railway inaugurated service between Montreal and Toronto in October of 1856. The following spring, it debuted an overnight sleeper service between the two cities. Although such trains would become commonplace in the next century, at the time, sleeping cars were state-of-the-art and something of a novelty. The *Montreal Leader* wrote glowingly: "Perhaps in no respect had science achieved results conferring more comfort on the traveler than are to be found on the night cars of the Grand Trunk Railway. Literally we are embodying the dreams of youth, when we read of the travels of Sinbad and of the Flying Horse. Who 20 years ago could have thought it possible that a party of Gentlemen would enter a comfortable saloon and after an hour's chat and a well-served supper each would take a rest upon a lounge and find himself next morning before breakfast time 300 or 400 miles from whence he started, with untired energy and fit for exertion?"

The enthusiasm for this new mode of travel was positively contagious. Never before had Canadians been treated to such speed and luxury.

---

link with a planned Canadian network, rather than an American one, the difficulties caused by incompatible rolling stock with existing American railways was not seen as a significant disadvantage. This thinking would soon prove flawed, but it would take decades before North American railroads solved incompatibility issues.

While the Atlantic & St Lawrence was under way, a much grander Canadian railway scheme was developing. Using British financing, planners conceived of a through railway that would span most of eastern Canada, ultimately connecting eastern cities with Chicago by way of Montreal. It was called the Grand Trunk Railway of Canada, as it was intended as Canada's trunk line, fashioned after the primary American trunk railroads. The Grand Trunk was designed to keep Canadian traffic along Canadian corridors, rather then letting it slip away to American routes, which had been a concern since the opening of the Erie Canal in 1825. In its day, it was to be the longest railway in the world. Like its Portland connection, the Atlantic & St Lawrence, the Grand Trunk was built to broad gauge. The Grand Trunk had its sights on Portland as well, and it leased the Atlantic & St Lawrence route shortly after the line opened.

The Grand Trunk connected Montreal and Toronto in 1856 and, by 1860, provided a through route between Portland, Maine, and Chicago. Progress toward the Maritimes was slower. Animosities among the different colonies were not conducive to a through line, and the sparsely settled Maritimes were an inauspicious environment for railway development. Nova Scotia developed a few short lines, but several years would pass before these disconnected lines would be joined with other Canadian railways.

AMERICAN CIVIL WAR FEARS

Ultimately, the Civil War forced Canadian railroad builders into action. This conflict aroused a great concern in Canada: there were fears that Union forces might try to annex Canadian territory, or simply invade outright. These fears inspired politicians and railway builders to promote the Intercolonial Railway, which eventually reached the port of Halifax, Nova Scotia, thus strengthening the Canadian political position, albeit years after the conclusion of the American Civil War. In the meantime, Canadians faced a more daunting task: building a railroad to the Pacific coast to unify the

▶ The Canadian National's wide range of services is portrayed on the cover of its timetables. In addition to streamlined passenger trains, hauled by both steam and diesels, the railway also operated planes, steamships, and fancy hotels.

nation, in order to fend off growing American interest in the ripe open lands to the west.

As in the United States, Canadian railroad vision-aries had discussed the prospect of a transcontinental line for decades. In the 1830s, before Canada had any substantive railway mileage at all, there was serious discussion about building a railway clear across Canada. The prospect of such a transcontinental venture was far more daunting than in the United States. The distances were greater, on-line traffic

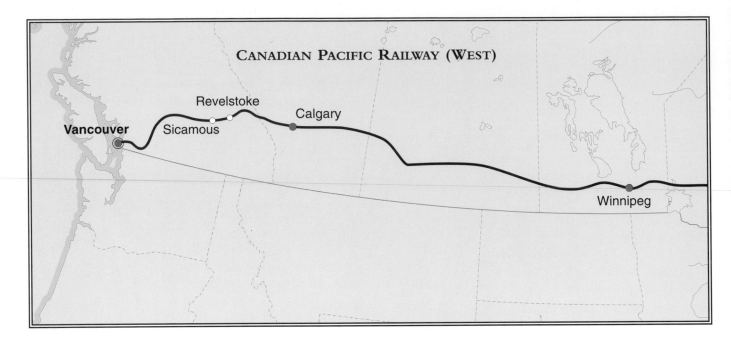

CANADIAN PACIFIC RAILWAY (WEST)

Vancouver · Sicamous · Revelstoke · Calgary · Winnipeg

▲ The Canadian Pacific Railway was built as more than just a financial enterprise, it was needed to solidify Canada's national identity. Unlike so-called transcontinental railways in the United States, the CPR truly joined Atlantic to Pacific.

potential was sparser, and the ability to raise funds domestically was practically non-existent. As a strictly commercial venture, a trans-Canadian railway to the Pacific seemed impossible.

American expansionist forces looked north-west and forced the issue politically. After the Civil War, some Americans, including the administration of President Grant, viewed western Canada as ripe for the taking. While it was unlikely that the United States would go to war for possession of Canadian territory, all other options were certainly being considered. The authorization of the Northern Pacific Railroad was in part designed to attract Canadian traffic and direct it into the United States, and, in the late 1860s, the Northern Pacific's financier, Jay Cooke, made little secret of his interest in western Canada.

The Alaska purchase of 1867 by the United States further fueled Canadian concerns about American territorial expansion. That same year, several Canadian colonies were joined, forming the Dominion of Canada, in a move to solidify Canada as a nation and strengthen its ties to Britain. The western provinces of Manitoba and British Columbia were initially

reluctant to join the newly formed Dominion and would only agree to join on the condition that a railway would be built to link them with the rest of Canada. Reflecting the opinion of his province at the time, Dr. J. S. Helmcken of British Colombia said, "We should be better off without Canada if we have no railway." A transcontinental line was promised, and, in 1870, Manitoba joined Canada, followed by British Columbia in 1871. Yet another decade passed before a serious effort to build a railway commenced. Political, financial, and geographical obstacles delayed the Canadian Pacific Railway; however, finally, in 1881, the line was under way. It climbed across the rocky and forbidding Canadian

---

The Alaska purchase of 1867 by the United States fueled Canadian concerns about American territorial expansion

---

Shield, long an impediment to travel across Canada, rolled across the prairies, and ascended the mighty Canadian Rockies, before reaching the coast.

By the 1880s, the skills of railroad building had been refined, and American railroads had demonstrated that it was possible to successfully construct and operate a line across a vast tract of wilderness.

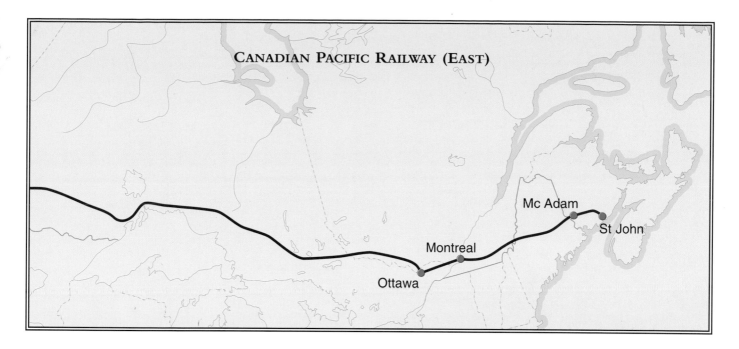

CANADIAN PACIFIC RAILWAY (EAST)

Mc Adam

St John

Montreal

Ottawa

Although the Canadian Pacific was discussed as a government-built project, ultimately the American mold of a privately managed company with a mix of government and private financing was deemed best suited for the task. Unlike the first American

▼ A set of Montreal Locomotive Works FPA/FPB diesel-electrics leads an eastbound Canadian Pacific Railway freight train along the rocky north shore of Lake Superior. This stretch of railway was among the most difficult to construct, and remains one of the scenic highlights of the network.

transcontinental, however, the first Canadian railroad to the Pacific was built under one management, thus avoiding the conflicts and inefficiencies demonstrated by the competition between the Union Pacific and the Central Pacific. The Canadian Pacific was awarded substantial land grants, in addition to government financial rewards as it built west. Most American land grant railroads were required to accept land grants in a checkerboard fashion along their right of way; however, the Canadian Pacific and subsequent lines could pick and choose their land as they best saw fit for development.

Once the Canadian Pacific was underway, progress was relatively swift, and the railroad to the Pacific coast was completed in 1885, several years ahead of schedule. Just four years later, the Canadian Pacific

Immigrants from eastern Canada, Britain, Ireland, and continental Europe, began settling the vast lands of western Canada

completed a line to the Atlantic Coast port of Saint John, New Brunswick, a railway that cut across the northern part of Maine. Finally, after years of discussion, surveying, and building, Canada had its own transcontinental railroad. A true transcontinental in every sense of the word – one company, operating one long, continuous line all the way from coast to coast – it was a triumph for Canada, discouraging American incursions, while bringing political stability and facilitating western settlement. Soon waves of immigrants from eastern Canada, as well as Britain, Ireland, and continental Europe, began settling the vast open lands of western Canada. With settlement came prosperity for the railroad and the nation.

The Canadian Pacific built a complex network of feeder routes and branch lines across Ontario, Manitoba, and Saskatchewan, allowing farmers all across

◄ **Here, the Canadian Pacific Railway's class P2 Mikado No. 5386 leads a freight train in the Canadian Rockies. The 2-8-2 Mikado type was one of the most common freight locomotives on the CPR, with over 300 in service – 174 of which were P2s.**

▲ The quiet station at Franz, Ontario, is the junction between the Canadian Pacific and Algoma Central lines. This 1960s view shows a typical heavyweight passenger car from the pre-streamlined era. In 2001 the Algoma Central still operated regular passenger service.

the fertile plains the benefits of railway transportation to ship their produce east. As the railroad grew busier, the Canadian Pacific made numerous improvements to its mainline. It added long sections of double track and eventually rebuilt its grade over Kicking Horse Pass in the Canadian Rockies. The original crossing of this pass involved an unacceptably steep 4.4 percent grade that required at least three locomotives for relatively short trains. The new line was built utilizing spiral tunnels to keep the maximum grade to a more acceptable 2.2 percent – the same maximum grade used on many American lines.

In its first two decades, the Canadian Pacific compnay enjoyed a near monopoly on Canadian transcontinental traffic. However, as might be expected, its dominant status lent itself to abuses and public resentment. By the early 20th century, other interests were building railway lines competing with the Canadian Pacific, much to the delight of shippers. The Canadian Pacific's first competition came from the Great Northern in the United States. This line, under the direction of James J. Hill, built a number of branch lines from the United States into Canadian Pacific territory in an effort to siphon off traffic. In 1879, the Great Northern linked St Paul, Minnesota, with Winnipeg, Manitoba.

RAILROAD RIVALRY

Domestic competition came after 1900 from the Canadian Northern, a line run by former Canadian Pacific contractors, which developed a network of tracks across the plains. It thrived in the shadow of the Canadian Pacific's unpopularity, as many people would bend over backward to assist their competitors – whomever they might be. For a time, it appeared the Canadian Northern would be a natural ally for the Grand Trunk and that the two companies might work together to construct a second transcontinental line in competition with the Canadian Pacific. However, this did not come to pass, for soon the two companies were competing with one another, pursuing independent Pacific ambitions. Instead, the Grand Trunk's new ally was a company called the Grand Trunk Pacific, which built a line west to Prince Rupert, British Columbia, reaching there in June 1914. Meanwhile, the Canadian Northern expanded its lines both east and west, reaching Vancouver, B.C., in early 1915.

WORKING ON THE RAILROAD
PRAIRIE TOWN

The rapid settlement of the Canadian prairie captured the imagination of F. A. Talbot, who wrote *The Making of a Great Canadian Railway*, chronicling the construction of the Grand Trunk Pacific and published three years before that line reached its western terminus in 1915. He describes in a colorful, almost comical, narrative the rapid coalescence of a town along the railway line: "The growth of a prairie town is a spectacle that cannot be paralleled in any other country. The location of the town is decided definitely, and in a few days the site has been split up by surveyors. Before they have settled down thoroughly to their work, one or two stray pioneers arrive and cast about, possibly assisting the surveyors in menial work … As the surveyors' work approaches completion, other stragglers appear on the scene, and before one can realize the fact, squatters appropriate attractive plots and run up their tents. In a few days a livery stable appears, which within easy distance a frontier hotel springs into existence.

"Two days later the place is overrun by investors and speculators … Within another two days, many a visitor has exchanged his cash for a piece of Canadian freehold, and before the week is out, a store, lumber yard, a variety of timber frame buildings serving as stores, a restaurant, barber's shop, possibly a newspaper, and private dwellings line the main thoroughfare. The complete change from barren, undulating vacant wilderness to a small village of 30 or 50 people has often been wrought in a week …

In this period postcard view of a cabin in the isolated mountain town of Fraser Lake, British Columbia, a group poses, with surveying equipment visible in the foreground. As the railroad rolled west, it brought settlement to previously virgin territory.

"If the town happens to be a divisional point, its progress is much more marked, for by the time the railway settles down to do business, the inhabitants may look forward confidently to the company spending something like $30,000 or £6,000 a month in wages among its employees stationed at that point. The elevator appears like magic beside the railway track, and the farmers around the town breathe freely, for here are the facilities for the disposal of their produce on the spot."

The duplication of routes (which exacerbated financial difficulties), the advent of World War I, and resultant changes in traffic flow meant the enormous investment in this duplicative infrastructure could not be sustained. The result was the nationalization of most of the new lines by the 1920s, including both the Canadian Northern and the Grand Trunk Pacific.

The last major line to join the new government-controlled Canadian National Railway was the Grand Trunk itself, in 1923. By this time, the Grand Trunk had a significant network of lines in the United States as well. After nationalization, its Chicago–Detroit mainline and related trackage became a subsidiary known as the Grand Trunk Western, while the Montreal–Portland route was operated by the Canadian National Railway under the Grand Trunk name. American lines controlled by the Canadian National Railways retained a fair amount of autonomy and maintained locomotives and equipment under their own names. The Canadian National's Central Vermont Railway ran from St Albans, Vermont, to New London, Connecticut, providing Montreal with another year-round port and giving the Canadian National access to the New York metropolitan area through steamship connections.

Nationalization did not include the Canadian Pacific, which maintained its independence. After 1923, Canada had just two massive Canadian rail systems – one private and one public – which served the majority of populated Canada. The Canadian Pacific became far more than just a Canadian railway. It took an interest in American railways, such as the Soo Line, which allowed it to tap Twin Cities and Chicago traffic. It also developed a chain of magnificent hotels, ran an international steamship company, was involved in mining, and later operated an airline, among other

◄ A track gang works on the Grand Trunk Pacific Railway circa 1914. Building a railroad across the vast Canadian wilderness was a daunting task.

► The Algoma Central is one of Ontario's most colorful railways, running from Sault Saint Marie to Hearst, and traversing some of the most remote and beautiful scenery in the province. Passengers riding the line are often treated to views of bears and other wildlife.

endeavors. Likewise, the Canadian National line diversified and became involved in a multitude of diverse enterprises, ranging from airlines to film-making, including one starring Buster Keaton.

Several lines remained independent from these gigantic railway systems. The governments of Ontario and British Columbia both built railroads northward into the interior of their provinces and chose to retain control of their lines, rather than convert them to privately run companies. The Temiskaming & Northern Ontario was constructed north from the city of North Bay, Ontario, reaching Moonsonee on James Bay in 1931. After World War II, this railroad changed its name to the Ontario Northland.

The Pacific Great Eastern began building northeast of North Vancouver, British Columbia, in 1912, and eventually its lines reached Driftwood, Dawson Creek, and Fort Nelson, B.C., close to the Yukon. The railroad is now known as BC Rail and, like the Ontario Northland, is not part of the Canadian National. Another Ontario railroad was the privately operated Algoma Central & Hudson Bay, which began construction just after the turn of the century and built a line connecting Sault Saint Marie with Hearst, Ontario, reaching its northern terminus in 1914. Now known as simply the Algoma Central, it is part of the Wisconsin Central network, an American-owned system.

The Canadian Northern was a latecomer to Montreal, arriving there on the eve of World War I. As a result, it was not afforded as easy an entry to the city as earlier railways. To reach its downtown Montreal terminal, it needed to build a three-mile (5km) long tunnel below Mt Royal. To avoid smoke problems in the long tunnel, the route was electrified, and this facilitated the development of a suburban electric service on its lines north of Montreal.

ELECTRIFICATION AND AFTER

Under the Canadian National, the electrified service was expanded, and eventually the majority of the Canadian National's Montreal terminal operations were under wire. A fleet of box-cab electric locomotives handled conventional trains, while electrically powered self-propelled passenger cars worked suburban runs. The electrification was scaled back after the introduction of diesel-electric locomotives in the 1950s. The original electrification system remained, along with many of the original locomotives, until the mid-1990s, when the entire system was overhauled. By that time, the Canadian National's vintage electric locomotives, some of which dated back to before World War I, were the oldest locomotives in continuous service in North America.

The early Canadian railways imported locomotives from Britain, and, as a result, many of these closely resembled machines used there. Eventually, as

the railways developed, they connected with American lines, and later locomotives were either built by American manufacturers, or in Canada using American-influenced designs. For many years, Canadian railroads built their own locomotives at company shops, in addition to purchasing them from domestic

builders and from the United States. From the beginning of the 20th century, most Canadian railways acquired their steam locomotives domestically.

The Canadian Locomotive Company of Kingston, Ontario, was among the oldest manufacturers in the country, its origins dating back to the mid-

◄ A new Montreal Locomotive Works 1,500-horsepower diesel road switcher poses for a publicity photograph on a turntable. The turntable is used to position locomotives inside the stalls of a roundhouse, each of which has its own short section of track.

a subsidiary of Alco (the American Locomotive Company). Before Montreal Locomotive Works began production in 1904, Canadian lines bought many of their locomotives from one of Alco's component companies in the United States, such as Schenectady or Brooks.

The Canadian Pacific founded its Angus Shops in Montreal in 1904 to help provide locomotives for its expanding system. In addition to its maintenance and repair duties, Angus Shops built about 700 locomotives for the Canadian Pacific and its subsidiaries over a 40-year period, which ended during World War II. After the war, the Canadian Pacific continued to buy some new steam, but embarked on a program to convert its operations to diesel.

After the war, the Canadian Pacific continued to buy new steam, but began converting its operations to diesel

Prior to World War I, just a few traditional North American steam locomotive types handled the majority of work on Canadian railways. The 4-4-0 "American Standard" had been especially popular in the early years, but, as in the case in the United States, larger and more powerful locomotives eventually superceded this type. The 4-6-0 Ten Wheeler was especially popular on both the Canadian Pacific and the Canadian National predecessor railroads.

As the 20th century progressed, the Canadian Pacific and the Canadian National took decidedly different paths in the development of their steam fleet. The Canadian Pacific was partial to compound locomotives when they were in vogue, to achieve greater efficiency. It even operated a handful of Mallets – the only articulated locomotives to serve in Canada. But the Canadian Pacific was also one of the first railways in North America to investigate

19th century. Over 100 years, the company made about 2,600 steam locomotives, largely for use on Canadian Pacific and Canadian National lines, although about 20 percent was exported.

Canada's largest commercial locomotive builder was the Montreal Locomotive Works, which was

▲ Canadian Pacific Railway 4-6-0 No. 560 was the railroad's first locomotive equipped with a superheater. The use of super-heated steam greatly improved efficiency, and was eventually a feature of most North American steam engines.

superheating, and it was to quick to see its advantages. As a result, it concluded that superheating was more effective than compounds and converted many of its compound types at a fairly early stage.

The Canadian Pacific preferred the 4-6-2 Pacific type for passenger work and owned more than 200 Pacifics. It later acquired a large roster of 4-6-4 "Hudsons," the most famous of which were the semistreamlined class that hauled Britain's King George VI and Queen Elizabeth across Canada in 1939. These locomotives became known as "Royal Hudsons," and carried embossed crowns. They were

handsome machines and undoubtedly the most familiar engines in Canada.

For operations over the Canadian Rockies, known for prolonged stretches of 2.2 percent grades, the Canadian Pacific acquired a fleet of 2-10-4s, which it called "Selkirks," rather than the American moniker "Texas" types. (Certainly, it would seem ridiculous for a Canadian line to be operating Texas locomotives.) Some were built with semistream-lined shrouds – the only 2-10-4s to receive such cosmetic treatment. They worked on both freight and passenger trains. During the 1930s, when fast light-weight trains were all the rage, the Canadian Pacific developed the 4-4-4 wheel arrangement with 84in (2,134mm) drivers for its fast passenger service, as an alternative to lightweight diesel streamliners. The Reading and Baltimore & Ohio in the United States

freight and local passenger service. As noted in Chapter 7, a handful of its 4-4-0s, built in the 1880s, remained active to the end of steam, their careers spanning more than 70 years. While the Canadian Pacific tried a pair of 4-8-2 Mountains, and later a pair of 4-8-4s, it was not taken with these two otherwise popular designs, and these types remained

---

Steam locomotives seemed to last forever on the Canadian Pacific – some 4-6-0s survived for more than five decades

---

orphans among the hoards of Pacifics, Hudsons, Mikados, and Consolidations.

The Canadian National's locomotive philosophy, in contrast to the Canadian Pacific's, favored the eight-coupled types, and, in addition to large numbers of 2-8-0s and 2-8-2s, the Canadian National operated a great many 4-8-2s and was one of the first to adopt the 4-8-4 type. Initially, the Canadian National referred to its 4-8-4s patriotically as "Confederations," but the use of this identification faded with time. The Canadian National and its American subsidiary the Grand Trunk Western had the largest fleet of 4-8-4s in North America – more than 200 locomotives. The Canadian National viewed the 4-8-4 as something of a universal locomotive and it was used in freight and passenger service on all mainlines in the system. While the railway's 4-8-4s were big locomotives,

had both experimented with this wheel arrangement without lasting success, but the Canadian Pacific made good use of its 4-4-4s, which it operated for many years. They were known as "Jubilees" to mark the 50th anniversary of the opening of the Canadian Pacific's line to the Pacific Ocean.

For the majority of its freight services, the Canadian Pacific relied on a large fleet of 2-8-0 Consolidations and 2-8-2 Mikados, in addition to its old 4-6-0s. It would seem that steam locomotives lasted forever on the Canadian Pacific: some of its 4-6-0s survived for more than five decades, working in

▶ A Canadian National 4-8-2 Mountain type leads a passenger train at Sunnyside, Toronto, on August 19, 1958. The Canadian National had no fewer than 80 Mountain types, as a precursor to its even larger fleet of 4-8-4 Northerns.

▲ While the Canadian National had the largest fleet of 4-8-4s ever built, its chief rival, the Canadian Pacific, owned just two of this type. These orphan locomotives spent most of their careers working the overnight sleepers – trains No. 21 and 22 – between Montreal and Toronto.

they had very light axle-loadings compared to similar engines on American lines, and as a result they were capable of running on many secondary lines. For passenger services, the Canadian National had a sizable fleet of 4-6-2 Pacifics, but only five 4-6-4 Hudsons, making that wheel arrangement nearly as unusual on the Canadian National as 4-8-2s and 4-8-4s were on the Canadian Pacific.

While most new railroad construction in the United States was completed by the mid-1920s, and American railroads were especially reluctant to build any new lines after the network began to decline in the 1930s, several completely new Canadian railways were built in relatively modern times. Among these were isolated lines in northern Quebec, designed to reach ore deposits beyond the Canadian Shield. The Quebec, North Shore & Labrador was built between 1951 and 1954, and it runs from Sept-Iles, Quebec, more than 350 miles (560km) north through the

▶ Nicholas Morant, the Canadian Pacific's chief photographer, captured one of the railway's big streamlined 2-10-4 Selkirks leading the Dominion along the Bow River at Massive, Alberta – not far from the popular resorts at Banff.

▲ The Canadian National's 4-8-4 Northerns were lightweight compared with most used in the United States. With the weight of the locomotive distributed over eight driving wheels, the load per axle was lower than comparable 4-6-4 Pacific types.

Newfoundland wilderness, to Schefferville, Quebec, with branches to Labrador City and Wabush Lake built later. Its primary commodity was iron ore, and it was known for operating some of the heaviest trains in the world, some weighing approximately 28,000 tons (25,400 tonnes), almost double what a modern American unit coal train would weigh. Although Schefferville closed in the 1980s, this railroad still operates an infrequent passenger service.

Another line, called the Cartier Railway, was built by the Quebec Cartier Mining Company in the early 1960s. It runs from Port-Cartier, Quebec, on the St Lawrence River west of Sept-Iles to Gagnon,

the heart of Lac-Jeannine iron-ore mining region, about 200 miles (320km) to the north. This remote line exists primarily for the transport of iron ore, and it operates like a gigantic conveyer belt. When the mines are running at capacity, the railroad runs five loaded ore trains every day. North of Port-Cartier, the railway runs through a scenic wildlife reserve, as it ascends the rocky Canadian Shield, crossing it at an altitude of more than 2000 ft (600m) above sea level. Other recently built lines in Canada include the Canadian Pacific's modern low-grade crossing of Rogers Pass in the Canadian Rockies, a line that features the longest railroad tunnel in North America,

▶ The featherweight 4-4-4 Jubilee locomotive was the Canadian Pacific's response to the advent of lightweight internal combustion streamliners in the United States. One of these fast machines is seen here at McAdam, New Brunswick, on February 6, 1957.

154

the 9.1-mile (14.65km) Mount MacDonald bore. This new line was opened in 1989 and is designed to handle westbound traffic, as the older route was retained for eastbound moves.

CANADIAN RAILWAYS TODAY

In many ways, contemporary Canadian railways mirror those now found in the United States. Today, they essentially employ the same types of locomotives, freight cars, and, to a lesser extent, passenger equipment as lines in the United States. Like the modern American network, Canadian railways now exist primarily to haul freight, while passenger services are relegated to a few suburban lines, a handful of intercity trains operated by VIA Rail – the Canadian

Despite a relatively lean passenger system, Canadian trains are maintained to a very high standard and enjoy good ridership

---

equivalent of Amtrak – and some private services, such as trains operated over the Algoma Central. Despite a relatively lean passenger system, Canadian trains are maintained to a very high standard and enjoy good ridership.

During the 1980s, both the Canadian National and the Canadian Pacific acquired American railroads and expanded their mileage in the United States. At the same time, both lines began spinning off secondary routes and branch lines in Canada. Routes in eastern Canada, particularly the Maritimes, were particularly susceptible to such schemes. As a result, today, the many lines east of Montreal are operated by short-line and regional railways instead of the Canadian National or Canadian Pacific. In the Canadian plains, changes in agriculture, notably wheat production, in recent years have resulted in the abandonment of numerous branch lines, and the once-vast network of branch lines is gradually being dismantled.

One of the biggest changes in the 1990s was the privatization of the Canadian National. Although the railroad name remains, the Canadian National is now

a publicly traded company. Recently, it entered into merger talks with American giant Burlington Northern Santa Fe. The merger was put on hold indefinitely when the American regulatory agency put a moratorium on railway mergers. Based on the

trend toward consolidation in the North American railroad industry, it would seem likely that some day the American and Canadian railroads will merge and form gigantic international systems stretching across North America, from Mexico to Canada.

▲ The Cartier Railway is an isolated line operating in northern Quebec for the sole purpose of serving one of the world's largest iron mines. A trio of M636/C636 diesel-electrics, each rated at 3,600-horsepower, leads a loaded ore train through the Sept-Iles–Port-Cartier wildlife area, in July, 1997.

157

$$=\equiv\mathbf{6}\equiv=$$

REACHING A PEAK

To counter competition from the road networks, the railroads introduced faster locomotives, which also helped cope with the dramatic increase in wartime traffic. Meanwhile, passengers traveled on exciting new streamlined trains.

In the days before the advent of motor trucks, the railroads comfortably enjoyed a near monopoly on most intercity freight business. Since it cost more money to run trains faster, railroads typically ran freight trains at a maximum of 20–30mph (32–48kph) on level stretches and much slower in the mountains. Freights were often held for hours to stay out of the way of passenger trains, and the average speed for a freight train was little more than 12mph (19kph). In reality, there had been little improvement in freight train speed from the dawn of the railway age until after World War I. Railroads had sought to run longer and heavier, but not necessarily faster trains. Nearly all freight locomotive development had been aimed at reducing the cost of haulage. Bigger, more powerful locomotive designs had allowed railroads to run longer, heavier freight trains. But these big, heavy trains still plodded along at the same very low speeds.

◄ **A Brooklyn Eastern District tank engine switches the Brooklyn car ferries at docks across the East River from Manhattan, New York. Freight cars were floated across the river on specialized barges fitted with tracks, and were known as car floats.**

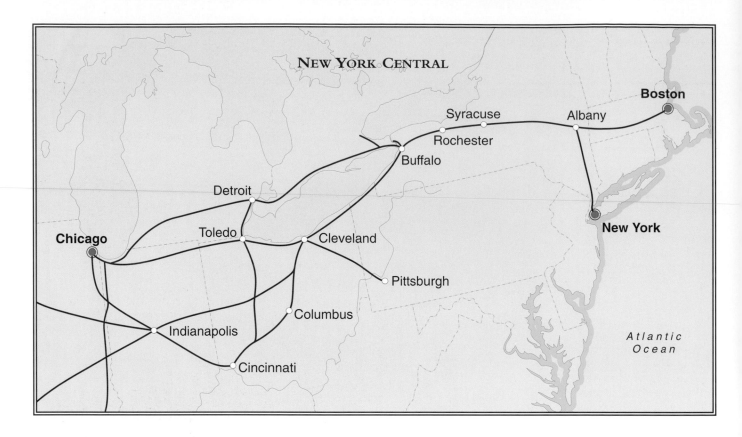

NEW YORK CENTRAL

▲ **The New York Central was one of the most important railroad systems in North America, serving the heart of the most populated and industrialized region of the US. Its affiliated lines included the Boston & Albany, Pittsburgh & Lake Erie, and Michigan Central.**

Following the end of World War I, North American railroads were experiencing an ever-greater pinch on their lucrative freight business from road trucks. Paved highways and improved engine designs had allowed for faster trucks. In response, some railroads defied traditional attitudes toward freight and operated them at near-passenger train speeds.

One of the foremost innovators was the "water level" New York Central, which had developed a four-track mainline that stretched from New York all the way to Chicago. Two of its four tracks were primarily dedicated to freight operations, thus allowing it to separate its freight and passenger traffic and minimize delays to both. Since the New York Central faced competition from all other modes, including other railroads, water transport, and now from highways, it needed to find ways to keep its shippers happy. It successfully speeded up its freight operation, running a network of fast freights on its water level lines. To haul

these trains, it employed modern 4-8-2 Mohawks, ideally suited for moving long trains quickly.

One area where the New York Central had difficulties raising its freight speeds was on its Boston & Albany mainline. This was Whistler's Western Railroad of Massachusetts, a pioneering mountain railroad with twisting curves and stiff grades that had long slowed the progress of trains between the Massachusetts and New York state capitals. It had long been where new and powerful locomotives were tested. In the 1890s, before the New York Central had taken control of the Boston & Albany, the railroad had tried cross-compound 4-8-0 Mastodons, known by railroad men as "Slam Bangs" for their uneven cylinder action. The New York Central had introduced huge 2-6-6-2 Mallets, followed by 2-10-2 "Santa Fe" types. Both of these powerful locomotives were able to move considerable tonnage over the Berkshire Hills, but were not known for speed.

▶ **For fast freight service, the New York Central developed the 4-8-2, which it called a Mohawk, rather than a Mountain type, and later refined as a powerful passenger locomotive. This L-3 Mohawk leads the *New England Wolverine* at Riverside, Massachusetts.**

In the 1920s, Lima was a newcomer to the big locomotive business and was looking for a way to increase its market share from the well-established locomotive builders Baldwin and Alco. Lima had enjoyed brisk business during the war and now wanted to increase its peacetime business. An inventive, visionary engineer named Will Woodard, who had variously worked for both of Lima's competitors, led the company's efforts. He had different ideas on how to build steam locomotives and defied conventional wisdom. Since the mid-19th century, most locomotives were either built to haul relatively light trains quickly or plod along with heavy tonnage. This was the difference between freight and passenger locomotives. While there were a variety of exceptions, and each railroad went about designing its locomotives to fit its services using its own parameters, the vast majority of heavy road locomotives in North America fit one of these two types of service.

A passenger locomotive typically had tall drivers for speed, which were not well suited to moving heavy trains. Freight locomotives had small drivers

▲ Railroads often interchanged freight cars among themselves. As a result, rolling stock from many lines would be seen on a long train. Here, Atlantic Coast Line and Santa Fe boxcars, far from their home rails, roll over the crossing at Campbell Hall, New York.

that were designed for maximum tractive effort and poorly suited for high speed. Heavy freight engines, particularly the big Mallets and 2-10-2 Santa Fes that had been all the rage during the 1905 to 1920 period, were essentially incapable of traveling at high speeds, even when hauling relatively light trains. A Mallet was limited to about 20mph (32kph) for several reasons: high back pressure on its large low-pressure cylinders, the lack of stability of the front engine, and small wheels with heavy reciprocating parts which pounded the track because of a force known in the industry as "dynamic augment." The 2-10-2s could move a little faster, but were still limited by the heavy pounding caused by their reciprocating parts. These locomotives had long, heavy main rods to reach all five sets of drivers. Another problem with these large locomotive types was that they did not have sufficient boiler capacity to maintain sustained high-speed running. Increasing the size of the boiler, specifically the firebox, was considered undesirable because it would make the weight of the engine prohibitively heavy.

EXPERIMENTAL DESIGNS

In the early 1920s, under the direction of Woodard, Lima built a series of experimental 2-8-2 Mikados for the New York Central with greater boiler capacity. The best of these were the H-10s, which could haul more tonnage than just about any other comparable locomotive on the railroad. Woodard's success with the Mikado led him to develop a whole new type of locomotive, a sort of "super Mikado." This new design used a 2-8-4 wheel arrangement and was the very first type to use a radial, weight-bearing four-wheel trailing truck. The larger trailing truck was necessary to distribute the weight of a significantly larger firebox — roughly a third larger than that used on H-10 Mikados. The larger firebox, combined with other energy-saving features such as a feedwater heater (which warmed the water entering the boiler using exhaust steam) and a booster engine (a small auxiliary engine that engages a trailing truck or tender truck) to help start a heavy train, gave this new locomotive a big advantage over traditional designs.

It was more powerful, more fuel efficient, and capable of sustaining comparably high speed while lifting heavy tonnage up a long, steep grade.

In 1924, Woodard demonstrated the advantage of his new type to the New York Central in a carefully orchestrated test on its Boston & Albany subsidiary. It was arranged to send two freights eastbound on the Boston & Albany: one was powered by Woodard's H-10 Mikado (then considered one of the very best locomotives on the railroad); the other, a slightly heavier train, was powered by the new 2-8-4 locomotive. The second train departed the yard about an hour after the first. In what seemed like no time at all, the new 2-8-4 had overtaken the Mikado that was hauling less tonnage. Best of all, the 2-8-4 used less fuel! The New York Central was very pleased and so was Lima. The new locomotive was named the Berkshire type, and the New York Central placed three successive orders for Berkshires for service over their namesake hills.

Woodard went on to expand upon the success of the Berkshire, and, in 1925, shortly after the success on the Boston & Albany, he sold a fleet of 2-10-4s to

▼ The Boston & Albany stretched across Massachusetts, connecting Boston with other large cities and towns on its way to Albany. After 1900, the B&A was a component of the New York Central, but it retained some autonomy through the end of the steam era.

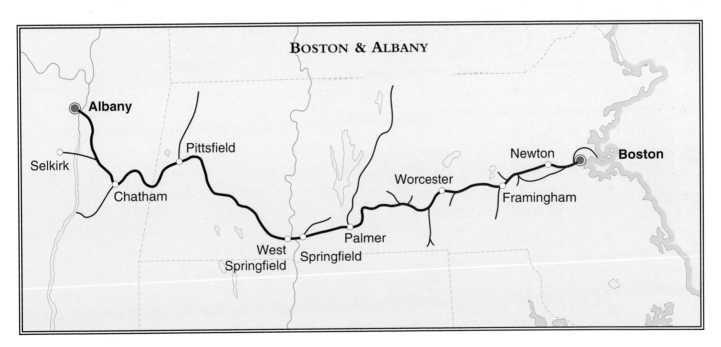

the Texas & Pacific. These big locomotives were essentially an expansion of the Berkshire type. Named after the T&P, they were designated Texas types. They overcame the limitations of the big, slow-moving 2-10-2s by employing significantly larger driving wheels, which were better counterbalanced and thus had less dynamic augment, permitting faster operation. To provide sufficient power to move five sets of drivers, the 2-10-4 had a massive boiler that operated at higher pressure than older locomotives. It was a winning combination.

▼ In an image of raw power, a Lima-built 2-8-2 Mikado leads a westbound New York Central freight train near Harrison, Ohio. In the 1920s, Lima revolutionized the locomotive business by pushing the limits of conventionally designed steam engines.

Woodard's initial innovation was just the beginning. Lima had effectively changed the way railroads looked at locomotives. Woodard called his innovation "Superpower" and soon all three builders were designing locomotives with large fireboxes carried by four-wheel trailing trucks. Lima had assured its place in the ranks of American locomotive builders, and its steam locomotives are generally held as some of the finest ever built on American soil. Other innovations helped promote more new designs. Advances in metallurgy resulted in a range of new lightweight alloy steels, which facilitated weight reduction for reciprocating parts. This, along with more advances in counterbalancing, permitted further reductions in dynamic augment. Better steels allowed for stronger boilers, which resulted in even higher working pressure and therefore greater power output.

In 1927, the New York Central and Alco worked to build a better passenger locomotive that used the Superpower principle. This was the 4-6-4 Hudson type, named for the mighty Hudson River, which the New York Central follows between New York City and Albany. The Hudson type was a significant improvement over the older 4-6-2 Pacific, allowing the New York Central to run longer passenger trains without compromising speed or the need to doublehead (use two locomotives) on a single train.

DEMISE OF THE MALLET
By the mid-1920s, the Mallet compound had largely fallen out of favor. The complexity of the plumbing needed to distribute high- and low-pressure steam required significantly more maintenance than simple locomotives, and, as with the earlier compounds, the cost advantages achieved through greater efficiency were often lost in the greater shop expense. More importantly, the Mallets were just too slow.

Railroads liked the concept of one huge locomotive under the control of a

▲ In 1938, H. W.
Pontin photographed a
Boston & Albany A-1b Berkshire
on "Englishman's Curve" in East Chatham,
New York. The B&A Berkshire was the first of Lima's
famous Superpower steam locomotives.

single throttle, and some lines took to rebuilding their Mallets as "simple" articulated engines. A simple articulated feeds high-pressure steam directly into all four cylinders, rather than using the complex compounding system. This requires a bigger boiler, as more steam is needed to keep the locomotive running, and more steam requires more fuel. So, as a result, a simple articulated was more expensive to operate than a Mallet, but cost less to maintain. Also, simple articulated locomotives were not affected by heavy back pressure and therefore were capable of running faster.

The Northern Pacific was the first to use the four-wheel trailing truck in the design of a simple articulated locomotive. It ordered a fleet of massive 2-8-8-4s for use in the Badlands of Montana and North Dakota. This gigantic locomotive, the largest

in the world when first built, was coined the "Yellowstone" type, and it was eventually employed on several lines around the United States.

Lima's Superpower concept was not the only solution offered to provide greater power. Alco had its own ideas for greater power, and it promoted three-cylinder designs. The three-cylinder compound had achieved popularity in Britain, but had not caught on in North America. Alco developed the three-cylinder simple engine in the 1920s, which it marketed with some success to railroads seeking more powerful, non-articulated locomotives. The third cylinder was located below the smokebox, between the two outside cylinders, and drove a cranked axle. A three-cylinder locomotive has more torque than conventional two-cylinder designs, which gives it an advantage hauling heavy trains up a grade.

Alco built 4-10-2s for the Southern Pacific and Union Pacific, and even larger 4-12-2s for the Union Pacific — a huge locomotive named appropriately the Union Pacific type after its only user. However, this locomotive with a wheelbase long

▲ The Baltimore & Ohio experimented with progressive loco-motive designs in the 1920 and 1930s in an effort to improve efficiency and performance. This 2-6-6-2 featured a water-tube firebox instead of a conventional fire-tube layout.

enough to accommodate 12 sets of drivers was not well suited to negotiating curves, and the Union Pacific found its 4-12-2s were best suited for level running across the prairies of Nebraska and eastern Wyoming. The Union Pacific's big 4-12-2s were not the largest non-articulated locomotives in the world. The Russians built an even larger locomotive with a 4-14-4 wheel arrangement. But some locomotives can get just too big, and that one did not perform well.

Other American railroads, such as the New Haven, operated fleets of more moderately proportioned three-cylinder locomotives. The New Haven employed its three-cylinder 4-8-2s on through freights, often assigning them to its Maybrook Line, where they would roll across the spindly, long, tall Poughkeepsie Bridge, which spanned the Hudson River Valley.

One of the greatest flaws of the conventional reciprocating steam locomotive is its inherent poor ability to convert heat into the rotary motion that propels the train. On typical American locomotives, only about six to eight percent of the energy consumed is actually used to move the locomotive. The rest is lost, an enormous waste considering the amount of coal used.

A few railroads took it upon themselves to explore new avenues of steam technology in an effort to improve the thermal efficiency of the engine and make a better locomotive. Eastern coal hauler Delaware & Hudson built a series of experi-

---

On typical American locomotives, only six to eight percent of the energy consumed is actually used to move the engine

---

mental very high-pressure compounds at its shops at Colonie, New York. One of these was a unique, triple expansion locomotive that featured three sets of cylinders – high, medium, and low pressure. While triple expansion engines had been common for other applications, the Delaware & Hudson's locomotive was the only one known in North America. The Delaware & Hudson was not alone in this avenue of research. The New York Central

► Moving heavy trains over steep grades required specialized locomotives. Here, a pair of Baldwin-built 2-8-8-0 Mallet compounds work as helpers, shoving on the rear of a B&O coal train ascending the Cranberry Grade at Terra Alta, West Virginia.

experimented with a high-pressure 4-8-4 compound, and the Canadian Pacific built a 2-10-4 with a multi-pressure boiler.

Beginning in the late 1920s, the Baltimore & Ohio, under the direction of Chief Mechanical Officer George H. Emerson, built a variety of experimental locomotives that used watertube fireboxes, instead of the more conventional firetube configuration. Then, in 1937, Emerson had the B&O's shops build the very first Duplex, a locomotive with a divided drive on a rigid frame. This locomotive, named after Emerson, used two complete sets of running gear, with the rear set of cylinders facing opposite the direction of travel. The advantages included lighter main rods and shorter piston thrusts, which theoretically would reduce dynamic augment and allow the locomotive to run at a faster speed. The *George H. Emerson* was the Baltimore & Ohio's only Duplex. Later, the Pennsylvania Railroad would explore the concept more thoroughly and with somewhat better results.

MORE SUPERPOWERED STEAM

While some lines experimented in steam efficiency, other lines ordered fleets of Superpower types. In 1927, several builders and several lines in both the United States and Canada developed locomotives using the 4-8-4 wheel arrangement. The first was the Northern Pacific, which was looking for a better 4-8-2 Mountain type to replace its 4-6-2 Pacifics on its long-distance passenger trains, including its famous *North Coast Limited*. The Northern Pacific had special

▲ The B&O's last experimental steam locomotive with a water-tube boiler was the *George H. Emerson,* named for its designer. It was also the first Duplex type, and used a 4-4-4-4 "divided-drive" wheel arrangement on a rigid frame. Compare this with the Pennsylvania Railroad's T1 seen on pages 204–205.

considerations because it burned a type of low-grade fuel, called "Rosebud" coal – sod, in some circles – known for its high ash content and low energy yield. It was this type of coal that inspired the development of the Northern Pacific's 2-8-8-4 Yellowstones and their cavernous fireboxes. Like its Yellowstones, the Northern Pacific's 4-8-4s, built by Alco, needed the four-wheel trailing truck to accommodate the enormous firebox and huge ashpans required to burn low-yield coal. The 4-8-4 is generally known as a Northern type after the Northern Pacific; however, many other lines developed their own moniker for this popular Superpower wheel arrangement.

Shortly after the Northern Pacific, the Santa Fe ordered 4-8-4s from Baldwin designed for fast passenger service. While impressive to look at, the real advantages of the Santa Fe's Northerns were a result of their spectacular efficiency. They could haul a third more train than the older 4-8-2 Mountains and burn less fuel doing it. This would be like buying a big new four-wheel drive sports utility vehicle and finding it got much better gas mileage than your old two-wheel-drive sedan! So, these were happy days on the Santa Fe. More 4-8-4s followed on that road and many others. Meanwhile, it also found use further north on Canadian National, another 4-8-4 pioneer, and ultimately the largest user of the type in North America (as discussed in Chapter 5).

The 4-8-4 became the most popular of all Super-power designs, and was developed into a variety of handsome, powerful machines, some of the most impressive locomotives ever made. Unlike most earlier wheel arrangements, the 4-8-4 was equally suited for both freight and passenger work. This made the 4-8-4 a truly dual-service locomotive like the American standard 4-4-0, 90 years earlier.

While all these new fabulous types of steam locomotives were seizing the day on American rails, a new type of motive power was emerging that would ultimately displace all steam power on North American rails. Internal combustion motors had been the bane of the railroad. It was the gasoline and distillate (a lower grade of fuel) engines that gave life to automobiles, trucks, and ultimately airplanes. However, the railroads had been experimenting with these motors, too.

A NEW TYPE OF ENGINE

First, they powered self-propelled railcars, such as the McKeen Wind Splitter, and later were used as prime movers in small switching locomotives. German inventor Rudolf Diesel had developed an internal combustion engine that worked on a compression principle. While early diesel engines were cumbersome and ponderous machines, as technology improved, the engines became more reliable and more compact. Early experimentation with diesel locomotives had proved troublesome, but, in 1925, the first successful commercially built diesel debuted. This was an ugly little box cab, No. 1000 for the Jersey Central, designed to run on industrial trackage in New York City, where strict smoke regulations stemming from the Park Avenue Tunnel disaster of 1902 forbid the use of steam locomotives. It was built by a consortium of Alco, General Electric, and engine manufacturer Ingersoll-Rand. By the late 1920s, a number of these odd critters were to be found burbling around in big city yards. They were typically used to comply with air quality regulations, not as a result of greater efficiency. Two lines experimented with road diesels: the New York Central,

which had one of the largest early fleets of boxcab switchers, and the Canadian National. Neither experiment amounted to much.

In the late 1920s, the United States Navy initiated research to develop practical diesel engines for use in submarines. This work ultimately produced a number of compact, lightweight, high-output diesels. In the early 1930s, General Motors, already one of the leading producers of automobiles, acquired the Winton Engine Company, a producer of distillate engines, and also one of its best customers, the Electro Motive Corporation (EMC). EMC was the leading manufacturer of gasoline electric railcars. Under General Motors, EMC set out to design a new type of diesel engine using new alloyed steels. This would prove to be one of the best engine designs of the era. The stage was set for a railway motive power revolution.

DARK DEPRESSION DAYS

The onset of the Great Depression decimated the railroads' business. Freight traffic – which had been fairly robust during the 1920s – tapered off, while passenger traffic – which had been weak – dropped precipitously. Money was tight and people did not travel. By the early 1930s, the railroads were in

▼ The 4-8-4 Northern was the most versatile and adaptable Superpower type. Between 1945 and 1947 the Reading Company built a fleet of 30 Northerns, using components from its old 2-8-0 Consolidation locomotives. Here, two Reading 4-8-4s march along in eastern Pennsylvania.

desperate financial straits. They curtailed expenses in every way they could. They trimmed back schedules, combined trains, and cut back their labor force. On some lines, laying off employees was a tough proposition. Railroads had developed a family outlook toward employment and this made it very difficult to simply let men go that had worked for the company their whole life.

While the Depression was tough on the railroads, it was really tough on the locomotive builders. While the locomotive business had tended to be cyclical, it totally bottomed out in the early 1930s. Most lines had stopped ordering new locomotives altogether. This was not surprising, as many lines had placed large orders in the 1920s and then watched in horror

---

Locomotives belched steam, smoke, and cinders, and passengers often felt like they had been on a tour of a coal mine

---

as their business evaporated. By the early 1930s, it was common to see long lines of locomotives stored in railroad yards and at shops. While most of the stored locomotives were old, some dating back to the beginning of the 20th century, others were fairly new. Meanwhile, the erecting halls at Baldwin's Eddystone plant and Alco's Schenectady works lay idle. To some in the business, it seemed like the end of the world. And, in some ways, it was. While these plants would get a second lease of life when World War II began, it would not last. The era of the steam locomotive was nearly over.

By the 1930s, railway travel was viewed as old-fashioned and stodgy. Most railroads provided passenger service in the same manner as they had for a generation. Trains used big, heavyweight passenger cars, painted in dull shades of "Pullman Green" – a dark, nearly black color – and "Tuscan" red – easily

mistaken for dirty brown. They were comfortable and conventional, but not very exciting.

Train speeds were moderate, but not fast. While some lines clipped along at top speeds of 70 and 80mph (112.7 and 128.7kph), trains had to stop often while locomotives were watered and filled with coal. Many lines needed to exchange engines on long runs, a procedure that killed time and slowed schedules.

▶ The Baltimore & Ohio was the first railroad to use stream-lined diesel-electric locomotives which could be disconnected from the fixed train set. This B&O train, with two early stream-lined Electro Motive diesels, is seen near Rockville, Maryland.

Train travel was a dirty business, too. All the romance of a ride on a steam train was lost on the woman whose pretty new dress was covered in cinders and ash. The Lackawanna's *Phoebe Snow* might have been hauled by a clean anthracite-burning locomotive, but most trains were not. Locomotives belched steam, smoke, and cinders, and, after a long trip, passengers often felt like they had been on a tour of a coal mine.

In the days when the railroad had been a vast improvement over traditional stage and canal travel, its flaws had been pardoned. After all, what's a little soot when you are riding in relative luxury, dining in the diner, and sleeping in the comparative comfort of a Pullman berth? And surely riding cross-country by train in a few days was vastly better than traveling for a month or more around Cape Horn by sailing ship.

However, with the advent of other forms of transport, notably the automobile, and more recently, air travel, trains were no longer seen as an exciting form of transportation.

Out of desperation, a few innovative lines attempted to make the railroad exciting again. They would introduce new trains that embodied some of the pleasurable qualities of automobile and air travel and attract people back to the rails. The advances in automotive and airline manufacturing techniques, plus the advent of compact high-output diesel engines combined with new streamlined styling, all coalesced in the early 1930s to help give railroad travel the boost it so desperately needed.

▼ The Burlington's shovel-nosed *Zephyrs* were introduced in 1934 and represented the epitome of high-speed passenger service. The *Pioneer Zephyr* was the first diesel-electric passenger train in North America and ushered in the age of the diesel-electric "streamliner."

The streamlined concept was nothing new – in fact, it dated back to the very first days of the railway. By streamlining, wind resistance is reduced, thus improving efficiency and permitting higher speeds. In 1865, one S. R. Calthrop patented a streamlined train design. Nearly three decades later, designer Frederick U. Adams published a book entitled *Atmospheric Resistance in Its Relation to the Speed of Trains*. In spring 1900, the Baltimore & Ohio – always a railroad interested in new concepts – gave the innovative Adams the opportunity to test his theories and build a wooden streamlined train. While a conventional 4-4-0 steam locomotive pulled it, the pioneering streamliner still attained a top speed of nearly 88mph (141.6kph). Sadly, this train came before its time and failed to meet the expectations set for it. McKeen's Wind Splitters gas-electrics also used a streamlined design, but generally did not travel fast enough for their sleek design to make any difference to their performance.

TRAVELERS' TALES
A ROYAL RATE

Sometimes those with greatest means enjoy the lowest fares. In short, it pays to be a VIP on the railroad. In his book, *The History of the Baltimore & Ohio*, author John F. Stover tells about how, in 1926, when America was enjoying great prosperity, Sam Hill helped make travel arrangements for Queen Marie of Romania during her visit to the United States. Sam Hill was not only a personal friend of the Queen, but also the son-in-law of the late, great James J. Hill (as it happens, Sam Hill married James J. Hill's daughter, Mary Hill).

Hill contacted Baltimore & Ohio president Daniel Willard, a man known for his considerable influence, to see if he could help arrange a lower rate for the royal family who were traveling across the United States. Such a matter was more difficult than it seems, because railroads were strictly regulated as to how much or, as the case may be, how little they could charge. Federal rules about giving away passes were not open to interpretation. In this regard, Willard's influence among railroad commissioners paid off, and he was able to get a new passenger rate authorized in an official capacity, specifically for "visiting royalty." This was truly a bargain, as it permitted the entire royal entourage to travel over each road that chose to adopt the rate for just one dollar. It is likely that the Queen and her guests were not subject to travel on the common day coach either!

In the late 1920s, there was a renewed interest in wind resistance and streamlined schemes, as a number of industrial design firms had begun promoting streamlining. Furthermore, the gas-electric rail car had been around for years – most railroads owned at least a few for branch line work – so the engineering concept behind the internal combustion engine was well founded and understood. The two ideas came together in the first streamliners.

The streamliner was born on two roads simultaneously as both the Union Pacific and Burlington had decided that new streamlined, high-speed, articulated internal combustion railcars might solve their passenger train problems. Once decided, each company wanted to have the first streamliner, but knew their competition was planning the same thing. A race was on to see which railroad would debut the first streamliner.

THE SLEEK NEW STREAMLINER

The Burlington train was built by the Budd Company and featured a sleek, shot-welded stainless steel streamlined body. The Union Pacific's train was manufactured by Pullman using a riveted lightweight aluminum body and painted in classy yellow and brown paint. Containing three cars, it weighed about the same as a single conventional heavyweight passenger car. Both trains were to be powered by new Winton internal combustion engines. While Winton had just perfected its powerful new diesel engine design, it was not yet ready for production. New technology often takes a while before it is reliable, and the bugs had not been worked out yet.

As it turned out, the Union Pacific train was ready first, several months before the new engine was ready to go. In order to beat the Burlington and get its train running first, the Union Pacific accepted a powerful Winton distillate engine – which uses spark plugs to initiate combustion, like an automobile gasoline engine – instead of waiting for the diesel. It thus made history on February 12, 1934, as the first American railroad operating a modern high-speed streamlined articulated train. Articulation meant the passenger cars shared a set of trucks and were semi-permanently coupled together. This reduced weight and slack between cars, permitting the train to run faster. It was designed for a top speed of 90mph (144.8kph)

► In the mid-1930s, the Rio Grande rebuilt several former Western Pacific dining cars, fitting them with modern interiors. This publicity view, from about 1939, shows the attractive Art Deco styling of a revamped Rio Grande lounge-diner.

and carried enough fuel to allow it to travel for hundreds of miles without stopping.

The Union Pacific named its train the *Streamliner* and sent it on a nationwide publicity tour, where it went from city to city thrilling the public and railroad officials alike. Unlike the traditional passenger train that everyone knew so well, this train was really new and exciting. Its streamlined contours, internal combustion power, and high speed made it the very vision of the future. Passengers were treated to a

The *Zephyr* was a marvel – a streamlined design so timeless that it still seems modern today, over 60 years after its debut

smooth ride and soundproofing that minimized the "clickety-clack" of the railroad tracks and other characteristic noises of railroad travel. The windows were sealed and coated to minimize glare, and the train was air-conditioned! We might take such amenities for granted today, but, in 1934, they were pure luxury.

Two months after the *Streamliner*'s debut, the Winton diesel was finally ready and installed in the Burlington Railroad's similarly articulated streamlined wonder. On April 7, 1934, the futuristic Burlington *Zephyr* made its national debut. The *Zephyr* was even more popular than the *Streamliner* and also made a well-publicized nationwide tour. Although not the first streamliner, the *Zephyr* can claim the more significant historical statistic of being the world's first successful diesel-electric passenger train, and it was the diesel engine that would ultimately revolutionize North American railroading.

According to Burlington historian Richard C. Overton, the Burlington president, Ralph Budd – not related to Edward Budd of the Budd Company – came up with the name *Zephyr* after reading Chaucer, who refers to the Greek god of the west

wind as "Zephyrus." This was also a symbol of renaissance. What better way to revitalize a western railway than with the power of Zephyrus!

The Zephyr was a marvel to behold, a streamlined design so timeless that it still seems modern today more than 60 years after its debut. While the Union Pacific's *Streamliner* featured an enormous grill that looked like a huge gaping mouth, the *Zephyr* featured a sharp, slanting shovel-nose front lined with windows for the operator (pp.172 and 179). The train skin was unpainted stainless steel with fluted sides. At the back was a fishtail, round-end observation car, where passengers could sit and watch the miles speed by. The *Zephyr's* shape was more than just styling – it was truly streamlined, having been designed in a wind tunnel. And it was a fast train, too. On its trial run from Edward Budd's Philadelphia plant, it hit a top speed of 104mph (167.4kph).

STREAMLINER MANIA

As the *Zephyr* toured the country, it entertained thousands of people. It was self-promotion in the finest style. The Burlington displayed the train first in Philadelphia where it was built and then all over its far-flung western system, making 16 stops along the way. Everywhere it went the train was a sensation; its progress made regular radio bulletins and the public

was excited to follow its progress. In June, 1934, the *Zephyr* rolled across the newly constructed Dotsero cut-off in the Colorado Rockies. This brand new line was the last link in the latest transcontinental route that included the recently completed Moffat Tunnel, a six-mile, 373-yd (9,997m) long bore through the Front Range. It was also one of the last new mainline links built in the United States.

The first two streamlined trains spawned a whole new era of American rail travel. Maury Klein, in his

◄ This intriguing platform view at Canton Junction, Massachusetts, on the New Haven Railroad in October, 1947 shows a gas-electric "doodle bug" car on the left, and a fast mainline passenger train on the right, led by one of New Haven's streamlined 4-6-4 *Shoreliner* steam locomotives.

▲ The Union Pacific's *Streamliner* draws a huge crowd at Denver, Colorado, during a 1934 publicity run. The distinctive-looking three-car Pullman-built train featured an aluminum body designed in a wind tunnel to minimize air resistance.

book *Union Pacific*, said of the streamliner, "in this first age of chic it was sleek, glamorous, and thoroughly modern, offering amenities once reserved only for the rich." While the Union Pacific and Burlington had anticipated additional streamlined trains even before the first streamliners had rolled out of the shop, the overwhelming popularity of the stream- liners resulted in both railroads racing to place orders for more trains.

Subsequent streamliners were longer and more powerful, and, by the mid-1930s, both lines had fleets of streamlined trains connecting a variety of cities in the Midwest and Far West. While the Union Pacific's original *Streamliner* was assigned the rela- tively obscure route over the old Kansas Pacific from Kansas City, Missouri, to Salina, Kansas, later trains were assigned to premier routes. The Union Pacific introduced the *City of Los Angeles* between Chicago and Los Angeles; the *City of Portland* between Chicago and Portland; the *City of San Francisco* over the traditional overland route via the Southern Pacific's Donner Pass; and the *City of Denver* connecting Chicago and Denver.

As true long-distance trains, these later streamliners were fully equipped with diners and sleeping cars. To maximize the effect of these new trains, the Union Pacific staged numerous stunts and special runs to

▲ It's been more than 40 years since the Burlington's stainless steel *Zephyrs* whisked passengers through Galesburg, Illinois, but this billboard advertising the town's annual "Railroad Days" festival still uses an image of a shovel-nose streamlined *Zephyr*.

attract publicity. In October, 1935, the Union Pacific's second streamliner sprinted coast to coast from Los Angeles to Grand Central Terminal in New York in just under 57 hours. This was nearly a full day faster than regularly scheduled trains and a new world record by a long shot. On another run, a streamliner zipped along at an average speed of 84mph (135.1kph) start to stop, covering a run more than 500 miles (800km) long. Impressive stuff in the days of steam!

Meanwhile, the Burlington Railroad's *Zephyr* had the starring role in a Hollywood production called *Silver Streak*, and the Burlington had introduced a host of its own streamlined trains. Its *Twin Cities Zephyr* raced across the prairies of northern Illinois and up the spectacular Mississippi Valley, connecting Chicago with Minneapolis–St Paul. The *Mark Twain Zephyr* – one of the few American trains with a literary name and a logical progression of its Chauceresque predecessor – operated between St Louis and Burlington, Iowa. Competing with the Union Pacific's *City of Denver* was the appropriately named *Denver Zephyr*.

Not to be left out, many other lines took to ordering streamlined trains. Some followed the mold of the Union Pacific and Burlington by ordering

◄ George C. Corey caught the New Haven's streamlined *Comet* in action at Canton Junction, Massachusetts. This unusual double-ended streamliner was painted blue and silver, and operated daily between Boston, Massachusetts, and Providence, Rhode Island.

copycat diesel-electric streamliners; others went about streamlining in different ways. New England's Boston & Maine ordered a Budd-built train nearly identical to those used on the Burlington. It initially ran as the *Flying Yankee*, connecting Boston and Portland. Although it held other runs in later years, the train is still known as the *Flying Yankee* and, more than 65 years after its introduction, remains one of the best remembered trains in the region. It was so popular that old-timers still talk about it today. The nearby New Haven Railroad had its own streamliner, a double-ended machine built by Goodyear and known as the *Comet*, which made several trips daily on the New Haven's Shoreline Route between

Boston and Providence, Rhode Island. The Illinois Central followed the Union Pacific prototype and ordered a Pullman streamliner that ran as the *Green Diamond*, an ungainly-looking beast likely to frighten small children.

THE MIGHTY *HIAWATHA*

Midwestern railroad the Milwaukee Road liked the streamliner concept, but the line was not too keen on all the new technology. So, it took a more traditional approach to streamlined trains and came up with one of the most successful trains in modern history – the *Hiawatha*. Rather than rely on outside vendors to build its streamliners, the Milwaukee Road made them at its own shops. However, it did order a small fleet of new steam locomotives from Alco specifically designed for its streamliner service. Initially it bought four tall-drivered 4-4-2 Atlantics, which were the first new steam locomotives to be

▼ **Streamlined trains offered a level of service and comfort not afforded by most conventional heavyweight trains. Passengers aboard the Burlington's *Denver Zephyr* were treated to an air-conditioned lounge, brightly lit and free of locomotive smoke.**

▲ The Milwaukee Road's famous *Hiawatha* at the company's namesake city in the 1960s. The "Skytop Lounge," pictured here, was one of the *Hiawatha*'s distinctive features in later years. It offered passengers a splendid view from the back of the train.

delivered with streamlined shrouds. In 1934, the New York Central had been the first American line to shroud a steam locomotive. It placed wind-resistant shrouds on one of its fast 4-6-4 Hudsons in an effort to improve performance.

The Milwaukee Road went with a steam-powered streamliner for very practical reasons. The use of locomotive-hauled trains offered flexibility of operation, and steam locomotives were cheaper to purchase, plus did not require special service facilities. Also, modern steam could produce high horsepower at top speeds. The Milwaukee Road's

Atlantics featured styling by Otto Kuhler, and, unlike the black paint worn by most American steamers, these were bright orange, gray, and maroon to match the lightweight streamlined cars they were designed to haul. The cars were truly modern, and each weighed a third less than conventional equipment to facilitate high-speed service. Marshall Field &

▲ Railroads were keen to promote their streamlined trains, and launched vigorous advertising campaigns depicting the luxuries that passengers could enjoy. This publicity photo shows passengers at the refreshment bar on a Union Pacific streamliner.

Company participated in the interior design. The cars had reclining seats that were more spacious and comfortable than regular coach seats. Interior coloring was the work of Karl F. Nystrom. Ceilings were flesh colored and walls were a handsome brown. Among the amenities was a cocktail bar – a real treat to passengers, since this came shortly after the repeal of Prohibition. The *Hiawatha's* ride was smoother and quieter than regular trains, and, as with the other streamliners, it was air-conditioned.

In preparation for the inauguration of the *Hiawatha*, the Milwaukee Road upgraded its Chicago–Milwaukee–Twin Cities mainline to 90mph (144.8kph) operation. It ran a test train on May 15, 1935, with the new equipment, and hit a speed of 112½mph (181kph) – the same speed that the New York Central's No. 999 was supposed to have reached 42 years earlier – and concluded the train was ready for service. Like the Union Pacific and Burlington streamliners, a *Hiawatha* train made a public tour acting as a publicity vehicle. Finally, on May 29, 1935, the *Hiawatha* made its debut. It was a smash hit, and soon trains were running up to nine cars long. That was about all the fast Atlantics could handle and still meet the tight schedule to which they were expected to adhere. The Milwaukee Road needed more powerful locomotives, and it ordered streamlined Hudsons with tall drivers that matched the speed of the Atlantics, but hauled longer consists. It was an investment that paid off for the railroad; soon the *Hiawathas* had the second-highest earnings of any passenger trains in the United States.

Today, what we find most amazing about the *Hiawathas* was their sustained speed. They were the fastest regularly scheduled steam-powered trains in the world and operated much faster than most American trains do today. The statistics are stunning. In some places, the *Hiawatha*s were required to maintain better than 100mph (160kph) between points, meaning they needed to run much faster than that to keep up the average speed. Jim Scribbins, author of *The Hiawatha Story*, said that he believes that the Hudsons operated at a maximum speed in excess of 120mph (190kph). Furthermore, the Milwaukee Road did not use any special technology to accomplish these feats, just very well-designed streamlined steam. If we could only ride these trains today!

MORE AND BETTER DIESELS

The success of the first streamliners demonstrated the practicality of diesel-electric power on the railroad and raised the awareness of railroad managers. Diesels could operate over greater distance at lower cost than steam. They required less maintenance, but had different shop requirements. Initially, some railroads were interested in the promise of diesels, but most still saw them just as gimmicks for running lightweight passenger trains. However, the streamliners

did establish General Motors' Electro Motive Corporation (later the Electro Motive Division) as a locomotive producer, and, despite the poor state of the locomotive industry during the Depression of the 1930s, EMC continued to invest in research and develop diesel-electric power and manufactured even better and more powerful diesels.

The very first streamliners had used diesel power cars that were semi-permanently coupled with the train set they were designed to haul. While this made for an aesthetically pleasing design in the form of a uniform train, it quickly proved impractical for daily operations. If a problem developed with the power car, the entire streamlined train needed to visit the shop. Later streamliners dispensed with semi-permanently coupled power cars and then with articulated consists altogether. Instead of fixed consists, the railroads ordered fleets of lightweight streamlined

▼ **The introduction of Electro-Motive Division's FT diesel-electric in 1939 revolutionized American freight railroading. FT diesels are identified by the row of four porthole windows on the side of the locomotive. This detail is not found on later F unit diesels.**

passenger cars, with the traditional trucks and couplers at each end and fleets of streamlined diesel-electric locomotives. Typically, these locomotives were painted and styled to run with a specific consist of cars. This more traditional arrangement of locomotives and cars gave the railroads much greater flexibility, allowing them to adjust the length of

streamlined trains in the same manner they would their conventional consists.

The Baltimore & Ohio was the first railroad to take delivery of streamlined diesels that were not part of a fixed train set – these were EMC's model EA, the first of what would become a standard line of passenger locomotives, the famous "E" units. At that

◄ Steam builder Alco introduced its own road diesel in 1940. Designated the DL-109, it featured a striking streamlining treatment by Otto Kuhler, the well-known industrial designer. The New Haven Railroad operated the largest fleet of DL-109s.

another great advantage to diesel-electric locomotives, something they shared with straight electrics: a single locomotive engineer could operate two or more locomotives from a single throttle, thus eliminating the need to assign a separate crew to each and every locomotive, as was required with steam. However, this arrangement created controversy between railroad unions and management. Railroad men were not happy with the fact that, by using diesels, railroads would be able to employ fewer

Railroad men were not happy with the fact that, by using diesels, railroads would be able to employ fewer locomotive engineers

locomotive engineers, and, in the early days, some unions insisted that an engineer, or at least a rider, be present on each and every locomotive. This practice then encouraged EMC to manufacture a set of locomotives with A and multiple B units, all carrying the same locomotive number, so the railroads could identify several "units" as one locomotive.

In the late 1930s, EMC's E units caught on quickly and many railroads ordered them to haul new streamlined passenger trains. By this time, EMC had begun building diesel switchers as well. Now that EMC had proven that the diesel-electric was an effective fast passenger engine, the company wanted to go after the largest section of the new locomotive market: freight locomotives. It refined its locomotive technology and developed a new more powerful and more reliable diesel engine to power its locomotives.

In 1939, it debuted a powerful, four-unit streamlined diesel, designated the "FT" – for freight. Like the streamliners a few years before, this new locomotive made an extensive nationwide tour. But it was not out just to impress the public, it was there to pull freight trains and impress railroad management. And

time, diesels were designed either with or without driver's cabs. Those with cabs were designated "A" units, those without were known as boosters, and designated "B" units. To make for a nice streamlined passenger consist, many railroads would assign a single A unit, followed by as many B units as was needed to give the train sufficient power. This was

it did! Soon many railroads were buying FTs in droves. Nor was EMC the only diesel builder. During the mid-1930s, long-time steam locomotive builder, Alco, developed its own line of diesel switchers. Then, on the heels of EMC's successful E unit, Alco came up with its own road diesel, an odd-looking machine styled by pioneering industrial designer Otto Kuhler.

Despite all these diesel doings in the 1930s, there was still a strong allegiance to steam power. Sure, diesel streamliners might be sprinting across the plains, reaching speeds of 90mph (144.8kph) or more, and, yes, there was a place for the odd diesel switcher here and there, but what about the rest of the freight and passenger trains? Even the Union Pacific, which had been the first to adopt an internal combustion streamliner, stayed with steam power for the bulk of its operations and went on to encourage the development of some of the very best modern steam locomotives ever designed. Other lines shunned the advent of diesels altogether, refusing to even allow them on the property for test runs and remaining loyal to steam power.

STEAM HOLDS ITS PLACE

Why this loyalty to steam? It was simple: steam was proven and established. Railroads and railroad men knew steam and had invested millions in shops and facilities to keep steam locomotives maintained. The culture of steam locomotive operation dated back right to the beginning of the railroads. Furthermore, the officials in charge of locomotive purchase were typically steam men who were often closely involved with the design and development of the locomotives to be used on their lines. They were reluctant to sacrifice this element of control for the savings afforded by diesels. Also, while it was true that diesels cost less to operate, initial costs were much greater. Moreover, modern steam could outperform diesels in raw power. While diesels had great initial power

◄ **Despite the development of road diesels in the 1930s, steam power continued to dominate railroad operations through World War II. Here, a Mikado and a Pacific "doublehead" a passenger train on the B&O at Terra Alta, West Virginia, in 1948.**

and were better at starting trains, it was hard to beat the raw power of a big steam locomotive. In fact, even the most powerful diesels being built today have yet to match the maximum output of a single late-era steam locomotive. In the 1930s, the best steam had yet to come. Alco, Lima, and Baldwin were still designing new locomotives, and there was more research yet into even better steam power.

In 1936, the Union Pacific and Alco developed a new wheel arrangement, the 4-6-6-4 "Challenger." This locomotive was a magnificent, powerful articulated machine that had overcome the failings of earlier articulated designs. The old Mallets, and even 1920s-vintage simple articulateds, were viewed as slow-speed locomotives. The Santa Fe had experimented with high-speed Mallets back in the World War I period without much success, but the Union Pacific's Challenger was truly a high-speed

▼ After the Union Pacific received its first flashy streamliners in 1934, it collaborated with Alco to create one of the most successful articulated locomotive designs, the 4-6-6-4 Challenger. This type of engine was designed for service at speeds of up to 70mph (112.7kph) on the railroad's mainline.

articulated. A four-wheel leading truck gave it good tracking ability, while a large boiler and firebox (supported by a four-wheel trailing truck) provided plenty of steam. It rode on tall drivers that were precision counterbalanced and incorporated a number of modern, energy-saving appliances.

NEW ARTICULATED TYPE

While older articulated designs were limited to a maximum of 30–40mph (48–64kph), the Challenger was designed to run at 70mph (112.7kph). It was intended as a dual-service locomotive and designed to work on both fast passenger trains and heavy freights. Unlike the Union Pacific's earlier 4-12-2s, which were restricted because of their long, inflexible wheelbase, the Challenger's articulated frame meant these locomotives could operate on mainlines all over the system. The type was a resounding success, and soon other lines were ordering them, too, including several eastern coal roads, such as the Delaware & Hudson.

On the eve of US involvement in World War II, the Union Pacific expanded the Challenger design into a 4-8-8-4, a monster of a locomotive known as a

"Big Boy." This gargantuan machine vies with the Chesapeake & Ohio's 2-6-6-6 Allegheny for title of the largest reciprocating steam locomotive ever built, and it was certainly among the most powerful. The Big Boy weighed 772,000lb (35,017kg) and developed 7,000 horsepower running at 40mph (64kph). Twenty five of these monsters were built, but, unlike the Challenger, the Big Boys were intended for a specific service. They were built to haul heavy freight over the Union Pacific's crossing of the Continental Divide between Cheyenne, Wyoming, and Salt Lake City, Utah. Here, they would lift long trains of perishable traffic – fruits and vegetables grown in the fertile valleys of California – up through Utah's Echo Canyon or slug it out over Wyoming's famous Sherman Hill with a mile or more of merchandise traffic behind them.

The Union Pacific also developed one of the best 4-8-4 Northern types ever to roll on American rails, or anywhere else for that matter. Despite the overwhelming success of its streamliners, the Union

▲ The Union Pacific's last new passenger steam locomotive was No. 844, a 4-8-4 Northern type built by Alco in 1944. This machine survived dieselization, and has remained active since it was made. Today the Union Pacific uses it for excursion service.

Pacific felt it needed a better passenger engine for conventional trains and ordered a fleet of 4-8-4s from Alco. The first of these arrived in 1937, three years after the *Streamliner* had made a name for itself. The Union Pacific's 4-8-4s were known as "800s" for the number series they were assigned. They were modern steam in every respect. Instead of conventional spoked driving wheels, they used an advanced wheel style, featured roller bearings on all reciprocating parts, and employed a variety of new alloy-steels on primary components.

The 800s were capable of great speed and designed for continuous operation at 90mph (144.8kph). On many occasions when trains needed to make up lost time, the 800s were "opened up" and run at well over 100mph (161kph). While they did

▲ A headlight of a westbound freight appears on the horizon, as the signal for an eastbound freight gives an "approach" indication – meaning that the next signal will be a red light. These Centralized Traffic Control (CTC) signals at Solitude, Utah, are remotely operated from several hundred miles away.

not run as fast as the Milwaukee Road's *Hiawatha* Hudsons and Atlantics in daily service, they were certainly capable of rivaling those speeds. One of these great locomotives racing across the Nebraska Plains with an 18-car passenger train at more than

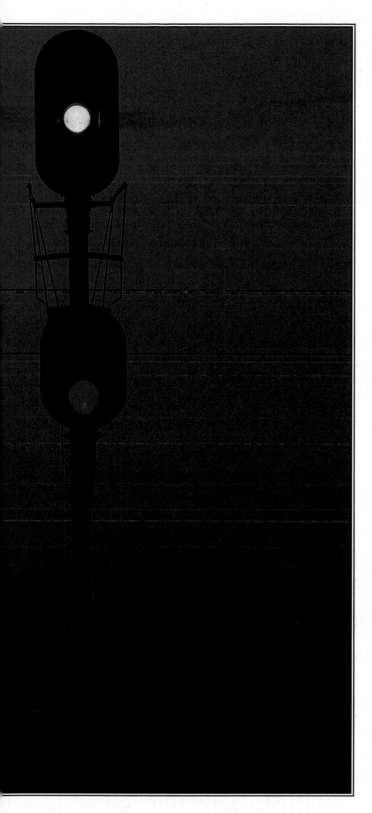

doomed by its inferior distillate engine and was cut up for scrap during World War II, when its aluminum body was especially valuable for airplanes. The railroad's other early streamliners survived longer, but most were taken out of service in the 1950s and replaced by the more conventional diesel-hauled streamlined consists introduced in later years. Yet the 800s – and other Union Pacific steam – soldiered on through the 1950s. One of the Union Pacific's 800s, No. 844, was never retired at all, and on rare occasions it still runs today.

During the 1930s, the Pennsylvania Railroad took a dim view of the advent of the diesel. It was not that the company did not think that the diesel could perform well; on the contrary, it had witnessed the

---

Traffic was picking up in the late 1930s, as the American economy gradually recovered from the worst years of the Depression

---

performance of early diesels with calculated alarm. The Pennsylvania was one of the few railroads known for designing and building its own steam. Its Altoona Shops had been respected as one of the best locomotive builders in the world. While, during the late 1920s and early 1930s, Pennsylvania had focused its efforts on its extensive mainline electrification schemes, it still had a vested interest in steam power, as it was the nation's largest coal hauler. So, when other railroads started ordering EMC E units, the Pennsylvania Railroad started to design a better, faster, and more powerful steam locomotive, with the help of the large steam locomotive builders. After several years of research and development, the Pennsylvania unveiled its super streamlined S1 Duplex, a fantastic-looking divided-drive machine designed for speed and performance. Unfortunately, it was too big to be of much use on the Pennsylvania Railroad and did not spend much time hauling trains. The Pennsylvania went on to build a fleet of more practical Duplex locomotives based on the S1 design experience after World War II (as discussed in Chapter 7).

100mph (161kph) was surely a sight to behold! The 800s outlasted the early streamliners, too.

It is ironic that the "trains of the future" met the scrapheap ahead of steam. The Union Pacific's initial *Streamliner* had a remarkably short career. It was

▲ During World War II, American railroads were saturated with freight and passenger traffic. This Illinois Central Berkshire type leads an oil train southbound at Waverly, Kentucky, in 1943. Petroleum rationing during the war made such cargo especially precious.

In the late 1930s, events in Europe pointed toward a renewed conflict, and the American railroads began taking steps to improve their infrastructure in the event of US involvement in another large war. The railroads had been especially unhappy with the results of government control during World War I, and they wanted to avoid a repeat of that debacle. Traffic was

picking up in the late 1930s, as the American economy gradually recovered from the worst years of the Depression. Freight and passenger traffic was rising, and, as mentioned, railroads had started to buy new locomotives again. They also began to rehire furloughed employees and make significant investment in rehabilitating lines in need of repair.

The onset of fighting in Europe with Germany's invasion of Poland in 1939, and its subsequent war with England and France, caused traffic to rise dramatically on American lines. This was nothing, however, compared to the deluge of business

were more than 30 years old, having been stricken from the roster and cast aside as scrap, were restored and pressed back into service. The locomotive builders, which a decade earlier had not been able to sell a single locomotive, were now building locomotives as fast as they could – both steam and diesel.

However, while the war generated huge amounts of traffic, it also resulted in tight restrictions on what and how much new equipment the railroads could purchase. The War Production Board (WPB) had to authorize railroad acquisitions, and it fundamentally altered what railroads purchased during the war. Many lines desperately wanted new Electro Motive FTs. But the manufacture of diesels used crucial

---

The war promoted the continuation of steam, and builders made thousands of locomotives for domestic use and export

---

commodities needed for military applications such as copper wire and, more importantly, diesel engines themselves – remember, they had originally been designed for submarines. So, many roads that requested new diesels were ordered to buy steam locomotives instead. The WPB also placed restrictions on new designs, often insisting that lines stay with established successful locomotive types, rather than waste time and money on untried types. The Pennsylvania Railroad, for example, was anxious to build fleets of freight and passenger Duplex types, but was told to acquire 2-10-4 Texas types instead. Adding insult to injury on the part of Pennsylvania engineers, they were told to adopt a Chesapeake & Ohio design, rather then something of their own. Hence the war actually promoted the continuation of steam, and builders made thousands of steam locomotives for the both the domestic and export markets.

It is difficult to comprehend how quickly the railroads were deluged with traffic, but it is important to understand how well they handled it. The ability of American railroads to quickly accommodate the tide of traffic thrust upon them with minimal government intervention was a tribute to the skilled people

dumped upon the railroads two years later, following the Japanese bombing of Pearl Harbor on December 7, 1941, an event that precipitated US involvement in the war. Over the next four years, the industrial might of the United States stirred into an unprecedented frenzy of activity. The railroads rose to the occasion and carried an avalanche of traffic which suddenly poured onto their rails. Routes that had been quiet for years were saturated with traffic. Equipment that had been languishing for years on sidings or in yards was shopped and put to use. And old locomotives – steam engines – some of which

▲ The Central Vermont owned a small fleet of 2-10-4 Texas types, which it assigned to freight service between St Albans and Brattleboro, Vermont. Here, the class leader, No. 700, hauls freight at Montpelier Junction, Vermont.

that managed and worked on them. The prewar rehabilitation and improvements were crucial to this vital success story. Had the railroads failed and bogged down, in the way that they had during World War I, it is doubtful that the United States could have mobilized as quickly and effectively as it did.

The Southern Railway, one of the principal lines in the southeast United States, carried 6.25 billion ton miles of freight in 1938. By 1942, this figure had doubled, and, in 1943, it had reached 15.5 billion ton miles. That's a lot of freight!

The Richmond, Fredricksburg & Potomac (RF&P) was a crucial double-track bridge line that effectively linked north and south, connecting the Pennsylvania Railroad and the Baltimore & Ohio with the Seaboard Air Line and the Atlantic Coast Line, among other southern routes. The RF&P handled numerous passenger trains running between eastern seaboard cities and points in Florida. It was also the primary corridor for fruit and other agricultural products moving from Florida and other southern states to the Northeast. Daily refrigerator trains loaded with oranges made their way over the RF&P.

Vacationers and oranges, however, were not the most important traffic in wartime. The RF&P was a key route for troop trains and a host of military materiel. In 1940, just before US involvement in the war, the RF&P accommodated an average of 19 freight and 38 passenger trains daily. Three years later, that figure jumped to 46 freight trains and 57 passenger trains daily. One of the line's busiest days occurred on April 21, 1943, when the railroad handled some 131 trains.

While counting trains is one measure of traffic flow, it does not tell the whole story. Not only did RF&P run many more trains, but they were much longer and heavier, too. By 1943, the railroad's passenger traffic had multiplied five-and-a-half times over prewar levels; its freight traffic increased three-and-a-half times in the same period. This is just one example, but in many ways typical of the traffic boom experienced nationwide.

NEW SIGNALING SYSTEMS

One way railroads were able to squeeze more trains over their lines was the introduction of relay interlocked Centralized Traffic Control (CTC) signaling systems. The advent of CTC permitted the remote automation of train authorization. On lines equipped with CTC, lineside signals gave trains permission to occupy track without the need of written train orders or timetable permission. This greatly simplified and speeded up dispatching procedures and eliminated the need for telegraph operators on the ground to copy and hand up orders to trains. Most CTC systems also featured remotely controlled automatic switches, which permitted the dispatcher to control routing automatically. The effectiveness of CTC essentially gave older, single-track mainlines 75 percent the capacity of a double-track line and added an important element of flexibility. The first CTC installations occurred in the late 1920s, and, during the 1930s, railroads invested in CTC to eliminate traditional bottlenecks and increase capacity. During World War II, numerous CTC projects were implemented to help busy lines cope with extreme saturation.

One line that greatly benefited from CTC was the Southern Pacific, which was by far the busiest railroad in the West during the war and the third heaviest used line in the entire United States, just after the two eastern giants, the Pennsylvania

Railroad and the New York Central. Unlike the two eastern lines, which were blessed with multiple-track mainlines and relatively easy profiles, the Southern Pacific was faced with some of the toughest mountain grades in the United States. Much is said about the Pennsylvania Railroad's celebrated Horseshoe Curve crossing of the Alleghenies, but this grade is not nearly as steep or as long as many on the Southern Pacific, and, where the Pennsylvania had the luxury of four mainline tracks, the Southern Pacific often had just one.

During the war, the Southern Pacific installed CTC on its mountain bottlenecks, equipping its Oregon Cascade crossing, the Coast Line's Cuesta Grade, and its sinuous mountain line through the California Tehachapi Mountains. The latter was a route shared with tenant railroad, Santa Fe, and known for its famous "Loop," where the tracks make a full circle to cross right over each other in order to gain elevation. During the height of the war, this rugged mountain line, which wound and wiggled its way up from the San Joaquin Valley over Tehachapi Summit into the high desert, accommodated an average of 60 moves daily, including trains and light helper moves.

On a mountain line such as Tehachapi, long freights would often require several helpers distributed throughout the train. These were extra locomotives required to move the tonnage up steep grades. After the train attained the summit, the helpers were removed and sent back down to the bottom of the grade, where they would repeat the process. Since helpers running light (without a train) would tie up the single-track mainline, they would often accumulate at the top of the hill. If all the available helpers ended up at the summit, eventually there would be none left to move loaded trains, so it was crucial to maintain a balance of power and the CTC system was especially good at this.

Secretary of Defense George C. Marshall said, "Two world wars have demonstrated the critical importance of our transportation system to national defense, particularly the railroads. Our ability to get men and supplies to where needed has been a fundamental reason for our military successes."

7

DECLINE AND METAMORPHOSIS

Eager to maintain the success of the war years, the railroads
built a new generation of diesel-electrics. Freight remained
lucrative, but interurban passenger numbers fell; suburban
services became profitable instead.

The railroads emerged from World War II with a
sense of false optimism and illusory hope.
During the war, American railroads demonstrated their incredible ability to accommodate
vast quantities of freight and human traffic. They had
risen from the depths of the Depression to serve the
nation at a time of need, and they had done so

◄ In the late 1980s, American railroads began ordering locomotives
with "wide-nose" safety cabs, providing crews with a safer and
more comfortable environment. Here, a 4,000-horsepower General
Electric diesel leads a Santa Fe freight over California's Cajon Pass.

admirably. Had the railroads not been prepared for
the war, the United States may not have been victo-
rious. The war strained the railroads' infrastructure,
but generated enormous revenues. The postwar prosperity that followed provided the railroads with
capital needed for improvements, and companies that
had suffered during the Depression were finally able
largely to overcome their pressing financial woes. The
railroads were ready, willing, and able to handle all the
transportation demands of a powerful peacetime
United States, and they were gearing up to remake
their mark in transportation.

War Emergency Train Schedules

Effective August 1, 1945—Form 1001

▲ During the war, American railroads carried record amounts of freight and passenger traffic, and issued emergency schedules giving details of extra trains. A streamlined New York Central 4-6-4 Hudson graces the cover of this special 1945 timetable.

Even before the war was over, American railroads were planning their postwar strategy. When the war finally ended, the railroads were quick to make a massive investment in their future. Although traffic tapered off as the fighting came to a close, it did remain robust for a few years. Now, with money at hand, the railroads were quick to embrace the new technologies introduced and proven in the years before the war. They behaved rather like a kid in a toyshop with his birthday money. They placed huge orders for new locomotives, acquired new passenger

fleets, equipped lines with new signaling systems, built new freight yards, and introduced a host of new services.

One of the railroads' first priorities was to re-equip their locomotive fleets. The phenomenal traffic of the war had worn out fleets of aging steam locomotives, many of which were more than two decades old when the war started, and some much older than that. On the eve of the war, the diesel had demonstrated its practicality and cost savings, but the war delayed the large-scale acquisition of diesels as the War Production Board (WPB) limited the production of diesels and encouraged many lines to purchase new steam locomotives. Now they had the money and the builders were ready to accept their orders.

NEW LOCOMOTIVES

During the war, General Motors' EMD had refined their diesel-electric designs and introduced new and improved diesel-electric locomotives in each major service category. These were more powerful, more reliable, and more efficient than prewar and wartime models. The traditional locomotive builders, Alco and Baldwin, had also developed new designs and intended to claim their share of the diesel market. A newcomer to the locomotive business, Fairbanks-Morse – long associated with supplying railroad equipment – designed and built its first production locomotives during the war. In wartime, Fairbanks-Morse had been responsible for providing diesel engines for Navy submarines. As the market for submarine engines slowed, the company began looking for new markets for its distinctive opposed piston engine and decided to enter the locomotive market.

Many lines flooded the market with locomotive orders, and locomotive builders, especially EMD, soon had more business than they could handle. Most American lines were anxious to dispose of their aging steam fleets in order to enjoy the greater efficiency offered by diesels. Diesels also offered hope for the future. The railroads wanted to rid themselves of their reputation as an antique, stodgy industry. In the eyes of both the riding public and investors, the railroads wanted to appear modern, progressive, and efficient. The quicker they could be rid of smoke-belching steamers and get the new colorful, racy-looking diesels online, hauling their best trains, the better their image would be.

While the initial cost of converting to diesel power was very expensive, long-term cost savings were enormous. Diesel locomotives cost more than steam locomotives on a unit-per-unit basis, and

diesels required new shop facilities. However, diesels required far less labor than steam. Where steam locomotives typically needed hours of attention daily and a variety of routine but complex, time-consuming, labor-intensive maintenance, diesels could operate for thousands of miles with only the basic necessities:

▼ Steam locomotives required large maintenance forces to keep them in good running order. Diesels, on the other hand, required relatively little routine care. Here, inside the steam shop at Chama, New Mexico, two Mikados are being repaired.

▲ Compared with steam locomotives, diesels provided a clean, modern working environment for crews. In this 1940-era publicity photo, a Baltimore & Ohio engineer checks the time while running an Electro Motive E unit hauling the New York section of the *Capitol Limited* from Chicago.

fuel, water, and sand (to provide adhesion when the wheels slipped). Thus, diesel locomotives typically spent less time in the shop and enjoyed much greater availability (time ready to work trains) than most steam locomotives ever did. Diesels could also travel further and did not need to be exchanged as often as steam (although some late-era steam locomotives were regularly operating for a thousand miles or more on a single mainline run). Diesels were less specialized than steam, and often one type of diesel could perform a variety of duties.

Diesels offered many of the performance advantages of electric locomotives without the massive investment in supporting infrastructure that electric locomotives required. The performance characteristics of diesel locomotives allowed them to provide maximum power when starting a train – something steam locomotives could never do. This allowed railroads to run longer trains and eliminate many "helper" districts – where extra locomotives were needed. Like electrics, diesel locomotives could operate in tandem, allowing railroads to employ a single crew for several

locomotives and eliminate extra crews used for "doubleheading." Railroads found they could run longer freight trains with diesels, which also potentially reduced the number of crews.

As a result of these advantages, railroads found they needed far fewer diesel locomotives to do the same amount of work as steam. More importantly, railroads required far fewer employees. While it would take years to take full advantage of these savings, railroads were anxious to begin implementing diesels as soon as they could.

TRANSITION YEARS

The United States was the first nation to use diesel locomotives in regular revenue service, the first nation to mass-produce them, and the first large nation whose railroads completely replaced their traditional steam power with diesels. American railroads eradicated steam from regular operations a decade or more before most western European countries and more than a generation ahead of many developing and communist nations. Canadian railroads were quick to follow the lead of American lines and completed dieselization a few years after their American counterparts. Yet, on most North American lines, the transition did not occur overnight.

Some railroads had embraced diesel power early for specific operations, but retained steam for others. Western lines such as the Union Pacific and the Santa Fe were among the earliest users of diesel-electric passenger trains, introducing them in the mid-1930s, but continued to order new steam power through the war. The Santa Fe was among the first to eliminate totally steam operations on a portion of its mainline. In the early 1940s, the Santa Fe completely dieselized its arid desert crossing in southern California and western Arizona, although it continued to use steam on other lines well into the 1950s. Likewise, the diesel pioneering Union Pacific was among the last large railroads to dispense with steam, and, through the late 1950s, it kept a fleet of its largest locomotives, the massive 4-8-8-4 Big Boys, in standby service to accommodate seasonal traffic rushes.

Many railroads gradually phased out steam by introducing diesel operation to one division at a

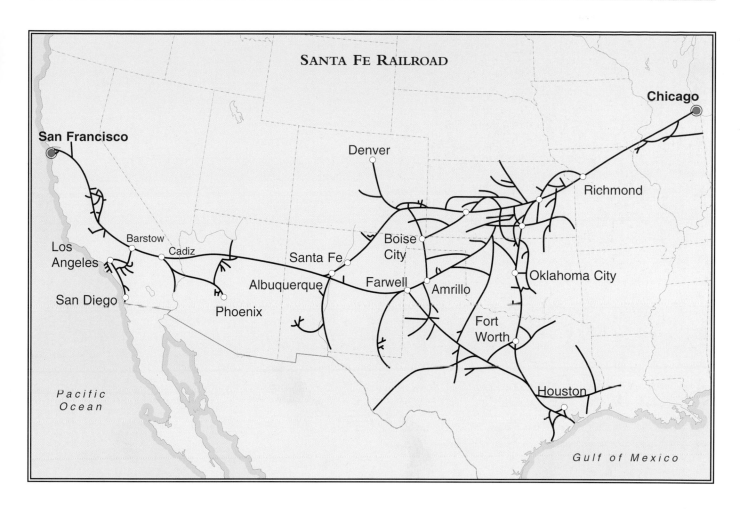

SANTA FE RAILROAD

▲ The Santa Fe was one of the best-known lines in the West. It connected Chicago with Texas and California, and included a multitude of secondary routes in the Southwest. Today, the Santa Fe is a component of the Burlington Northern Santa Fe Railway.

time, or by assigning diesels to high-priority trains, slowly bumping steam to less and less important traffic. Often the first jobs given to diesels were switching services at terminals and in yards. Premier passenger services were typically the next to get flashy new diesels, then fast freight trains or mountain lines where diesels would generate the most immediate cost savings. Often the last hold-outs for steam were as reserve locomotives (as in the case of the Union Pacific) or in suburban passenger services where steam was well suited to tight scheduling. Steam locomotives can accelerate rapidly, making them ideal for passenger trains that start and stop frequently. Thus, at the end of the steam era, there were several situations where late-era modern locomotives, designed to haul named passenger trains,

had been reduced to local passenger service or even to hauling local freights.

STEAM "COMMUTES"

Such was the case on the Southern Pacific, which had dieselized the majority of its mainline operations by the early to mid-1950s, but which retained steam until 1957 on its Bay Area suburban services. Every afternoon, a parade of steam-powered "commute" trains would depart San Francisco's Third & Townsend terminal for the run down the peninsula to San Jose behind modern Lima Northerns, locomotives that had been built and designed to haul the *Daylight* and other named passenger trains. As a result, steam and diesels often coexisted for years, working different assignments.

The Central Vermont, a rural New England subsidiary of the Canadian National, operated its through freights with modern diesels from its Canadian parent, while assigning its own aged 2-8-0 Consolidations to its local and wayfreights (a freight

▲ The coal-hauling Chesapeake & Ohio was among the last rail-roads to order new steam power. This 4-8-4 was built by Lima in 1948, and lasted only a few years in revenue service before being replaced by diesels. Today, it is used for mainline excursions.

that delivers local shipments). The Central Vermont was one of the last railways in southern New England to use steam regularly. The nearby Boston & Maine had purchased a fleet of Electro Motive FTs in the early 1940s for mainline freight service, and was quick to dieselize much of its freight and

passenger lines after the war. Yet, it retained a small fleet of antique 2-6-0 Moguls until 1956 for use on its suburban passenger trains operating out of Boston's North Station.

Some railways were compelled to continue steam operations on lines where conversion to diesel warranted a greater expense than was deemed prac-tical. The Canadian Pacific maintained a small number of 4-4-0 Americans built in the 1880s until the early 1960s, to serve lightly built branch lines in rural Quebec and New Brunswick. These lines

the first major railroads to discontinue steam was the Gulf, Mobile & Ohio (formed in 1940 by the merger of the Gulf, Mobile & Northern and the Mobile & Ohio, and which added the Chicago & Alton line in 1947), which discontinued its last steam operations in October 1949.

LAST GASP FOR STEAM

Not all railroads were immediately anxious to abandon steam power. Several of the largest railroads maintained their long-time allegiance to steam power for a few years after the war. The two biggest eastern lines, the Pennsylvania and the New York Central, initially placed orders for postwar steam, hoping that their new, more efficient steam locomotives could

▲ The Canadian National's Central Vermont subsidiary was one of the last companies to operate mainline steam in New England. Here, a pair of its aged 2-8-0s doggedly climb State Line Hill in Monson, Massachusetts, in April, 1952.

needed substantial upgrading of bridges before diesels could operate over them. In the United States, a number of logging lines in the Appalachian Mountains, Deep South, California, and Pacific Northwest retained steam much later than larger railroads. Sometimes the cost of dieselization could not be justified at all and, when steam was finally discontinued, the railroad was abandoned as well.

Other lines were quick to depose steam in favor of diesels and, within just a few years, had vanquished all of their steam locomotives. One of

▲ The Pennsylvania Railroad decided to build a modern steam locomotive that could rival diesels. Its Loewy-styled streamlined T1 Duplex used two complete sets of running gear on a rigid frame and was built for 100mph (161kph) operation. However, design flaws doomed the T1 to a short career.

match the performance and economy of diesel power. While steam proved that, in some situations, it could move trains as well as, or even better than, diesels, no accounting could justify the greater cost of steam locomotives.

Both railroads' postwar steam set records for performance. The Pennsylvania's mighty T1 Duplex was one of the fastest, most powerful passenger engines ever conceived. Designed during World War II after years of experimentation and testing that began with the S1 in the late 1930s (see Chapter 6), the Duplex was a direct response to the diesel-electric. The T1 Duplex was designed to haul an 880-ton (798-tonne) train at a top speed of 100mph (161kph). It was dressed in stylish shrouds styled by famed industrial designer Raymond Loewy. There are stories of the T1 racing passenger trains on level track in Indiana and Ohio at speeds well in excess of 100mph (161kph). The Pennsylvania Railroad also employed the Duplex concept on a fleet of new freight engines – enormously powerful machines designated class Q2.

The New York Central's more conventionally de-signed 4-8-4 "Niagara" was one of the finest steam locomotives ever built. It was a fast, powerful machine that set records for efficiency and service, working in both fast passenger service and heavy mainline freight service. It was a handsome machine, with a large boiler and just about every modern appliance available at the time. The Niagara used lightweight alloy steels for its reciprocating parts, featured roller bearings, and even employed aluminum for its cab and other auxiliaries in order to reduce the weight of the engine.

Despite the promise of the Duplexes and the Niagaras, both of these marvelous locomotives arrived on the scene too late to compete in the diesel world. The T1 suffered from design flaws which made it unpopular with management, and the Q2 never had the opportunity to mature. While the Niagaras performed admirably, they were simply more costly to operate than comparable diesel designs. Patience for steam had run out, and, despite these late-era advances and other innovations – such as the Penn-sylvania's brief experimentation with a steam turbine – both lines reversed their policy on locomotives shortly after the war and began the mass conversion to diesel-electric power.

A few other lines remained committed to steam for longer. The coal-hauling Chesapeake & Ohio,

▲ The Norfolk & Western continued to refine conventional steam designs into the 1950s, and was the last major railroad to give up on steam. It had an unusual relationship with steam; it built its own locomotives and was closely tied to the coal industry.

Norfolk & Western, and Midwestern Nickel Plate Road were among the last major railroads to acquire new steam and continued to place orders several years after most lines had developed an all-diesel outlook. The Norfolk & Western remained fully committed to steam power until 1954, when it finally succumbed to the cost-effectiveness of diesels.

This Pocahontas region coal hauler was a special case because of its unusual relationship to the steam locomotive. Unlike most railroads, which had purchased the majority of their locomotives from the three large steam builders, in the late steam era, the Norfolk & Western had built nearly all its own locomotives to its own highly refined designs. During the 1930s and 1940s, the Norfolk & Western had continued serious research into steam locomotive design at a time when few other railroads were investing in the technology. Rather than pursue radical designs such as the Pennsylvania Railroad's Duplexes, it

chose to hone conventional technology to perfection. It even chose to perfect the Mallet compound, years after most lines had abandoned the type in favor of simple articulated engines. Its locomotives were famous for performance and availability. When the first diesels were being demonstrated, they could not match Norfolk & Western steam, and, even if they could have, the highly independent Norfolk & Western would not have touched them.

DIESEL SUPREMACY

By 1954, diesel technology had matured, and even Norfolk & Western could resist no longer. It finally abandoned building its conventional locomotives in favor of diesels. Yet it made one final venture into steam power with the construction of a coal-fired, steam-electric turbine, prophetically named *Jawn Henry*, after the mythic black laborer who raced against a steam drill, only to die after winning the competition. Steam survived on the Norfolk & Western until 1960, and it was the last American line to use heavy steam in daily mainline freight service.

Toward the end of its steam operations, the Norfolk & Western attracted the interest of railroad photographers and enthusiasts around the world. Internationally known photographer O. Winston Link built his reputation on his unique nocturnal photographic tableaux depicting rural life and the Norfolk & Western's steam. Today, his railway images are some of the most recognized in the world.

Canadian railroads were slower to dieselize than most American lines. Both the Canadian Pacific and Canadian National were ordering new steam through World War II, and they did not fully dieselize until after most of their American counterparts. As a result, mainline steam survived on Canadian lines a few years longer than it did on most American railroads. As a result of this practice, some of the last mainline uses of steam in the United States actually occurred on Canadian lines or subsidiaries operating

▼ A Canadian Pacific 4-6-4 Hudson leads a passenger train out of Windsor Station in Montreal in the late 1950s. Canadian railways took a few years longer than most American lines to fully convert to diesel operation.

in the United States. For example, the Canadian Pacific's mainline between Montreal and St John, New Brunswick, skirted the top of Maine, and this line retained limited steam operation until 1960.

TRANSITION YEARS

The change from steam to diesel was far more than just a change in railroad motive power. The steam locomotive was the icon of the railroad, and, when it vanished, the railroad forever lost an essential element of its character. The loss of steam reflected a symbolic change in the role of the railroad in American life. The railroads abandoned steam in an effort to cut costs and remain competitive in a rapidly evolving transportation market. But, while steam locomotives were being replaced, the railroads' traffic was being eroded. Many people have the perception that soon after steam disappeared, the railroads vanished as well.

While familiar railroad companies may have remained, as did their tracks, in a fairly short span of time the railroad ceased to have an impact on the life

▲ In the early 1950s, US railroads made one last effort to attract passengers. Denver Union Station was once served by the Rio Grande, Rock Island, Union Pacific, Burlington, and Santa Fe. Today only Amtrak and the seasonal Rio Grande Ski train use the station.

operations. While trains still rolled through, they no longer stopped.

Coincident with the loss of steam was the mass desertion of the American passenger train. Railroads had been struggling with declining passenger ridership and revenues since before World War I. Rural branch lines were the first to feel the effects of competition. First, it was the electric interurbans, then other modes. During the 1920s, the railroad faced greater competition from motor buses and growing private automobile ownership. The Great Depression had a disastrous effect on rail ridership and travel in general. Many people simply did not have the resources to travel at all and ridership figures plummeted. The development of the streamliner temporarily reversed this trend on mainline services, but had little effect on branch lines and secondary runs where the operation of flashy, high-speed services was impractical, and branch line trains were typically the first to go. World War II had a great effect on rail ridership, as people flocked back to trains in record numbers. Many railroads hoped to capitalize on these gains in the postwar environment and invested millions of dollars in new passenger equipment after the war.

HOPES FOR RAIL RENAISSANCE

Railroads hoped there would be a revival of rail travel in the United States. Many railroads boosted service levels, shortened running times, and debuted beautiful new streamlined passenger trains. The Southern Pacific was the largest passenger carrier in the West, and it made an enormous investment in rebuilding its passenger fleet. Its *Daylight* streamliners introduced in the mid-1930s were some of the most profitable passenger trains in the United States, and, based on their successes, the Southern Pacific greatly expanded its streamlined services. The other western lines improved their services as well. The Union Pacific continued to expand the high-speed streamlined runs that it had introduced with its famous *Streamliner* in 1934. Likewise, the Santa Fe introduced a host of new Budd-built stainless steel trains, expanding on its successful *Super Chief*. The Northern Pacific and Great Northern lines, which had ignored the prewar stream-

of the average American. With steam went the small town engine house, local roundhouses, and regional shops. In many communities where the railroad had long been the principal employer, the railroad was now just a dividing line through town, its buildings and facilities hollow, lifeless shells of their former vitality. Small towns such as West Brookfield, Massachusetts, or Gold Run, California, which once hosted watering facilities, crucial to the daily operation of the railroad, now had no importance to railroad

lined movement, added deluxe transcontinental streamlined runs to their schedules. In the east, the passenger train had many proponents, and lines such as the New York Central and Chesapeake & Ohio also made significant investments revamping their passenger train fleets.

One of the most interesting developments was the introduction of the dome car, which carried an elevated glass-topped lounge, specifically designed for passengers to relax and observe the scenery. The first dome cars were debuted in the late 1940s, and, by the early 1950s, many western railroads were using them, along with a handful of eastern lines. Restrictive clearances on many eastern roads precluded the use of domes. Most lines left seating in the domes open, allowing passengers to come and go as they pleased. One of the most popular and most famous of all dome trains was the Chicago to Oakland, California, *California Zephyr*, a deluxe streamliner jointly operated by the Burlington, Rio

▲ The Western Pacific Railroad's herald advertised the line as the Feather River Route. Its most famous train was the original *California Zephyr,* which connected the cities of Chicago and Oakland from 1950 to 1970.

▲ The *California Zephyr,* introduced in 1950, was operated by the Burlington, Rio Grande, and Western Pacific railroads. One of the scenic highlights of the route was the Feather River Canyon in California's Sierra Nevada Mountains.

Grande, and Western Pacific. This train traversed some of the most spectacular scenery in the West. While making its way to California via Denver and Salt Lake City, it crossed the Colorado Front Range and California's Feather River Canyon in daylight, to the delight of passengers. The streamlined dome car was a marvelous success, but sadly it was short lived.

ROAD AND AIR COMPETITION

During the prosperity of the late 1940s and early 1950s, Americans were buying new automobiles as fast as they could. Meanwhile, commercial airlines were making serious inroads with both domestic and international services. While the railroads had been able to retain some of the traffic gains they had won back during the war, by the mid-1950s, ridership continued to taper off, and, as ridership dropped, revenues plummeted. Many lines, such as the Southern Pacific, were unable to justify the massive investment they had just made in new equipment. New passenger diesels and streamliners had not proven a good long-term investment. While some trains were profitable, many were not, and the future did not look promising. In order to check their losses, railroads began to discontinue some mainline runs and combined services to better reflect the level of ridership. At first, flagship trains such as the New York Central's *Twentieth Century Limited* remained unchanged; instead, railroads focused their cost cutting on secondary mainline trains.

Traditionally, railroads had operated several different types of long-distance services. Flagship trains were generally the best known, most prestigious, and most expensive to ride. Next on the schedule were more economical runs, designed to cater to the average traveler. These trains would still carry popular names and maintain expedited schedules, but would be more affordable than the flagship. In addition to long-distance services, railroads operated local trains, based in smaller cities, serving the general population. Local runs operated in varying frequency from once or twice a day, to hourly or better, depending on the population density. It was often the lightly patronized local trains and all-stops long-distance trains that were the first to be cut.

A serious blow to long-distance passenger services was the building of the Interstate Highway system, initiated in the mid-1950s

Next would be the economy "express" trains, which, as ridership continued to decline, were typically combined with the more prestigious "Limiteds."

Federal and local laws made it difficult for railroads to discontinue trains, even ones that had little or no ridership. Even when railroads were running nearly empty trains, at first they found it difficult to convince Federal regulators to permit discontinuance.

A serious blow to privately operated long-distance railroad passenger services was the building of the Interstate Highway system, initiated by President

▶ Passengers aboard the *California Zephyr* were treated to the view from Budd-built Vista Domes. One could enjoy a most pleasurable train trip watching the rolling panorama from a reclining chair in a Vista Dome. The view from a 737 just isn't the same.

Eisenhower in the mid-1950s, and the introduction of commercial jets. These new modes precipitated a further drop in ridership, from which the railroads could not escape.

Some railroads chose to maintain their services as best they could, accepting unprofitable services as a civic obligation or writing them off as positive publicity, and gradually trimming services to reflect ridership, but not allowing the quality of service to deteriorate. This attitude may seem odd today, but there was an age-old belief in railroad circles that a line's flagship train reflected the health of the company as a whole. If a company permitted its flagship to deteriorate, it meant the company was not

---

Traditional passenger services no longer met the needs of the modern traveler, who needed frequent, convenient services

---

doing well. In fairness, there was something to be said for this economic indicator.

One line that did not fully subscribe to this philosophy was the Southern Pacific. When it felt that passengers had deserted its trains, it took draconian measures and hacked service levels. This was in part a business decision, but the SP also felt betrayed by the public's abandonment of the railroad. The Southern Pacific had provided what it honestly believed were some of the "most beautiful passenger trains in the world," and yet people still would not ride them anymore.

Some railroads tried gimmicks to attract passengers back to the rails. In the mid-1950s, a new wave of sexy lightweight trains debuted, in the hope that they would have the same effect that the 1930s streamliners had had. The New York Central introduced its *Train-X*, while the Boston & Maine and the New Haven introduced low-slung streamlined *Talgo* trains. General Motors introduced its futuristic *Aerotrains*, which variously operated on the Pennsylvania, New York Central, and Union Pacific. While the *Aerotrain's* styling was imaginative, its ride was awful. Ultimately, these trains ended their short

service careers on Rock Island's Chicago suburban services. A decade later, the advent of true super high-speed passenger service in Japan spurred American research into high-speed technology. This proved a better strategy than lightweight train gimmicks. Eventually, high-speed technology was introduced in regular service in the Northeast and in eastern Canada.

One of the problems with traditional passenger services was that they no longer met the needs of the modern traveler. The railroads were still trying to sell the deluxe long-distance services with sleeping cars, diners, and lounges. On most lines, these trains only operated a few times a day at best. What passengers really needed were service frequency and travel

▲ In 1938, the New York Central debuted its all-new, stream-lined *Twentieth Century Limited*. Among the most famous trains in the United States, it was featured in numerous Holly-wood films, including Hitchcock's *North by Northwest*.

convenience. Another factor that contributed to declining passenger demand was the deterioration of American cities and their public transit systems. Railroads were still serving traditional downtown terminals. By the 1960s, these once-opulent structures had become seedy, run-down monstrosities. Railroad hotels, which a generation earlier had been considered among the finest places to stay, reflected the overall decline of the American inner city. Throughout the United States, train stations, which

had been designed as welcoming gateways to begin or end one's journey, had deteriorated into dark, decrepit, possibly unsafe buildings.

Throughout the 1950s and the 1960s, the cycle of decline spiraled downward. Fewer trains and reduced service further discouraged ridership. By the mid-1960s, nearly all passenger trains in North America were losing money. One of the problems has been attributed to a cost accounting system that distributed the burden of basic passenger infrastructure, such as stations and terminal facilities, over the few remaining trains, raising the cost of operating each individual train as cuts were implemented. In the late 1960s, the railroads lost mail and package express services, which had a further negative effect on the

TRAVELERS' TALES
A DAY LATE AND ON SCHEDULE

The days of precision timekeeping on American railroads have long since passed. Since the majority of the US railroad network is designed for heavy freight operations that do not require strict timetables, it is now very difficult to maintain long-distance passenger schedules. Long-distance trains often run an hour or two late, despite padded schedules that help trains make up lost time. Nowhere is this more acute than in the West, where some Amtrak passenger trains have to cover more than 2,000 miles (3,218km) between terminals. In the winter, storms and heavy freight traffic frequently conspire to delay Amtrak, and efforts to maintain tight schedules can prove frustrating. Since Amtrak rarely owns or operates the tracks it runs on, its trains are subject to the will and priorities of its host railroads – priorities that don't always hold Amtrak in the highest regard.

In the winter of 1994, Amtrak was having a particularly difficult time with its *California Zephyr*, which operates between Chicago, Denver, and Oakland (California), crossing several mountain ranges and long stretches of lonely desert. Heavy freight traffic on the Southern Pacific's former Rio Grande lines west of Denver, combined with extremely bad weather, ruined Amtrak's best efforts at keeping the *Zephyr* to schedule. For several weeks the train would routinely arrive at Oakland many hours behind time. By February, it seemed that every day the train was running a little later. One clear morning, after racing across the Nevada desert, Amtrak No. 5, the *California Zephyr*, pulled into Sparks yard, near Reno, Nevada, exactly at its posted time. This was an unusual event indeed, given the train's recent performance. The yardmaster, from his perch in the Sparks tower, radioed the engineer of the train with enthusiasm:

"Number five, you're right on schedule today!"
The engineer replied somewhat gloomily:
"Yeah, it's a pity we're 24 hours late!"

---

bottom line. Many passenger trains had relied on the extra revenue from mail and express to cover costs, and, when this revenue vanished, it was the last blow.

Railroads began to discontinue their once famous flagship trains. In 1961, Lehigh Valley dropped its *Black Diamond*. In 1967, the New York Central's *Twentieth Century* made its final run. Even the celebrated *California Zephyr* was finally discontinued in 1970. Some trains went out in style, discontinued before their image was tarnished; others suffered the indignity of gradual deterioration. The loss of these great trains was demoralizing. The public's reaction varied from ambivalence to outrage. But simply eliminating some unprofitable passenger runs had not solved the railroad's problems.

By the late 1950s and early 1960s, many major railroads were in deep financial trouble and not just because of sagging passenger revenue. Generally lines in the far West remained healthy, while the large eastern lines that had once been the showcase of the industry and among the wealthiest companies in the world were showing signs of decline. Some were losing millions of dollars a year. The decline of the railroads was the result of many factors, and there were a variety of deterioration scenarios.

FINANCIAL WOES

The gradual decline of heavy industry in the Northeast and Midwest, a general switch from coal to oil as home heating fuel, the rapid construction of the Interstate and other highway systems, plus inexpensive gasoline and diesel fuel for automobiles and trucks – all contributed to the diminishing revenues of eastern lines. As freight markets had shifted, the inherent inflexibility of the railroad network made it difficult for railroads to compete. The railroad culture of moving freight was equally damaging. While the railroads had made an effort to speed up freight service in the 1920s, and, by the 1950s, many lines were operating some expedited freight schedules, the vast majority of freight trains still moved very slowly compared to over-the-road trucks. Innovations such as intermodal transport using piggyback cars may have had a significant impact in the postwar era, but this business generally had a lower profit margin than traditional carload traffic. And while some lines enjoyed greater volumes, railroads' market share of intercity freight declined.

Compounding the companies' financial difficulties were inequities with their vast, inefficient labor force, which by virtue of legislation passed decades earlier was largely inflexible and protected by powerful unions. A variety of laws and agreements

mandated five- and six-person freight train operating crews. These agreements dated back decades when the lack of modern safety equipment required that many people on a train for safe operation. Other agreements required that railroads change crews roughly every 100 miles (161km), a practice that made sense in an earlier era, but was obsolete with the introduction of diesel locomotives and faster train schedules.

Rate structures were also inflexible, as the railroads were tightly bound by regulations stemming

▼ In the 1950s, the railroads tried to repeat the success of the first streamlined trains that had been introduced two decades earlier. This articulated *Talgo* train, made by American Car & Foundry, is seen on display at Springfield, Massachusetts, in 1954. *Talgo* technology was imported from Spain.

▲ During the 1960s, many famous trains were discontinued. The Pennsylvania Railroad's *Broadway Limited* is seen here on its last night as an all-Pullman sleeper train. While the Broadway name was maintained, the service was downgraded, and the railroad was never really the same.

from abuses — real and perceived — that occurred at the end of the 19th century. Often railroads were legally obligated to carry traffic that was at best marginally profitable and maintain lines that had virtually no sustainable traffic, while they were directly and indirectly prohibited from pursuing new profitable business ventures because of antiquated anti-monopoly regulations.

So, by the late 1960s, vast yards that had classified thousands of freight cars lay underutilized, disused, or abandoned. The railroads that had built multiple-track mainlines to accommodate a mix of heavy freight and passenger traffic were finding they barely had enough business to justify a single line, let alone the expense of maintaining a complicated infrastructure. In the anthracite coal region of eastern

the Pittsburgh, Shawmut & Northern, and a few of the last remaining electric interurbans, the Class I railroads – the major lines – had held on benefiting from the general economic prosperity of the postwar economy. The first relatively significant railroad to succumb was anthracite hauler New York, Ontario & Western, a line known by its initials "O&W," which had come to stand for "Old & Weary."

The O&W served the Catskill region of upstate New York, with lines into the anthracite region of Pennsylvania. It reached the New York metro area by virtue of trackage rights on the New York Central's West Shore route. While the O&W had had its moments of prosperity, it had never been a healthy line, as other routes better served most of its territory. After the war, the O&W had attempted to modernize by dieselizing its operations and installing a modern Centralized Traffic Control signaling system to cut operating costs on its mainlines. These

---

Austerity prevailed in an industry once typified by abundant riches and opulence. A cost-conscious attitude prevailed

---

efforts helped a little at first, but it was still losing money. O&W discontinued all passenger operations in the early 1950s and a few years later gave up entirely. In 1957, the railroad completely shut down; its locomotives and equipment were auctioned off and its tracks torn up, save for a few short segments which were picked up by other lines. It was the first large liquidation of a railroad in modern times.

Austerity prevailed in an industry once typified by abundant riches and opulence. A cost-conscious attitude prevailed. The colorful streamlined diesel locomotives gave way to utilitarian road switchers. From the early 1950s, railroads started to favor Electro Motive "General Purpose" and Alco RS2 and RS3 road switchers, instead of the handsomely designed streamlined EMD F units and Alco FAs that had dominated new purchases just a few years earlier. By the early 1960s, nearly all new locomotives were being built in road-switcher configurations.

Pennsylvania, which once had enough traffic to sustain a variety of competing railroads, barely enough traffic was generated to feed one road by the mid-1960s. Yet most of the traditional companies maintained tracks in that region. In so many cases, railroads competed with each other for an ever-shrinking market, while the highway grabbed new business in new areas.

This situation could not continue, and, by the late 1950s, railroads started to go bankrupt. While some small lines had shut down after World War II, such as

▲ This Queen Anne-style station at Oakland, Maryland, is among the finest on the Baltimore & Ohio's line from Cumberland, Maryland, to St Louis. While beautifully restored, it has not seen a revenue passenger train in decades, yet the tracks remain busy with coal traffic.

At the same time, the business began to contract, and weakened builders dropped out of the market. Unable to compete with diesel giant EMD, Baldwin and Fairbanks-Morse had exited the locomotive business in the mid-1950s, while Alco struggled on for a few more years. By the 1960s, new high horse-power locomotives were all the rage. Railroads had enjoyed the benefits of diesel operations and were running ever-longer freights. Some of these trains required as many as 10 locomotives. To reduce the number of locomotives on a freight, the railroads needed significantly more powerful engines, and two lines – the Southern Pacific and the Rio Grande –

even went so far as to import German-built diesel hydraulics in an effort to find a more powerful motive power solution. The locomotive builders – EMD, Alco, and newcomer to the heavy-haul diesel-electric business, General Electric – introduced successively more powerful single-unit designs. In 1966, EMD's SD45 debuted, a powerful six-axle locomotive that delivered a whopping 3,600 horsepower, nearly three times the output of EMD's original prewar FT units. Railroad paint schemes were simplified to basic colors, as the complicated multi-color schemes featured on postwar diesels faded into memory.

DEPOTS DISAPPEAR

Railroads took other draconian measures reflecting their need to cut losses and streamline their plant. The decline of the passenger train had rendered many traditional stations surplus and unnecessary for routine operations. Tax laws were unsympathetic to the architectural significance of these historic buildings, and railroads had a tax liability for such structures whether they were generating revenue or not. So, railroads were quick to dispose of station properties any way they could.

Some were sold to private concerns, a few were sold to the cities they had once served, but all too many were demolished. The most famous, and most

▼ In the early 1960s, passengers gather at track 16 at Penn Station, New York, to ride the final run of Lehigh Valley's *Maple Leaf*, bound for Toronto, Ontario. Within a few years the grand old Penn Station would be demolished and replaced by an inferior structure.

controversial, station demolition, and certainly one of the most tragic, was the Pennsylvania's destruction of its crown jewel, which had been designed as a monument to itself and the gateway to the nation's largest city: Pennsylvania Station, New York. Despite protests, the Pennsylvania Railroad demolished the building superstructure between 1963 and 1965 to make room for a new revenue-generating Madison Square Garden above the tracks. It was a move symbolic of the state of the railroad.

One solution to trimming losses was railroad consolidation. While there had been a few mergers since World War I, most of the railroads operating in the 1950s had not significantly changed their route map in nearly two generations. A variety of consolidation scenarios had been discussed for years, but very little had actually been done. In 1960, two arch competitors, the Erie and the Delaware, Lackawanna & Western – route of the *Phoebe Snow* – merged to form Erie Lackawanna. These two lines had made some consolidations a few years earlier, but more were to follow. In several places, duplicative routes were abandoned and facilities combined. It was the first big merger in the East, but not the last. Soon many lines were discussing mergers, in the West as well as the East.

The largest and most significant merger was the pairing of the two gargantuan rival empires, the Pennsylvania and the New York Central. These two railroad giants had been bitter foes, operating parallel systems that competed for market share nearly everywhere they went. They had vied for control of neighboring lines, built into each other's territory, and raced each other for the fastest New York to Chicago passenger train. In December, 1968, the two lines were joined to form the Penn-Central. A few months later, the Penn-Central was coerced by

▲ In a striking vision of modern railroading, a Santa Fe intermodal train, led by three high-horsepower diesel-electric locomotives, catches the glint of the setting sun at Williams Junction, Arizona.

the Federal government to accept the bankrupt New Haven as part of its system.

The joining of the two largest eastern railroads was doomed from the start. The Penn-Central was rife with internal woes and burgeoning financial problems. Any hopes at attaining better efficiency through consolidation were dashed, as the total inability of the component railroads to cooperate with one another became apparent. Old allegiances die hard, and employees of the two lines fought with one another internally for control.

Among the Penn-Central's problems was its mounting passenger deficit. It was the largest single intercity passenger carrier in the United States, and it was losing millions of dollars a month on its passenger trains. Finally, the Federal government stepped in to relieve the railroads of their passenger obligations. So, from the chaos of the ill-fated Penn-Central merger

The joining of the two largest eastern railroads, the Pennsylvania and the New York Central, was doomed from the start

and the long, slow decline of the intercity passenger train, Amtrak was born on May 1, 1971. This effectively nationalized the American passenger network, but simultaneously cut roughly half the national route mileage. With the creation of Amtrak, most railroads became freight-only businesses, although a few lines such as the Southern and the Rio Grande held on to their passenger trains for a few years more.

Dressed in patriotic colors, Amtrak set out to operate and maintain the nation's intercity passenger trains, albeit under the perpetual storm of conflicting political agendas. On more than one occasion, Amtrak has faced oblivion on the guillotine of Federal budget cuts, but, despite cutbacks, it has managed to survive for three decades. Today, Amtrak carries more than 20 million passengers a year, most of them riding trains on a few heavily traveled corridors, such as in the Northeast on former Penn-Central lines. Elsewhere, Amtrak offers a skeletal passenger network, typically providing just a single train daily. Some routes are only afforded tri-weekly service, and many relatively large cities are served at odd hours, or not at all. While Amtrak has come to own some of its lines, many Amtrak trains run on tracks of the freight railroads. As a result, they are frequently subject to delays that are beyond Amtrak's immediate control.

AMTRAK INNOVATION

In recent times, Amtrak has invested in new, modern equipment that is comfortable and rather spacious. Despite perpetual deficits that are covered by the Federal Government, Amtrak is one of the least subsidized passenger rail networks in the world, and it is working toward financial independence from government subsidy. Amtrak must survive in a culture that is dominated by and codependent with the automobile and a heavily subsidized highway culture. One of Amtrak's most recent and progressive innovations is its high-speed *Acela Express* service, which introduced 150mph (240kph) trains to the northeast corridor in late 2000, representing a vast improvement to intercity services between Boston, New York, Philadelphia, Baltimore, and Washington. The *Acela Express* trains use modern tilting technology designed to give passengers a smooth, comfortable ride, even at high speeds. The ability to tilt counters the effects of centrifugal forces in curves.

The story of the American freight train is rather different than that of the passenger train. An often-asked question is, "Why doesn't the United States make better use of its railroads?" The answer is, it does

make good use of railroads – moving freight, rather than people. Today's freight railroads move more freight than they did at the height of World War II, a fact that would surprise most people. The railroads do this with fewer companies, fewer lines, fewer employees, and fewer locomotives. Today, core mainlines handle the bulk of the intercity freight traffic. Trains are often more than a mile or two (1.5–3km) long, and carry everything from coal, grain, and new automobiles, to electronics and foreign imports.

In the East and Midwest, the railroads underwent a traumatic transformation in the 1970s and 1980s. The creation of Amtrak did not save the Penn-Central, and that line made world news as the largest corporate bankruptcy ever in 1971. By the mid-1970s, most of the Eastern railroads were bankrupt. In 1976, the government bailed the railroad companies out, by consolidating all of the bankrupt lines in a single large carrier called Conrail that operated with Federal subsidy to cover deficits. Under Conrail, many routes were abandoned and consolidated, trimming away redundant and surplus track and route structure.

In the late 1970s, other lines were faltering as well. The Milwaukee Road and Rock Island both

▲ The old Soo Line operated through Minnesota, Wisconsin, and upper Michigan, connecting Sault Saint Marie with other Midwestern gateways. In later years, the Soo Line expanded, taking over a variety of lines, including those of the old Milwaukee Road.

▲ In the 1970s, the Burlington Northern tapped the coal fields in Wyoming's Powder River Basin. Today this region sees more than 100 coal trains daily. This SD70MAC is working on a coal train ascending Crawford Hill, Nebraska, in 1995.

succumbed to their financial burdens. While the Milwaukee Road was trimmed back, reorganized, and eventually merged with the Soo Line, the Rock Island was liquidated. Its locomotives and lines were sold off. Some routes were picked up by competing railroads; others were abandoned and ripped up.

During the 1970s, these gigantic railroad failures made it obvious that serious action must be taken or the whole industry might collapse. Legislation was enacted that freed the railroads from many of the restrictive burdens that had plagued them in recent decades. This allowed the railroads to better compete with the highways for freight traffic. Unprofitable business was dropped, which resulted in further route abandonment. Railroads simplified their labor rules, resulting in the discontinuance of time-honored but ineffective traditions such as the operation of cabooses.

since. Ever-larger railroad networks were assembled from the traditional Class 1 railroads. During this time, most of the historic railroad names vanished into corporate amalgams that convey little of their heritage. It was a renewed era of empire building, as late 20th century rail barons pieced together vast transportation empires that would have made the

---

During the 1970s, legislation was enacted that freed the railroads from many of the restrictive burdens that had plagued them

---

likes of Jay Gould and Edward H. Harriman envious. Since the early 1980s, western giant the Union Pacific has steadily expanded, first buying the Missouri Pacific and Western Pacific, then the old Katy, Chicago & North Western, and finally the Southern Pacific. A host of railroads in the southeast consolidated to form the Seaboard System, which then merged with the C&O/B&O Chessie system, forming the homogeneous sounding CSX. The once-bankrupt Conrail lines that had proven such a burden during the 1970s had become a financial success by the mid-1980s and returned to the private sector. In 1999, the Conrail system was split up and sold, its respective parts operated by CSX or Norfolk Southern (formed by a merger of the Norfolk & Western and Southern Railway). By the year 2000, six massive railways, including the Canadian National and the Canadian Pacific, represented the majority of mainline rail mileage in North America, with more mergers expected.

Shortlines are small railroads that typically operate a branch line, or a network of secondary railroad lines, and feed a larger system. There have always been shortlines, but, with the consolidation of the large carriers, many branch lines and other secondary routes were deemed surplus and sold off. This created hundreds of new shortline railroads all throughout North America.

In the 1980s, a new breed of railroad emerged: the regional line. Most of these regional railways were secondary mainlines, or surplus networks, disposed

Although the Penn-Central had proven disastrous, other mergers were more successful. In the West, the merger in 1970 of the Hill lines – those railroads once under the influence of the late James J. Hill – to form the giant Burlington Northern system had proven reasonably successful. Other consolidations, such as the joining of the Baltimore & Ohio and the Chesapeake & Ohio, had also proven viable. The deregulation of the railroad industry in the late 1970s and early 1980s sparked a maelstrom of merger activity that has continued ever

of by the larger railroads. Unlike the shortline, a regional railroad is typically more than 300 miles (480km) long and often operates mainline trains. The Wisconsin Central – a new company with an historical name – is primarily comprised of former Soo Line mainlines and branches, and is one of the largest and most successful regional railroads in the United States. The advantage of a line such as the Wisconsin Central is that it can provide a higher level of customer service

---

The freight railroads continue to enjoy robust traffic levels, thanks to deregulation and advanced technologies

---

and operate at a lower cost than a traditional Class 1 railroad. Regional lines have to be able to exploit creative business practices to attract freight business back to the railroads that the larger lines have not even thought possible. The success of some regional railroads, combined with changes in railway labor practices, saw a number of regional lines purchased back by the larger carriers in the 1990s. Lines such as the Chicago, Central & Pacific, which had been spun off by the Illinois Central Gulf in the mid-1980s, was re-acquired by a leaner, trimmer, more profitable Illinois Central (sans Gulf) in the mid-1990s.

Heavy traffic warrants more powerful locomotives. Diesel locomotive technology was gradually advanced through the 1970s, 1980s, and 1990s, introducing a variety of improvements such as more powerful engines, more effective electrical systems, and microprocessor controls. The two remaining large locomotive manufacturers, General Motors's Electro Motive Division and General Electric, have competed fiercely for market share.

Externally, locomotives' designs over the years have changed only a little and reflect a boxy, utilitarian aesthetic. But, inside, they become gradually more and more powerful. The biggest external change to locomotive design in recent years was the introduction of the wide-nose safety-cab. This style of cab, used in Canada since the 1970s, became popular in the United States in the early 1990s, and

it is now prevalent on most new freight locomotives. Internally, the most significant innovation was the introduction of three-phase alternating current traction motor technology, which has allowed for a significant increase in pulling power and braking ability. Two modern AC traction diesels of today can handle the same tonnage as four 1970s-era locomotives, or eight 1950s-era locomotives.

The freight railroads continue to enjoy robust traffic levels, thanks to deregulation and advanced technologies. Many states and cities around the United States have developed commuter and suburban passenger carriers. These passenger-hauling

lines accommodate thousands of commuters traveling from the suburbs into the cities every day. Some commuter lines, such as the Long Island Rail Road, have always served in this capacity. Other lines, such as the Los Angeles Metro Link, are relatively recent phenomena. Nearly all commuter lines have demonstrated great successes in moving people and prove that railway transport is still a practical and valid way to travel in the United States.

The combination of growing freight traffic and thriving suburban lines has had a dramatic effect on railroads. During the past decade, there has been a substantial amount of investment in the network.

▲ After World War II, American railroads looked to the diesel-electric locomotive to solve their power woes. Diesels were expensive, but cost-effective in the long run. The Atlantic Coast Line engine pictured on the left is on loan to the Norfolk & Western, the last American railroad to use steam on a large scale.

Lines have been rebuilt and track capacity expanded. The days of retrenchment and consolidation have ended. Double-track lines, reduced to single track in the 1970s, have been restored. A few routes that were closed or abandoned have been reopened and rebuilt. While much progress still needs to be made, American railroads have a solid role in its transportation future.

PRESERVING THE PAST

As early as the 1920s, aficionados began organizing "fan trips"
on lines closed to regular services, and today, narrow-gauge
lines continue to be restored as scenic routes for tourists.
Enthusiasts can visit scores of sites to view vintage equipment.

L ocomotives have always had a place in the
public imagination, and, because of this, there
has always been some sense of railway preservation and history. In an inverse relationship to
the decline of railways, nostalgia for railways has
grown and preservation efforts have gained momen-
tum. Most railway preservation in North America has

occurred in the past 50 years. Today, there are hundreds of railway sites, representing every period of
railway development, from the earliest days right up
to the present. Some sites are well funded, reflecting a
high standard of preservation, presentation, and interpretation. Others are run at grass roots level, often the
inspiration of concerned communities or individuals.
In several significant instances, railroads themselves
have been closely involved in setting aside historical
equipment and structures for preservation, restoring
old locomotives, and operating historic locomotives
on excursions. Railroads initiated many of the earliest

◄ Valley Railroad No. 40, a 2-8-2 Mikado, waits for passengers
to board an excursion train at Essex, Connecticut, in December,
1996. The Valley Railroad is one of many successful tourist
railways that offer excursions using vintage equipment.

▲ From the 1930s, groups of railroad enthusiasts began chartering train trips for the sheer pleasure of riding trains. This "Reading Ramble" excursion at Shamokin, Pennsylvania, in the early 1960s was typical of its day.

preservation efforts, often as a way of promoting their own history and celebrating the successes of their operations over the years.

Modern railway preservation had its origins in the early 1920s. The Railway & Locomotive Historical Society was organized in 1921 and began publishing regular bulletins on railroad history. In the 1930s, enthusiast groups emerged and began organizing "fan trips" over lines closed to regular services and circle trips that allowed people to ride over one route and back on another. These trips often would use different or exotic equipment, giving railway enthusiasts a chance to experience something out of the ordinary. The fan trip offered a train ride for the pure pleasure of it, and fan trips have become a popular way of experiencing railroad. Every year, dozens of fan trips operate all over the United States and Canada using a variety of equipment.

By the 1930s, the rural branch line and the electric interurban were rapidly disappearing from the North American scene. Many fan trips of the period focused on these operations, giving enthusiasts a ride over lines that may have lost regular passenger service or were about to be abandoned altogether. Between the mid-1920s and the mid-1930s, a great many of these lightly used railways had already seen their last runs. Rural branch line passenger trains had long been poor revenue performers, and railways, which had made every effort to trim the costs of these services, were quick to apply to discontinue services when ridership plummeted during the

Depression. Interurban electric railways, which had emerged in the 1890s and expanded rapidly all across the United States thereafter, began to recede as quickly as they had been built once automobiles became affordable and rural roads were improved in the 1920s. The Great Depression put the final stroke on most of these electric lines, but also spurred the earliest serious preservation efforts.

TROLLEY MUSEUMS

The first instances of private individuals spending their own money toward railway preservation was in New England during the late 1930s and mid-1940s, when three different groups moved to acquire cars and rights of way from discontinued interurban lines. These three efforts eventually emerged as the Seashore Trolley Museum in Kennebunkport, Maine; the Connecticut Trolley Museum at Warehouse Point (East Windsor), Connecticut; and the Shore Line Trolley Museum at East Haven, Connecticut.

Initially, these preservation efforts did little more than save a few cars from scrapping and secure a short section of track or right of way. Later, as funding grew, more equipment was restored and regular operations begun. Now these three New England electric railways all have sizeable fleets of beautifully restored cars, some of which operate regularly on restored trackage, providing an historic railway experience that both entertains and educates the general public. These pioneering efforts set an important precedent, and many other electric railway museums followed their example. Today, there are numerous trolley museums all around the country that have preserved hundreds of interurban and street railway cars, locomotives, and other equipment.

▼ A pair of electric trolley cars traverse the streets of Montreal, Quebec, in the late 1950s, shortly before the end of regular streetcar service. The demise of this mode of transport in North America led to the development of trolley museums.

The cable-powered streetcar originated in San Francisco and, as it happens, has lasted longer there than anywhere else. A number of American cities once featured cable car networks, including New York City and Seattle, Washington. While usually associated with steep hills, the most extensive of all cable car networks was actually located in the billiard table-flat city of Chicago.

San Francisco's cable car network was once operated by a variety of different companies on different routes. As electric traction and later motor buses became more popular, the city's cable car routes were gradually trimmed back. In later years, all routes came under the control of the San Francisco Municipal Railway, which operates most of the public transit in the city. By World War II, the cable system was in tatters, and service was totally discontinued for a period during the war. After the war, service was restored on three lines. The enormous popularity of the cable car made it a tourist attraction and one of San Francisco's eclectic trademarks. But, by the early 1980s, the cable car network was completely worn out. The below-ground cables that hauled the cars up the city's precipitously steep hills had become prone to snapping. Although not as much dangerous as inconvenient, it was deemed the cable car network should either be overhauled or discontinued. Happily, San Francisco opted to rehabilitate the network.

While some of the terminals were altered to better cater to the tourist trade, the cable cars continue today and are one of the United States' best known historic rail operations. Among the sites on this unique railway is the cable car museum and powerhouse. Here, people can view the gigantic wheels that turn the metal cables that propel the cable cars.

Another declining area of the American railroad was that of the

◄ One of San Francisco's famous cable cars is viewed from a window in the Cable Car Museum. At one time, several American cities had extensive cable car networks. Today, only a small portion of San Francisco's remains.

narrow gauge (see Chapter 3), which, by 1940, was on the verge of extinction. Narrow-gauge lines had been popular with train-riding enthusiasts long before organized groups had focused their efforts on excursions. They were remote, rural, scenic, and quirky; qualities that made them endearing to enthusiasts, while being a hindrance to railroad operations.

DISAPPEARING NARROW GAUGE

The last Maine 2ft (610mm) gauge lines struggled through the Depression and finally expired on the eve of US involvement in World War II. While the railroads were liquidated and abandoned, a few of their Forney steam locomotives were saved from scrapping by a sympathetic individual who moved them to southeastern Massachusetts, where they worked at a private railway located in a cranberry bog at South Carver, Massachusetts, called Edaville. Here, they survived for many years, entertaining tourists and enthusiasts of all ages. Eventually most of the locomotives returned to Maine, and today several independent efforts are under way to restore 2ft (61mm) gauge lines and equipment. A museum in Portland, Maine, has a short section of narrow-gauge track, while, further north, another group has restored part of the Wiscasset, Waterville & Farmington line. In the year 2000, it began steam service. Likewise, a small portion of the narrow-gauge Monson Railroad is under restoration.

These examples of railway preservation are among the most remarkable, since they stem from some of the earliest private attempts at saving locomotives from scrap and resulted in the re-creation of an aspect of American railways that was almost completely lost.

The North American narrow-gauge movement had its beginnings in Colorado, with General Palmer's Denver & Rio Grande. Ultimately, this pioneering railway had the most extensive network of narrow-gauge lines in North America, connecting

▲ The Rio Grande narrow gauge was dearly loved by aficionados, who flocked to ride the railroad's diminutive steam trains in the Colorado Rockies – despite the company's best efforts to discontinue these services. Nowadays, a couple of narrow-gauge lines survive as tourist railways.

many towns and cities in Colorado, New Mexico, and Utah. Other narrow-gauge railways had once prospered here, too; however, by the 1950s, the day of American narrow-gauge railway was rapidly coming to a close. The remaining lines were a remnant of a once vast and prosperous network.

ROCKY MOUNTAIN LINES

Most of the narrow-gauge routes had either been converted to standard gauge or abandoned and removed. But a few of the old Denver & Rio Grande lines survived as they had been built, and in their waning days had attracted photographers, writers, and innumerable enthusiasts. Some came to ride the last of the narrow-gauge passenger trains, others to capture the last of a colorful era. Railroad enthusiast and author Lucius Beebe wrote extensively on the charm of the Rocky Mountain narrow-gauge lines.

By the 1940s, the narrow-gauge routes were an anachronism, representative of railway operations of an earlier generation. They embodied the spirit and character of the western railway in the days of the frontier and had changed little from the railroad scene of the early 1900s. This was a place where time moved slowly and change was imperceptible. Steam locomotives were small and quaint, and depots,

> By the 1940s, the narrow-gauge routes were an anachronism, representative of railway operations of an earlier generation

roundhouses, and railroad shops were still standing much as they were built – 70 years earlier. The rail-roaders tended to be friendly and engaging. But, perhaps best of all, these lines traversed some of the most spectacular, awe-inspiring scenery in the world: deep canyons, towering mountain peaks more than 14,000ft (4,200m) above sea level, and broad, open, unspoiled vistas.

In the 1950s, Robert Richardson recognized the significance of the narrow gauge and initiated a personal effort to preserve steam locomotives and rolling stock. There were few precedents for such heroic actions, and he paved the way for more ambitious preservation. Ultimately, his collection became the basis for the Colorado Railroad Museum at Golden.

Passenger trains were often the first to go on marginal railway lines. One of the last regular sched-uled passenger trains on the Rio Grande's narrow-gauge network was the thrice-weekly steam-powered mixed train that carried both freight and passengers between Durango and Silverton in southwest Colorado. Despite attempts to rid itself of the obliga-tion to run the train, the Rio Grande was forced by the Federal government to continue the operation.

▶ **A Durango & Silverton narrow-gauge excursion train negotiates a narrow shelf in Colorado's glorious Animus River Canyon. This former Rio Grande route is now privately operated and carries more than 200,000 passengers a year.**

The train wound its way through the narrow, sinuous Animas River Canyon, far away from paved roads and human habitation. In places, the tracks clung to a rock shelf high above the Animus River, with vertical cliffs looming even higher above the tracks. By the early 1950s, railroad enthusiasts and tourists had discovered the charm of this run, and, as the awareness of the Silverton line spread, ridership swelled. At first, the railroad resisted this unexpected growth in traffic, but ultimately it embraced the tourist trade and boosted the service by fixing up the trains, decorating the cars in bright yellow paint and promoting the service as a tourist attraction and a ride to yesteryear.

The overwhelming scenic attraction of the line and the quaint equipment attracted a growth in ridership, defying the national trend of rail passenger decline. Yet it was just that decline of the American train that really fueled the success of the Durango &

Silverton, and many other tourist train rides. As the railroad passenger train disappeared from public service, the concept of riding a train was transformed from a necessity to a romantic, nostalgic experience. Where an earlier generation may have regarded an all-day

---

As the passenger train disappeared, the concept of riding a train was transformed from a necessity to a nostalgic experience

---

train trip in rickety wooden cars behind dirty, coal-burning steam locomotives as an ordeal, it was now considered a pleasant way to spend a summer holiday.

The popularity of the Durango & Silverton grew, and, by the late 1960s, it was the only passenger train left on the Rio Grande that was actually generating revenue. When Rio Grande finally abandoned the

◄ A Baldwin-built former Rio Grande class K-36 Mikado powers a Cumbres & Toltec excursion train near Chama, New Mexico. The Cumbres & Toltec Scenic Railroad operates over 64 miles (103km) of the former Rio Grande narrow gauge in Colorado and New Mexico.

under way to save the lines from being totally scrapped. It had been recognized that the narrow gauge was integral to the development of Colorado and northern New Mexico, and that the railroad had an important place in western history. While large portions of the narrow-gauge route were ultimately abandoned and the track lifted, in 1970, the states of New Mexico and Colorado joined to save a 64-mile (103km) segment of Rio Grande narrow-gauge line that ran between Antonito, Colorado, and Chama, New Mexico.

This sinuous, steeply graded route roughly follows the state line as it hugs the rim of the scenic Toltec Gorge and crosses the 10,016ft (3,053m) high Cumbres Pass. Rio Grande steam locomotives and other equipment, including steam-powered Leslie rotary snow plows, were preserved along with the railroad. Today, the railroad and related properties are known as the Cumbres & Toltec Scenic Railroad,

▼ The classic depot at Chama, New Mexico, is now served by the Cumbres & Toltec Scenic Railroad. This quaint mountain town lies at the base of the west slope of the line that surmounts Cumbres Pass at an elevation of 10,016ft (3,053m) above sea level.

remainder of its 3ft (904mm) gauge network, it retained the Durango to Silverton branch for excursion service. Eventually, the railroad sold the line to another company, and today the line is known as the Durango & Silverton Narrow Gauge Railroad. It operates as many as four or five steam-hauled round trips daily in the summer and carries an estimated 200,000 passengers annually, making the line one of the most successful tourist trains in the United States.

In the late 1960s, when the Rio Grande closed the last of its freight-hauling narrow-gauge lines, isolating the Durango & Silverton line from the rest of the network, a preservation movement was already

DENVER 344 M. CHAMA ELEV. 7863 FT.

◀ **The Durango & Silverton narrow gauge, built to serve the mining industry, is one of the last remnants of William Jackson Palmer's Rio Grande empire. Most of the Colorado narrow gauge was either converted or abandoned. Today the D&S is a tourist line.**

and are owned by Colorado and New Mexico. It is listed on the National Register of historic places, and train service is contracted to a private operator.

The Cumbres & Toltec is supported by a dedicated group of volunteers, the Friends of the Cumbres & Toltec, who have been crucial to the preservation of the line. They maintain and restore the aged railway equipment to a high degree of historical authenticity. In season, two trains are operated every day. One departs Chama, the other from Antonito, and they meet at Osier in the Toltec Gorge. While the Cumbres & Toltec does not attract as many passengers as the Silverton line does, it offers one of the best railway rides in North America and, perhaps more importantly, one of the most authentic traditional railway experiences.

Unlike many museums that offer a sanitized interpretation of history, the Cumbres & Toltec's shops at Chama are the real thing: dirt, grease, soot, cinders, and live steam. On a summer morning, you can wander down to the engine facility in Chama, located across the tracks from the passenger station. Here, in the warm glow of the rising sun, you will find two or more original Rio Grande 2-8-2 Mikados steaming, as they are serviced for their morning run over Cumbres Pass. Ashes are dumped from the ashpans below the firebox, valve gear is lubricated with old-fashioned oil canisters, and then the locomotives are inspected and moved into position for watering at the large, wooden water tank that sits just north of the shops. This scene, once common all across the United States at small town roundhouses and railroad shops, is now the exclusive domain of a handful of places such as Chama, preserved and saved from progress and the ravages of time. If you visit, you leave the modern world for a few minutes and experience the steam age for real, as it was more than seven decades ago.

The 3ft (904mm) gauge East Broad Top is the East Coast equivalent of the Rocky Mountain preserved narrow-gauge lines. This rustic Pennsylvanian coal-hauling line was constructed at roughly the same time as the Colorado lines, in the 1870s and 1880s. Like the Rio Grande, East Broad Top survived until the mid-1950s as a common carrier. It suffered in the 1940s when the bulk of its traffic dried up, and, by 1956, the line was forced to close.

The whole railroad – track, structures, locomotives, and rolling stock – was sold to Pennsylvania scrap dealer Nick Kovalchick. Instead of dismantling the railroad, he let it stand idle for a few years, before, in 1960, he began operating excursion trains on a short section of track at Orbisonia, Pennsyl-

Rockhill is one of the few places where one can experience what a steam operation would have been like

vania. The train rides proved popular and have continued ever since. It is a classic example of a private preservation effort and one of the best preserved traditional steam railroads in the United States. What makes it especially significant is that most of the equipment and structures are indigenous to the site and were not collected from a variety of different sources, as is the case with many historic railways. The roundhouse and shops at Rockhill Furnace look much the way they would have in 1900. Inside the roundhouse is East Broad Top's entire fleet of six narrow-gauge 2-8-2 Mikados, four of which run. In addition, the railroad's gas-electric passenger car has been preserved and restored to operation. It is the best example of a 1920s-era gas-electric car in the United States.

Like Chama, Rockhill furnace retains the atmosphere and charm of a small town railroad facility. It is one of the few places left where one can experience what a steam operation would have been like in the first half of the 20th century. East Broad Top is a time machine and a national treasure.

While the electric railway and narrow-gauge preservation efforts are some of the earliest and most authentic examples of railway preservation in

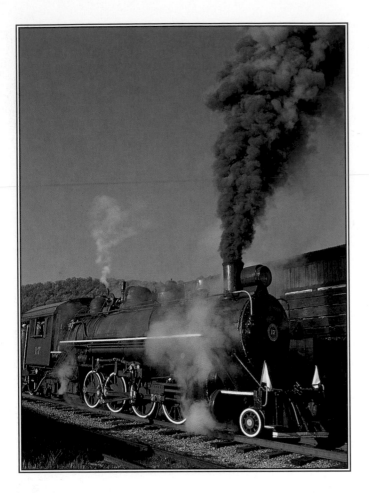

▲ East Broad Top No. 17 is steamed up and ready to go at Rockhill Furnace, Pennsylvania. This marvelous narrow-gauge Mikado operates for only a few days every year. When it comes out of the roundhouse, hundreds of people come to watch it.

North America, there are numerous examples of standard-gauge "steam railroad" preservation all across the continent.

One of the first and by far the best examples of conventional railroad preservation is the Baltimore & Ohio Railroad Museum in Baltimore, Maryland – a museum started by the railroad. Baltimore, one of the first cities in the United States actively to embrace the railroad, was also one of the first to recognize the historical significance of railroad history. The Baltimore & Ohio practically invented railroad preservation, and it actively preserved pieces of its historic equipment in the 19th century at a time when few other companies saw any value in saving old railroad equipment. Today, the Baltimore & Ohio's early efforts are the foundation of

the Baltimore & Ohio Railroad Museum collection. While the museum is no longer directly affiliated with CSX Transportation – the B&O's present-day corporate successor – the museum collection largely represents equipment operated by the railroads and its affiliates, including the Central Railroad of New Jersey, the Chesapeake & Ohio, and the Western Maryland.

The Baltimore & Ohio Railroad Museum grounds are centered on the 1851 Mt Clare Station and a beautifully restored 1880s-era covered roundhouse. This well-lit circular building is one of the finest of its kind in North America. The gems in the museum's collection include one of Phineas Davis's Grasshoppers, built in the 1830s (see Chapter 1) and the oldest passenger car in North America. The collection is also well represented by more modern yet historically significant items, such as the Central Railroad of New Jersey 1000, often described as the world's first commercially successful diesel-electric locomotive. Outside the roundhouse are other interesting locomotives, including a Chesapeake & Ohio streamlined 4-6-4 Hudson type – one of only a few American streamlined steam locomotives to escape scrapping, and one of the first streamlined diesels, B&O No. 51.

DECLINE SPURS PRESERVATION

At the beginning of the 1950s, most American railroads were still using steam locomotives, although by that time most had begun to purchase large numbers of diesels. In the next decade that would change, and, by 1960, virtually all steam locomotives had been retired. The omnipresent locomotive that had built North America was suddenly gone from the landscape. Yet the significance of the steam locomotive and the railroad in the rapid development of North America cannot be underplayed.

Neither the United States nor Canada would exist as integrated nations if it had not been for the steam locomotive and railway networks. This is

▶ The Baltimore & Ohio Railroad Museum in Baltimore is one of the finest railway museums in the United States. This 1880s-era covered roundhouse (so-called because of its circular shape) contains one of the best collections of steam locomotives in the country.

especially obvious in the West where communities were founded to serve the railroad. Both railroad companies and towns have recognized this fact, and many lines offered their retired locomotives for display. Of the estimated 175,000 locomotives built in the United States, roughly 1,800 were preserved. Some of these are now housed in museums such as the Baltimore & Ohio Railroad Museum in Baltimore, or on railways such as the Durango & Silverton, but a great number of them are displayed by communities which owe their existence to the railroad. These locomotives are typically in parks, railway yards, or at stations.

Some lines were very generous in this regard, notably the western railroads: the Southern Pacific, Union Pacific, and Burlington donated dozens of locomotives. Smaller lines such as the Soo Line and

◀ **In the early 1990s, the first Baldwin-built 4-8-4 Northern type, Santa Fe Railway No. 3751, was returned to operation after years of restoration work. The locomotive is seen here being serviced at Needles, California, on its way to Chicago.**

▲ **Steamtown is one of Scranton, Pennsylvania's greatest tourist attractions, converting the city's rich industrial history into a museum for everyone to enjoy. The former Lackawanna Railroad shops have been imaginatively adapted for public access.**

the Duluth, Missabe & Iron Range also provided locomotives to the towns along their lines. As a result, all across the western United States and Canada there are locomotives on display for public enjoyment. Many are well preserved, often sheltered beneath a roof, and painted to avoid rusting and deterioration. Of these better kept locomotives, some have been reclaimed and restored to operation, even after decades of resting in parks. Sadly, not all locomotives have been so well treated. Ambivalence among civic leaders and the public at large has led to the neglect and vandalism of preserved locomotives. Some are in poor shape, rusty and forlorn, while yet others have been scrapped many years after their siblings met the same fate.

Steam locomotive museums were virtually unheard of prior to 1960, but today, enthusiasts and railroad

companies have developed sites all over the country where full-sized, standard-gauge locomotives are on display or in active excursion service.

In addition to donating locomotives for local display, several railroads made a conscious effort to set aside significant locomotives for preservation. Toward the end of its steam operations, the Pennsylvania Railroad saved nearly one of every class of locomotive and stored them at its roundhouse in Emporium, Pennsylvania. The Pennsylvania Railroad's locomotive fleet was more than simple motive power – it was a profile of the company's engineering ingenuity and a matter of considerable pride to the road. The Pennsylvania was one of a few American railroads in the modern era that designed and built its own locomotives on a large scale. While the Pennsylvania Railroad's collection is one of the most comprehensive preserved by an American railroad, it is not complete. There are no examples of its divided drive Duplex types or its sole direct-drive turbine. Also missing are its World War II–era Superpower 2-10-4 Texas types; all of these late-year locomotives were scrapped.

Today, much of the Pennsylvania Railroad's preserved steam fleet has been restored and is displayed along with examples of Pennsylvania's electric locomotives and other equipment at the Railroad Museum of Pennsylvania at Strasburg, one of the finest railroad museums in the United States. Its "Hall of Locomotives" was designed to resemble a classic 19th-century passenger terminal and houses more than a dozen locomotives. Among them are a K4s Pacific, the pride of the railroad's steam passenger fleet, and a handsome Raymond Loewy-styled GG1 electric. Among the more unusual locomotives featured are the DD-1 siderod electric (a ponderous-looking machine designed to haul trains through New York's Penn Tunnels) and examples of three primary types of logging locomotives – the Shay, Climax, and Heisler.

◄ **A Durango & Silverton train threads its way through a snow-filled rock cut on its run between its namesake towns. On this tourist railway, a trip that was once an endurance test is now an opportunity for vacationers to relive the glory days of steam.**

Although the Railroad Museum of Pennsylvania is primarily a static collection, it is adjacent to the southern terminus of the Strasburg Railroad, one of the oldest steam excursion railroads in North America. This nine-mile (14.5km) line has always been a private branch line. It made a successful transition from a common carrier business to tourist line, and it operates steam excursion trains over a scenic route through Pennsylvania Dutch country to the

Pennsylvania hosts an endless treasure of railroads. The state is laced with rail lines and more than two dozen museums

nearby town of Paradise. It maintains a collection of its own steam locomotives, including one of the last 4-8-0 Mastodons in the United States.

Pennsylvania hosts a seemingly endless treasure of railroads and railway preservation. The state is laced with numerous rail lines and more than two dozen museums and tourist roads. Not to be missed is the Steamtown National Historic Site in Scranton. This wonderful museum is now operated by the US National Park Service and ranks among the best railroad museums in North America. Steamtown was the inspiration of the late Nelson Blount, who began collecting steam locomotives at the end of the steam era. For many years, the Steamtown collection resided in Bellows Falls, Vermont, where excursions were operated over the Green Mountain Railroad to Chester, a scenic line once part of the Rutland Railroad. In the mid-1980s, the Steamtown collection was moved from Bellows Falls to Scranton, and is now housed in part of the old Delaware, Lackawanna & Western shops.

Steamtown has undertaken the restoration of many of its historic locomotives, which include a great variety of engines from all around the United States and Canada. The impressive site of a Union Pacific 4-8-8-4 Big Boy, which is displayed outside the shops, greets visitors. While Steamtown has one of the most impressive railway interpretive centers in the United States, it is a working museum, and, in addition to its steam shops, it operates a 27-mile (43.5km) excursion over the former Lackawanna mainline. Most other railway museums are located on secondary routes and branch lines, but Steamtown is one of the few museums in the United States that provides the public with a mainline experience. A significant portion of the Steamtown collection is made up of Canadian locomotives, at least two of which were serviceable until the 1990s.

▼ This former Grand Trunk 0-6-0 steam switcher is a star performer on the Conway Scenic Railroad in New Hampshire. Here, it poses on the turntable at the North Conway round-house; the turntable is used to rotate the locomotive.

Sacramento, the capital of California, was the original terminus of the first transcontinental railroad. A major railroad center for more than 125 years, it is also the location of another fine railway museum. Like the Railroad Museum of Pennsylvania, and the Baltimore & Ohio Museum in Baltimore, the California State Railroad Museum houses a unique, historically significant collection relevant to its region. Included are early examples of Southern Pacific and Central Pacific locomotives. Among them are the "C. P. Huntington" (a 4-2-4T) and the "Governor Stanford" Southern Pacific No. 1 (a Norris-built 4-4-0). Not be missed is Southern Pacific No. 4294, the last built and only remaining Southern Pacific cab–ahead articulated type. This huge locomotive represents several classes of locomotives designed to haul heavy freight over the Sierra Mountains. The collection is beautifully restored and magnificently displayed. Among the museum's other contributions to railway preservation and history are its extensive library and photographic archives.

MORE TRAIN RIDES

The decline of the privately operated passenger train, like the earlier disappearance of the electric interurbans, narrow-gauge lines, and steam locomotives, has provided inspiration for more railway preservation.

In 1971, most US railways turned over their passenger operations to Amtrak. A few years later, the two large Canadian rail systems, the Canadian National and the Canadian Pacific, gave their passenger trains to the government-supported VIA. With a few exceptions, the privately operated intercity passenger train had vanished.

While some historic train rides existed prior to the 1970s – such as the Durango & Silverton, the Strasburg, and Vermont's Steamtown – since the advent of Amtrak, there has been a great increase in new historic and tourist railways all across North America. These new preservation efforts

TRAVELERS' TALES
A LUCKY CHANGE OF TRAIN

In September 1950, Clark Johnson Jr was a young railway enthusiast heading from his home in the Twin Cities (Minneapolis/St Paul, Minnesota) to the National Model Railroad Association convention in Milwaukee, Wisconsin. He and about 20 other conventioneers were riding overnight on Chicago & North Western's *North Western Limited*, and hoped to get to Milwaukee by morning in order to catch a special excursion on the Milwaukee Electric Rapid Transit & Speed Rail – a suburban electric interurban line. Johnson recalls: "A lot of my friends were planning to ride. It would have been a lot of fun."

In the early morning hours, the *North Western Limited* paused at Merrillan, Wisconsin, a five-way junction in the northern part of the state.

"When our train pulled in, I saw a short local passenger train at the station. I thought it was the local run to Manitowoc. It had a little old Ten Wheeler [4-6-0], a couple of baggage cars, a mail car, and a lone coach. A friend and I made a quick decision to get off the through train to Milwaukee, and jump on this cross-country local instead. It didn't go where we were headed and it would not travel very fast, but it was a lot more interesting!"

The chance to ride such a classic train seemed more important than the model railroad convention and the special excursion. Here was a small piece of history. At one time, local passenger trains such as this one connected almost every town in the United States, but by 1949 they were a dying breed. Within a couple of years, the train would be canceled, the rails pulled up, and North Western's little Alco-built R-1 4-6-0, now sitting there at the Merrillan depot happily steaming away, would be cut up for scrap. As it turned out, Johnson's choice to climb onboard was a good one that may have saved his life.

Soon, he and his friend were riding through the pastoral Wisconsin scenery, listening to the music generated by the small locomotive pulling the train. As the local made its way east it paused at small, out-of-the-way stations, picking up mail and passengers, just as it had for decades.

"After we got on, we found that this train was only going as far as Kaukauna, and not making it all the way to Manitowoc. It didn't matter – we enjoyed the ride, not caring that we would miss the interurban special. When would we ever get back to ride a steam train like this? As it turned out, we never made it to Milwaukee, and it was lucky too! The excursion we had hoped to ride was involved in a terrible fatal accident when it collided head-on with another car at Hales Corners near Milwaukee. Ten or 11 people died in the crash, including a couple of my friends. If I had gone to Milwaukee I would have been on that excursion, and I might have been killed too."

Sometimes it pays to follow your intuition!

have taken a variety of different forms. Some are museums that focus on a specific historical period and strive for historical authenticity within definable parameters. Others are simply groups of railway enthusiasts who have gathered together historical railroad equipment, while entertaining the public and generating revenue by offering train rides. And some are merely businesses that sell the experience of a train ride to tourists, often with little concern for historical accuracy or authenticity. One popular type of train ride has been the dinner train, which typically uses antique railroad cars to provide a pleasant and authentic period setting for dinner parties. Some dinner trains roll along at a leisurely pace across the countryside; others are just static cars set up as theme restaurants.

The shedding of branch lines by the large principal (Class 1) railroads has also spawned railway

preservation. During the 1970s, 1980s, and 1990s, many secondary rail lines were abandoned or sold to shortline operators. Some new shortlines found a supplemental income by operating seasonal or weekend rail excursions. The most authentic of these closely resemble branch line passenger services of a bygone era, while others simply provide a pleasant jaunt in the country.

In Connecticut, the Valley Railroad began steam excursions on a disused former New Haven Railroad branch in July 1971, only a few months after Amtrak assumed intercity passenger operations. Based at Essex, the Valley Railroad is situated in the scenic Connecticut River Valley and has flourished as a popular tourist attraction. It has several steam locomotives, two of which operate, and features a handsome depot that conveys the feeling of a small town railway station. The Valley Railroad is situated in a rural location that is relatively close to several large population centers and other well-known tourist attractions.

Further north in New England is the Conway Scenic Railroad, which operates a former Boston & Maine branch line and, more recently, a portion of the exceptionally scenic former Maine Central Mountain Division, which crosses Crawford Notch. The Conway Scenic's base of operation is the Boston & Maine station and roundhouse at North Conway, New Hampshire, located at the foot of the White Mountains, an area blessed with a long tradition of tourism. This line operates a steam locomotive as well as several vintage diesels. The majority of its equipment comes from New England and eastern Canada, which gives the railroad a classic look, while still retaining its regional bias. In the morning, when former Grand Trunk 0-6-0 No. 7470 steams out of its stable, one can observe the spirit of a typical New England branch operation of a half century earlier.

While the Grand Trunk never operated to North Conway, it did serve towns just a few miles to the

north, and the proliferation of vintage Boston & Maine and Maine Central diesels lends to the atmosphere. Two different rides are offered: a relatively short ride behind steam and an all-day affair that takes passengers over the Notch and back. The Conway Scenic Railroad follows a good precedent for carrying passengers through the White Mountains. Not far away is the Mt Washington Cog Railway, the oldest continuously operated steam-powered railway in the United States. This line was built in 1869 specifically to haul passengers to the top of Mt Washington, 6,288ft (1,917m) above sea level.

The effect of the railroad on the communities it passed through has not been forgotten, and many traditional railroad towns now host historic railways. Cumberland, Maryland, has long served as a principal terminal for the Baltimore & Ohio and

---

During the 1970s, 1980s, and 1990s, many secondary rail lines were abandoned or sold to shortline operators

---

Western Maryland railroads. It is still the location of a major classification yard, locomotive shop, and terminal facility for CSX, and a stop on Amtrak's *Capitol Limited*. In recognition of its history, Cumberland (and nearby Wrigley, West Virginia) hosts the Western Maryland Scenic Railroad. Cumberland's old Western Maryland station, now a transportation museum, serves the historic train, which is often hauled by a restored 2-8-0 Consolidation. It makes a 32-mile (51.5km) round trip over the old Western Maryland mainline to Frostburg. The Western Maryland route ran parallel to the Baltimore & Ohio's, but was discontinued as a through line in the 1970s, following a disastrous flood that damaged portions of the line.

The Midwest is home to numerous sites of steam railway preservation. Small lines, such as the Kettle Moraine Railway, which operates a four-mile (6.4km) section of former Milwaukee Road branch line, keep the steam tradition alive. Other sites have an array of different types of regional equipment.

◄ **The Western Maryland Scenic Railroad operates a short stretch of the old Western Maryland route west of Cumberland, Maryland. A great deal of the Western Maryland mainline was abandoned in the 1970s following severe flood damage.**

► Union Pacific steam locomotives Nos. 844 and 3985 approach Sand Pass, Nevada, in April, 1991, on an excursion to Sacramento, California, for RailFair '91, an event commemorating the 10th anniversary of the opening of the Sacramento Railroad Museum.

One important aspect of American railway preservation is the continued involvement of the railroads themselves. Railroads have maintained close ties with their past by operating historic equipment or permitting public excursions over their lines using vintage locomotives and cars. Some lines have been more open to excursions than others. Not all railroads embrace excursions, particularly if such adventures threaten to disrupt profit-making operations. American railroads remain private companies, the primary goal of which is earning income for their stock-holders, not pleasing railroad enthusiasts, historians, and the general public. So, despite the

One important aspect of American railway preservation is the continued involvement of the railroads themselves

popularity of historic excursions, some lines have declined to operate them.

The Union Pacific is one the largest American railroads and also one of the most history-conscious lines. While its business is primarily the transport of heavy freight — and lots of it — it has always kept its heritage in mind. At the end of steam, the Union Pacific, in addition to providing retired locomotives to towns and organizations, retained several of its steam locomotives for its own use. One locomotive, its 4-8-4 Northern type No. 844, has never been retired, and it has remained serviceable on the Union Pacific since it was built. This locomotive has often been called upon to run excursions and provide publicity for the company, and has traveled widely across the railroad's network. In the early 1980s, the Union Pacific added another active steam locomotive to its fleet — a restored 4-6-6-4 Challenger, No. 3985. This huge articulated locomotive is just slightly smaller than the famous Union Pacific

Big Boy, and it is now the largest operating steam locomotive in the world. Not as well known as these two famous showpieces are several other locomotives that the Union Pacific keeps at its roundhouse in Cheyenne, Wyoming. These engines are not currently on public display, nor are they in a museum. They are on railroad property, but someday they, too, could be brought back to steam.

The Union Pacific's railway preservation efforts go beyond its dedication to steam. Railroad history did not end with the passing of steam, and today many people fondly remember the locomotives and trains of the diesel era. The Union Pacific was one of the pioneers of the streamlined passenger train, and it still maintains a significant fleet of historical streamlined passenger cars and has reacquired and rebuilt a matching set of Electro Motive E9 diesels. These locomotives are used along with its steam fleet in excursion service and to haul the companies' executive trains. The general public is often just as thrilled to see a reincarnated "City of Los Angeles" flash by behind the E9s, as they are to see one of the Union Pacific's steam excursions.

Throughout the United States and Canada, there are several large mainline steam locomotives available for excursions. Some of these locomotives are too big and too heavy to allow for operation on the branch lines typically operated by railroad museums and tourist lines. In recent years, the Milwaukee Road 261, an Alco-built 4-8-4 Northern based in Minneapolis, Minnesota, has enjoyed a productive career. This locomotive has operated a number of mainline trips on the Burlington Northern Santa Fe routes, and it has been a regular visitor at Galesburg, Illinois' "Railroad Days" festival – a popular event that celebrates the town's railroad heritage.

One of the most popular operating mainline excursion locomotives in the United States has been the Southern Pacific's magnificent streamlined 4-8-4 Northern type No. 4449. A 1941 product of Lima, it is arguably one of the finest Northerns ever built. Designed to haul the flashy *Daylight* passenger trains – which were painted red, orange, silver, and black – the locomotive is often known as simply "the Daylight." In 2000, No. 4449 was repainted in darker colors for work on the Burlington Northern Santa Fe's employee appreciation specials that operated in the Pacific Northwest that year.

PRESERVATION IN CANADA

North of the border, The Canadian Pacific and the Canadian National operated mainline steam longer than the majority of their counterparts in the United States. In the 1960s and early 1970s, after it had discontinued regular steam operations, the Canadian National operated numerous excursions with steam locomotives.

Today, there are more than 30 major railway preservation sites across the whole of Canada, displaying and operating a great variety of historic equipment. The Canadian Railway Museum at Saint Constant, Quebec, near Montreal, is the nation's largest. It is home to some of the oldest locomotives in the country, including what is described as a replica of the *John Molson*. The original was one of the locomotives imported from Dundee, Scotland, in the 1840s. The museum also features a number of electric streetcars from Montreal.

The National Museum of Science & Technology in Ottawa is home to several significant steam locomotives, including one of the Canadian Pacific's famed Royal Hudsons and a streamlined Canadian National 4-8-4 Northern type. Another Royal Hudson regularly operates on BC Rail, typically powering a scenic 80-mile (130km) round-trip journey through the spectacular scenery of British Columbia.

While the North American railroad system has evolved into a modern freight hauler, railway preservation at all levels – from the simple restoration of an old depot or caboose, to the operation of an authentically restored mainline steam-powered passenger train – has helped keep the spirit and history of the golden era of American railroads alive. As long as there is an interest in railways, people will flock to see the relics of this colorful and bygone age.

► **The rails of the former Canadian National Railway in Nova Scotia catch the glint of the setting sun. With over 170 years of history, North American railroads continue to play a vital role in transportation – and to serve as a reminder of our rich heritage.**

BIBLIOGRAPHY

Books

BEEBE, LUCIUS: *The Overland Limited;* Howell-North Books, Berkeley, California, 1963.

BERTON, PIERRE: *The Last Spike: The Great Railway 1881–1885;* McClelland and Stewart, Toronto, 1971.

BLACK, ROBERT C. III: *The Railroads of the Confederacy;* University of North Carolina Press, North Carolina, 1952.

BRUCE, ALFRED W.: *The Steam Locomotive in America;* W. W. Norton & Co., New York, 1952.

BUSH, DONALD J.: *The Streamlined Decade;* George Braziller, New York, 1975.

CASEY, ROBERT J. AND W. A. S. DOUGLAS: *The Lackawanna Story;* McGraw-Hill, New York, 1951.

CHURELLA, ALBERT, J.: *From Steam to Diesel;* Princeton University Press, New Jersey, 1998.

CURRIE, A. W.: *The Grand Trunk Railway of Canada;* University of Toronto Press, Toronto, 1957.

DORSEY, EDWARD BATES: *English and American Railroads Compared;* New York, 1887.

DRURY, GEORGE H.: *Guide to North American Steam Locomotives;* Kalmbach, Milwaukee, 1993.

DUBIN, ARTHUR D.: *Some Classic Trains;* Kalmbach, Milwaukee, 1964.

DUBIN, ARTHUR D.: *More Classic Trains;* Kalmbach, Milwaukee, 1974.

FARRINGTON, JR., KIP, S.: *Railroads at War;* Coward McCann, New York, 1944.

FARRINGTON, JR., KIP, S.: *Railroading from the Rear End;* Coward McCann, New York, 1946.

GRODINSKY, JULIUS: *Jay Gould – His Business Career 1867–1892;* University of Pennsylvania Press, Philadelphia, 1957.

HEDGES, JAMES B.: *The Federal Railway Land Subsidy Policy of Canada;* Cambridge, Massachusetts, 1934.

HARLOW, ALVIN F.: *Steelways of New England;* Creative Age Press, New York, 1946.

HARLOW, ALVIN F.: *The Road of the Century;* Creative Age Press, New York, 1947.

HILTON, GEORGE W.: *American Narrow Gauge Railroads;* Stanford University Press, California, 1990.

KLEIN, MAURY: *Union Pacific, Vols. I &II;* Doubleday, New York, 1989.

LAMB, W. KAYE: *History of the Canadian Pacific Railway;* Macmillan, New York, 1977.

MARSHALL, JAMES: *Santa Fe— The Railroad That Built an Empire;* New York, 1945.

MIDDLETON, WILLIAM D.: *When the Steam Railroads Electrified;* Kalmbach, Milwaukee, 1974.

MIDDLETON, WILLIAM D.: *Grand Central . . . the World's Greatest Railway Terminal;* Golden West Books, San Marino, California, 1977.

MORGAN, DAVID P.: *Steam's Finest Hour;* Kalmbach, Milwaukee, 1959.

PEARSON, J.P.: *Railways and Scenery Vol 1;* Cassell & Co., London, 1932.

OVERTON, RICHARD C.: *Burlington Route;* Alfred A. Knopf, New York, 1965.

QUIETT, GLENN CHESNEY.: *They Built the West;* Appleton Century, New York, 1934.

SIGNOR, JOHN R.: *Tehachapi;* Golden West Books, San Marino, California, 1983.

SHEARER, FREDERICK E.: *The Pacific Tourist,* Bounty Books, New York, 1970.

SINCLAIR, ANGUS: *Development of the Locomotive Engine;* Angus Sinclair Publishing, New York, 1907.

SOLOMON, BRIAN: *The American Steam Locomotive;* Motorbooks, Osceola, Wisconsin, 1998.

SOLOMON, BRIAN: *Trains of the Old West;* Metro Books, New York, 1998.

STEVENS, G. R.: *History of the Canadian National Railways;* Macmillan, New York, 1973.

STILGOE, JOHN R.: *Metropolitan Corridor;* Yale University Press, Connecticut, 1983.

STOVER, JOHN F.: *The Life and Decline of the American Railroad;* New York Oxford University Press, New York, 1970.

SWENGEL, FRANK M.: *The American Steam Locomotive: Volume 1, Evolution;* Midwest Rail Publications, Davenport, Iowa, 1967.

TAYLOR, GEORGE ROGERS: *The American Railroad Network 1861–1890;* Cambridge, Massachusetts, 1956.

WHITE, JOHN H., JR.: *Early American Locomotives;* Dover, Toronto, 1979.

WHITE, JOHN H., JR.: *The American Railroad Freight Car;* John Hopkins, Baltimore, 1993.

Periodicals

Locomotive & Railway Preservation; Waukesha, Wisconsin. [no longer published]

Rail News; Waukesha, Wisconsin. [no longer published]

Railroad History (formerly *Railway and Locomotive Historical Society Bulletin*); Boston, Massachusetts.

Railway Age; Chicago and New York.

Railway Gazette, 1870–1908; New York.

Official Guide to the Railways; New York.

Trains; Waukesha, Wisconsin.

Vintage Rails; Waukesha, Wisconsin. [no longer published]

ACKNOWLEDGEMENTS

This book was made possible with the help and generosity of many people who assisted in its preparation and production. I often consult professional railroaders, fellow authors, historians, and railroad photographers, who have led me to interesting places, pointed out significant locomotives, trains, and facilities, recommended books and articles, and offered photographic advice. I owe the most to my father, Richard J. Solomon, who introduced me to railroading when I was a child, and has traveled with me on many occasions. He has also given me unlimited access to his railroad library and photo archive, and provided editorial help. My long time mentor, Robert A. Buck, has also fostered my interest in railroads, and assisted with photo research and fact checking. Colin Garratt of the Milepost 92 1/2 Library encouraged me to work on the book. John Gruber, a fellow author, has been very helpful, supplying articles, artwork, and photographs,

and providing lodging while I was doing research at libraries in Madison, Wisconsin. Mike Gardner was especially generous with his darkroom facilities, which I used to print a number of old photographs used in the text. I reviewed thousands of photographs for this project, so thanks to: Jay Williams, H. Bentley Crouch, Robert W. Jones, Milepost 92 1/2 Picture Library, John P. Hankey, George S. Pitarys, J. R. Quinn, Brian L. Jennison, Bob's Photos, and George C. Corey for access to their photo collections. Lori Swingle of the Denver Public Library assisted with photographs from the Otto Perry collection. Special thanks to Dennis LeBeau for access to the Bullard photo archive; and Michael Sullivan for access to his railway memorabilia. Doug Moore has helped on several occasions with making duplicate photographs. Thanks also to Sally Harper and Jill Fornary of Amber Books for their editing and suggestions.

INDEX

PICTURE CREDITS